# LESLIE MARMON SILKO

*A Study of the Short Fiction*

## Also available in Twayne's Studies in Short Fiction Series

Twayne publishes studies of all major short-story writers worldwide. For a complete list, contact the Publisher directly.

*Twayne's Studies in Short Fiction*

Gary Scharnhorst and Eric Haralson,
General Editors

Leslie Marmon Silko
*Photograph by Lee Marmon. Reproduced by permission.*

# LESLIE MARMON SILKO

*A Study of the Short Fiction*

*Helen Jaskoski*

*TWAYNE PUBLISHERS*
*An Imprint of Simon & Schuster Macmillan*
*New York*

*PRENTICE HALL INTERNATIONAL*
*London Mexico City New Delhi Singapore Sydney Toronto*

*Twayne's Studies in Short Fiction Series, No. 71*

Copyright © 1998 by Twayne Publishers

Twayne Publishers
An Imprint of Simon & Schuster Macmillan
1633 Broadway
New York, NY 10019

## Library of Congress Cataloging-in-Publication Data

Jaskoski, Helen.
  Leslie Marmon Silko : a study of the short fiction / Helen
Jaskoski.
      p.    cm. — (Twayne's studies in short fiction ; no. 71)
  Includes bibliographical references and index.
  ISBN 0-8057-0868-5
  1. Silko, Leslie, 1948–    —Criticism and interpretation.
  2. Women and literature—Southwest, New—History—20th century.
  3. Western stories—History and criticism.   4. Indians of North
America in literature.   5. Laguna Indians in literature.
  6. Southwest, New—In literature.   I. Title.   II. Series.
  PS3569.I44Z75    1998
  813'.54—dc21                                                97-36410
                                                                CIP

This paper meets the requirements of ANSI/NISO Z3948-1992 (Permanence of Paper).

10 9 8 7 6 5 4 3 2 1

Printed in the United States of America

*For Dan*

# Contents

## Contents

# Preface

The State of New Mexico has designated Leslie Marmon Silko as a living cultural treasure; in her early 30s she was the recipient of a MacArthur "genius" award; she has been counted as one of the 135 most important women writers in the history of the world;[1] and she has received many other awards for her writing. Her fiction has appeared in anthologies and on college reading lists under the headings of writing by women, by American Indians, by Western writers, by American writers, by prizewinning authors.

As a young child she spoke Keresan, a language few people have ever heard of. Her writings are suffused with the landscape and traditions of the southwestern pueblos where her Laguna ancestors lived for centuries and where she grew up, and she has reflected frequently on both her American Indian background and her sense of herself as an individual on many borders—linguistic, cultural, and social. Yet despite what seems to be an extremely local and particular material, the honors enumerated above testify to the power of her writing to reach and inspire people who have no knowledge at all of the special milieu so carefully and lovingly rendered in her work.

The power of that writing has inspired this book.

So has the belief that Silko's writing deserves attention for its artistry, its backgrounds, and its genesis. My readings of these stories have grown out of 20 years of teaching them and reflect the approaches I have devised to help my students make sense of the texts and of their responses to them. Silko's prose is lucid and deceptively transparent, and her short fiction lacks the structural experimentation of her longer works, even as it finds a place in her most experimental book, *Storyteller*. That transparency can be beguiling, and it is easy to forget that there is a writer manipulating the words the reader finds so moving; it is not unusual to see students and even scholars heatedly take sides with or against Silko's characters as if they were real people whose positions on things required evaluation, or as if a single character's point of view exhausted the possibilities a given story raises. But to miss the textuality of these tales, their manipulation of point of view and writerly device, is to lose a great deal of their meaning and almost all of their humor. If there is a major emphasis in my readings here, it is just this attempt to articulate the nuances of narrative texture, in the hope that bringing out what speaks to me in these stories will open up their eloquence and passion to others.

Many people have given generously of their time, interest, encouragement and expertise to make this book possible. It is a privilege to thank Lee Marmon for permission to use his own photograph of his daughter Leslie for the frontispiece in this volume. The copy of the photograph used here was provided by Robert M. Nelson, and Bob has given much more besides in the last 10 years: constant friendship, encouragement and moral support, notes on Silko's biography and Laguna geography, and his always valuable insights into Silko's work; his writings on Silko in *Place and Vision* and elsewhere are essential reading.[2] I owe special thanks to the contributors of the essays and interviews in this volume, for reprint permissions and for much more. A. LaVonne Brown Ruoff and Lawrence J. Evers, who organized and directed extraordinarily rich and challenging NEH seminars, have been the best of mentors to me as to many; LaVonne considerately provided the revised version of her classic early study of Silko's short fiction, and Larry encouraged my contact with Leslie Silko besides permitting reprint of both his interview and his essay. Kate Shanley's kindness in allowing reprint of her essay matches her other kindnesses over the years. Likewise, Lee Francis and Elaine Jahner included their personal encouragement with their generous permission to reprint. Dean Rader, whose essay appears here for the first time, was patient and good humored through several revisions. To James Thorson, one of Silko's own mentors at the University of New Mexico, I owe thanks for his invaluable help with the chronology. Kenneth Roemer graciously sent a preview copy of the entry on Silko in the *Dictionary of Literary Biography*. Whatever errors or omissions may be found here are entirely my own. Gary Scharnhorst, Twayne's short fiction series editor, was encouraging from the beginning of this project, and Anne C. Davidson of Twayne has been unfailingly supportive and pleasant. Cal Barksdale at Arcade Publishers was prompt and helpful in securing reprint permission for the quotations from *Storyteller*. Two grants from California State University Fullerton supported the initial proposal for the book and final preparation of the manuscript; for this support, as for the NEH summer stipend and summer seminar grants that permitted my earliest work on Silko and other American

Indian authors, I am thankful. Last and most important, my gratitude always to Dan Brown, my husband, the best part of my life.

## Notes

1. "Leslie Marmon Silko," in *Great Women Writers: The Lives and Works of 135 of the World's Most Important Women Writers, from Antiquity to the Present*, ed. Frank Northen Magill (New York: Holt and Co., 1994), 495–99.

2. Robert M. Nelson, *Place and Vision: The Function of Landscape in Native American Fiction* (New York: Peter Lang, 1995).

# Acknowledgments

Grateful acknowledgment is made for permission to print or reprint the following items:

Photograph of Leslie Marmon Silko by Lee Marmon, reprinted by permission of Lee Marmon.

*Storyteller.* Copyright © 1981 by Leslie Marmon Silko; quotations reprinted from *Storyteller,* by Leslie Marmon Silko, published by Seaver Books, New York, New York, by permission of Arcade Publishing and Seaver Books.

"A Conversation with Leslie Marmon Silko," © 1976, and "The Killing of a New Mexican State Trooper: Ways of Telling an Historical Event," © 1984 by Lawrence J. Evers; reprinted by permission of Lawrence J. Evers.

Excerpt from "The Novel and Oral Tradition: An Interview with Leslie Marmon Silko." © 1981, reprinted by permission of Elaine Jahner.

"Two Interviews with Leslie Marmon Silko." © 1981, reprinted by permission of *American Studies in Scandinavia.*

"Dealing (with) Coyote: Sexuality and Trickery in 'Coyote Holds a Full House in His Hands,' " published here for the first time by permission of Dean Rader.

"Ritual and Renewal: Keres Traditions in the Short Fiction of Leslie Silko," by A. LaVonne Brown Ruoff. © 1979 by MELUS, The Society for the Study of the Multi-ethnic Literature of the United States; reprinted by permission of MELUS and of A. LaVonne Brown Ruoff.

*Acknowledgments*

"The Devil's Domain: Leslie Silko's 'Storyteller,' " by Kate Shanley Vangen. © 1984; reprinted by permission of Kathryn Shanley.

"A Note on 'Tony's Story' in Laguna Context," by permission of Lee Francis.

*Part 1*

# THE SHORT FICTION

# Introduction: The Southwest

> Where I come from is like this
>     the warmth, the fragrance, the silence.
> Blue sky and rainclouds in the distance
>     we ride together
>         past cliffs with stories and songs
>         painted on rock.
>             700 years ago.
>             —Leslie Marmon Silko, "Slim Man Canyon"[1]

All but one of Leslie Silko's short stories are set in the Southwest, more specifically in northern New Mexico, where her childhood home, Laguna Pueblo, is located. Nothing in her fiction is stronger than her sense of belonging to this landscape, and of its belonging to her. In her interviews and essays she emphasizes that self, land, and community are united by presence at a place whose meaning is expressed and internalized through story. The physical, mythical, and historical landscape is endowed with numinous and unique significance: "The narratives linked with prominent features of the landscape . . . delineate the complexities of the relationship that human beings must maintain with the surrounding natural world. . . . What I enjoyed most as a child was standing at the site of an incident recounted in one of the ancient stories. . . . That was when the stories worked best, because then I could . . . visualize myself as being located *within* the story being told."[2] What was true for the young Silko listening to traditional Keresan stories being told by her kinswomen holds as well for the reader of her fiction: it is essential to be able, so far as possible, to visualize oneself inside the landscape—including the historical and sociocultural landscape—of the particular corner of the Southwest where all but one of these stories take place. Any reading of the stories must take into account at least something of the physical and cultural geography of this region.

The upper Rio Grande valley is an arid plateau about a mile in elevation at the southern end of the Rocky Mountains. The climate is hot in summer, cold and often snowy in winter. Rainfall is uncertain and precious; the rainy season comes in late summer, and snow precipitation also replenishes streams and underground aquifers.

Culturally, the area has apparently always been a borderland shared and contested among differing cultures. Most prominent at the time of European entry were the people whom the Spaniards designated as the Pueblo Indians, in recognition of their permanent settlements in city-states of stone and adobe houses built on the plains or, more dramatically, on the isolating mesas. The pueblo called Laguna, birthplace and childhood home of Leslie Marmon Silko, is one of these.

The pueblos of the northern Rio Grande valley form the northern frontier of the great agricultural civilizations of central Mexico. Their economy was based for centuries on floodplain agriculture augmented by irrigation; complex and intimate relationships with the specifics of the land and its ecology were necessary for successful environmental management. Astronomical science was highly developed and used to determine the times for seasonal activities such as the building and taking down of the temporary dams that flooded the fields in preparation for planting. Corn was the staple crop, an essential and sacred food. Pueblo historian Joe Sando notes that "[e]very kind of corn was grown by the natives of the New World. . . . The United States Department of Agriculture has listed 1,112 species of native plants which furnished food for American Indians in North America, and the Pueblos used many of these wild plant species."[3] Traditional Pueblo narratives and songs reflect the people's preoccupation with subsistence through rainfall and successful crops, and are suffused with references to corn and water.

At the north and east of this frontier live the peoples of the Great Basin and southern plains. The Ute and the Havasupai peoples to the north developed a complex lifeway based on hunting and gathering, and to the east the Comanches and Kiowas exploited the mobility afforded by the introduction of the horse and became premier buffalo hunters of the southern plains. Many Pueblo traditional stories record interactions with these peoples. Last to arrive before the Europeans were the Navajos and Apaches, speakers of a language called Athabascan, who adapted technology acquired through their contact with the Pueblos and, later, Europeans and who developed highly distinctive pastoral/farming cultures.

The Spanish were the first Europeans to enter the area; the earliest expeditions, led by Fray Marcos de Niza in 1539 and Coronado in 1540, sought wealthy cities as sources of tribute, but later settlers established a colonial economy based on ranching and agriculture. The Spaniards had most direct contact with the Pueblos, less with the more nomadic Navajos and Apaches. Catholic missionaries directed most of their efforts toward the Pueblo peoples, and a Catholic presence is visible in the Indian pueblos as well as in the Spanish-speaking communities of New Mexico. According to Sando, "Although most Pueblo people have been nominally Catholic for more than three hundred years, the native religion is the basis of their system of belief. The two systems are maintained by a process which Pueblo scholar Alfonso Ortiz once described as 'compartmentalization.' . . . [The different religions are] mutually distinct socio-ceremonial systems" (Sando, 23). The area was part of New Spain from the 1500s until it was made part of the newly independent country of Mexico in 1821. This change made little difference in the ongoing appropriation of Indian lands and other wealth, although there was a decline in the influence of the Catholic Church. Although many New Mexicans distinguish between the Spanish-American descendants of the early colonizers and the Mexicans who immigrated north at a later date, Silko tends to use the term *Mexican* to refer generally to any Spanish-speaking persons.

In 1848 when the Treaty of Guadalupe Hidalgo transferred the territory to the United States, the American or "Anglo" presence became dominant in the region's government and economy. The imposition of a capitalist economy and a culture that privileges individualism onto the more communitarian indigenous and Hispanic societies continues to create both friction and fruitful encounter in this frontier contact zone. What has remained stable is the land and its ecology. The preservation of land from erosion, access to water and grazing land, mineral extraction, energy production, depletion of forests, urbanization, and the complications of the nuclear age from uranium mining to the development of atomic weapons are all contested issues.

Silko's family history has been bound up with the history of Laguna Pueblo for over a century, ever since two Marmon brothers moved there from the Midwest, married Laguna women, and settled in the community; over the years the Marmon family seems to have exerted considerable influence on the political, religious, and economic affairs of the pueblo. This is the context of Leslie Silko's writings, and an acquaintance with the basic geography and historical background of the area enables the reader to make sense of much that is otherwise obscure or overlooked in her writings.

# The Stories in *Storyteller*

## Introduction

The eight short stories for which Leslie Silko is best known and that represent her finest work in this form appear in the mixed-genre book titled *Storyteller*.[4] Although each of the eight stories had been published previously, and some had appeared in more than one collection, their placement in *Storyteller* with the various texts that surround them gives them a context that enriches the reading of any individual story. Besides short stories, the book includes redactions of traditional Pueblo myths and tales, fragments of letters to non-Laguna correspondents, poems, and autobiographical and family-history vignettes; there are also 26 photographs strategically placed throughout the volume. Genre classification for the book varies; most libraries catalog it as fiction, but Arnold Krupat treats it as autobiography, and Linda Danielson suggests a poetic reading.[5]

*Storyteller* is a self-reflexive work that takes both form and theme from the traditional relationship between storyteller and audience. In so doing, it challenges every reader to assume the role of storyteller's audience in cocreating text and context. For the non-Indian reader, the process will result in a radical de-centering, enabling a refocusing of signification from a putatively marginal perspective. Indeed, the book calls into question whole categories of "center" and "margin," prodding the reader to rethink the means by which such positioning is itself accomplished.[6]

*Storyteller* simultaneously addresses two different audiences, Laguna and non-Laguna. Cultural boundaries and integrity consistently figure in Silko's philosophy and practice. In an important early essay she criticizes writers like Gary Snyder and Oliver LaFarge for improperly assuming a right to claim Indian materials as their own.[7] With respect to her Laguna audience, then, Silko's task is to validate her claim to the elder's role of teacher: she must establish her right to tell Laguna stories. In addressing a non-Laguna, non-Indian audience, the text invites the reader to participate in creating its meaning, yet it must do so without violating the integrity of cultural materials by complicity in an invalid appropriation. Mediation requires boundaries; assimilation erases distinction and destroys otherness.

Silko's strategy for accomplishing these complicated addresses and interchanges is to reverse a (theoretical) historical development whereby oral story became transformed into written fiction and the function of the author displaced the performance of the storyteller. Michel Foucault's discussion of the concept of author offers a relevant paradigm for Silko's undertaking. Although *Storyteller* conforms to the "author-functions" that Foucault says are the only real constituents of the author, it proposes to displace the absent author with the presence of the text *as* storyteller.[8] *Storyteller* sets out to reinvent the written text as the traditional storyteller.

Such a reinvention involves a radical reconstitution of audience as well as of author. Unlike writing, storytelling is fundamentally a communal activity, one that requires both teller and audience. As Silko puts it, "Storytelling always includes the audience and the listeners, and, in fact, a great deal of the story is believed to be inside the listener, and the storyteller's role is to draw the story out of the listeners."[9] *Storyteller* includes the advice of Hopi elder Helen Sekaquaptewa in *I'isaw and the Birds:* "You must be very quiet and listen respectfully. Otherwise the storyteller might get upset and pout and not say another word all night" (254). Another translation of Helen's words affirms even more strongly the constitutive role of the audience in the storytelling situation: "It is known that the storyteller is touchy. If you *do not answer* she may pout and not tell a story" (my emphasis).[10] In *Storyteller* the author's text continually promises to revoke the frozen certitude of writing and devolve into the dynamic uncertainty of live performance. The reader, then, must assume the constitutive, creative task of the storyteller's audience.

One of many paradigms in *Storyteller* for the storytelling performance is found in Silko's retelling of a tale given to her by her aunt Susie, the story of Waithea, a little girl who runs away from her mother and whose clothes are transformed into butterflies. As Silko develops the text, she presents first a passage of reminiscence about Aunt Susie's background and education; the story proper follows. However, the author takes care to embed the story of Waithea within a framing account of her aunt's storytelling, and Silko incorporates within the tale details of Aunt Susie's demeanor and expression, as well as interpolated explanations of Laguna words: "Yashtoah is the hardened crust on corn meal mush / that curls up. / The very name 'yashtoah' means / it's sort of curled-up, you know, dried, / just as mush dries on top" (8). The story embodies the complexities of audience participation just outlined .

The situation and Aunt Susie's intent are clearly didactic: Aunt Susie instructs her audience in Keres[11] language, geography, and history, contextualizing for the real little girl the marvelous experience of the legendary little girl. Silko's own role is complex. In the text, young Leslie's figurative presence in the story models the reader's role with respect to the book *Storyteller:* the reader takes the part of listener/learner to the text's teller/teacher. Silko as author, on the other hand, displaces Aunt Susie as transmitter—and teacher—of the text, yet as author she is inevitably absent. Contradicting this absence, the text as presence performs the storytelling function.

Using this story as a model for the book, we may say that following the narrative and absorbing the contextual information are the activities *Storyteller* requires of the reader. This is what, conventionally, storytellers' audiences do—and how they learn. But the retelling of a traditional story near the end of *Storyteller* gives further directions for still more active participation in constituting the text. "Skeleton Fixer," which Silko notes is "A Piece of a Bigger Story" (245), offers a version of the ubiquitous bungling host tale "collection."[12] In the opening of Silko's story an unidentified woman finds "[w]ords like bones / scattered all over the place" (242). Old Man Badger comes along and reconnects the bones, fitting together even the ones that are not clearly recognizable, until—surprise!—"Old Coyote Woman jumped up / and took off running" (246). The story of "Skeleton Fixer" recapitulates the process of fragmentation and reconstitution required of the *Storyteller* reader, who must negotiate the apparently scattered, unrelated, and fragmentary texts and illustrations dispersed throughout the book in order to coinvent the story. The synthesizing operation the reader undertakes will change with each rereading, just as each storytelling situation offers a new version of the "skeleton text."

To understand the relationship between Silko's theorizing about storytelling and the short stories in *Storyteller,* it is helpful to have some sense of how the storytelling theme is played out within the total structure of the book. In a brief anecdote at the center of the book the author recalls stopping to chat with Nora, a neighbor in the village. Nora's children have brought home a library book with one of Leslie's poems in it. "We all enjoyed it so much," Nora says, "but . . . the way my grandpa used to tell it is longer" (110). Silko responds with a brief analysis of the distinction between writing and storytelling: "Yes, that's the trouble with writing. . . . You can't go on and on the way we do when we tell stories around here. People who aren't used to it get tired" (110). The vignette brings the Laguna audience into the text, acknowledging the intertextuality of Silko's written and oral materials—even as it suggests to the non-Laguna reader how much is silent in the book. Nevertheless, *Storyteller* does set out to recapture a sense of the recursive and elaborative "going on and on" of oral storytelling, as it plays and replays themes of hunting, planting, rain bringing, witchcraft, and of course storytelling itself.

Silko's address to her Laguna audience also involves functions of legitimation and authentication. Deep respect for elders as carriers of truth and tradition characterizes Laguna—and other American Indian—values. Silko's Laguna audience might remark the audacity of a young woman who claims the important role of storyteller. A parallel example of a woman artist introducing innovation from within a traditional role is that of Helen Cordero, originator of the popular "storyteller" statuettes.[13] Leslie Silko's transformation of the storyteller role into the medium of print may be compared with Helen Cordero's stylistic and thematic innovations in figural pottery. Silko and Cordero (both members of Keresan-speaking pueblos) present their appropriation of material traditionally reserved for elders or males as affirmation rather than critique of tradition. *Storyteller* may be read as a document supporting Silko's claim to the storytelling role, and validating in particular her assumption of the role of Laguna (American Indian) storyteller.

Silko's criticism of Snyder and LaFarge asserts in the strongest terms the background required for the authentic storyteller: "We are taught to remember who we are: our ancestors, our origins. We must know the place we came from because it has shaped us and continues to make us who we are" ("Attack," 213). One of the functions of the family history portions of *Storyteller* is to authenticate Leslie Silko's claim to the materials she includes in the book. The introduction of Aunt Susie, then, not only contextualizes the story of Waithea for the non-Indian reader and provides a paradigm for the storytelling experience, it also documents the Laguna genealogy of the story and thereby validates the teller/author and her right to reproduce the text.

The non-Indian audience likewise appears in *Storyteller* explicitly in the inclusion of Lawson Inada and James Wright. Letters addressed to these two writers also elaborate the didactic and contextualizing functions of storytelling. In writing to Inada, Silko describes the relationship of storytelling to place, illustrating how and why "we must know the place we came from":

> I remember the stories they used to tell us about places that were meadows full of flowers or about canyons that had wide clear streams. I remember our amazement; . . . the places they spoke of were dry and covered with tumbleweeds. . . . But I understand now. I will remember this September like they remembered the meadows and streams; I will talk about the yellow beeweed solid on all the hills, and maybe my grandchildren will also be amazed and wonder what has become of the fields of wild asters and all the little toads that sang in the evening." (170)

Stories are important not (just) because they describe an ideal world or an imaginary one, but because in a material sense they offer crucial information about the real, physical world. The stories Leslie heard and the ones she will tell about Dripping Springs contain essential knowledge, hidden by drought from direct observation, about this "place where she comes from."[14]

The letter to James Wright also teaches by example the importance of storytelling. In it Silko reflects on rooster stories told in her family, on the complicated genealogy of family and story through which she has inherited a particular rooster anecdote, and on the connection between rooster stories of the past, like the one about Aunt Lillie and Grandpa Marmon's rooster, and stories of her own rooster in the present (226–27). Like other brief self-contained passages in *Storyteller*, the letter fragment recapitulates in miniature the exuberant abundance of the whole book.[15] The letters to Inada and Wright also have a mediating function. Non-Indian readers learn that the text includes them. *Storyteller* addresses them (us) directly and holds out expectations for their (our) participation.

Implicit in the careful delineation of genealogy of story and storyteller is the related project of reclaiming Laguna (and other Native American) materials from outsiders who have appropriated them. Silko comments in *Storyteller* on ethnographers' collections of Laguna materials. Prefacing a redaction of a story told by her great-grandfather Marmon to Franz Boas and Elsie Clews Parsons, she maintains that "Boas, as it turns out / was tone-deaf / and the Laguna language is tonal / so it is fortunate he allowed Ms. Parsons / to do the actual collecting of the stories" (254). This emic critique of the ethnographic record aims to displace the authenticating function from the outsider—ethnographer, linguist, anthropologist—and reclaim it for the subject's own storytelling voice. The attribution of tone deafness that Silko makes here is problematic and contested, perhaps one more example of the divergence, disagreement, and argument inherent in "oral tradition." Whether or not the real Franz Boas was in fact tone-deaf, the vignette has a metaliterary as well as authenticating function: it can be read as a cautionary story providing implicit warning to the "tone-deaf" critic who, though perhaps well-intentioned, may engage in the colonizing activity of interpreting a work in ways inappropriate to its context.

The synthesizing activity required of the reader of *Storyteller* postulates a relational dynamic that requires maintenance of difference. That is, the text mediates Indian culture to the non-Indian reader precisely by its delineation of boundaries between Indian and non-Indian. Such boundary maintenance implies another project of reclamation and reinvention: the constitution of an Indian identity.

It is no secret that *Indian* is a construct of the non-Indian world. Anishinabe (Ojibwa) writer Gerald Vizenor deconstructs "the Indian" as an invention that European(ized) society uses to mask its failure to perceive the particular and the human.[16] Hopi linguist Emory Sekaquaptewa offers the notion "Indian" as a mediating agent, a bridge to be left behind in the encounter with specific tribal reality.[17] I see Leslie Silko's construction of "Indian" emerging in response to the perception of "non-Indian"; her embrace of Plains Indian and Cherokee as well as Laguna ancestors supports the self-construction of an "Indian" identity.[18] Thus Silko proposes to reappropriate the designation of "Indian" from within. *Storyteller*, by reinventing the stories and storytellers of Laguna culture and inventing the reader-listener for them, reclaims and reinvents "the Indian" as well.

Like the recuperation of Laguna texts long buried in anthropological volumes, Leslie Silko's invention of an Indian identity reasserts essential values that she distinguishes from and places over against the other, the Anglo—white—world. In affirming "Indian" as a meaningful concept, *Storyteller* finds the perceptible locus of difference in language. In particular the eight short stories in *Storyteller* examine difference in order to postulate Indian identity. The stories focus on protagonists and settings from different cultures: an Eskimo woman, an aged Navajo woman, a Laguna man visiting a Hopi village, a young soldier returning to an unspecified pueblo, the Apache Geronimo. These diverse characters share a perception of their difference from a powerful, threatening world that speaks a different language. The short stories of *Storyteller* de-center the non-Indian reader through language and point of view. Written in English, they are written against English. In every case the reader is inducted by way of the central consciousness into the world of the Other, the putatively marginal.

Kenneth Roemer points out how reconsidering supposedly marginal texts—his example being American Indian texts—can offer insight, available in no other way, into all literature.[19] Silko offers the figure of her great-grandfather Marmon, who is pictured in three photographs in *Storyteller*, as a paradigm for the kind of transformation she extols. All she knows of the man, she says, are the stories told in the family and the photographs in which "[h]e stands with his darker sons / and behind the wire-rim glasses he wore / I see in his eyes / he had come to understand this world / differently" (256). *Storyteller* asserts that stories provide for any reader the possibility of transformation into someone who "sees differently" that the author attributes to her great-grandfather.

This is the theme central to many of the contemporary story-poems in *Storyteller* as well as the retellings of traditional Pueblo stories. "The Storyteller's Escape" is one of Silko's own poem-stories, and it models the process of continuity and transformation by which stories are kept alive and handed on when people become storytellers. The speaker introduces an old woman and tells us that she "has been on every journey / and she knows all the escape stories" (247); the old woman has become a storyteller by, in her own words, "turning around / for the last look ... so I could tell where these dear ones stopped" (248). Pursued by enemies and weakened by age, the old woman cannot go on. But then a child repeats the old storyteller's act: "A'moo'ooh, the child looked back" (250). Through the child's act of sympathetic imagination, the old woman returns: "This is the story she told, / the child who looked back, / the old teller's escape—the story she was thinking of" (253). The old storyteller makes her way home as part of the child's account, to remain a living part of the community constituted by stories.

"The Storyteller's Escape," in the last pages of *Storyteller*, invites the reader back to Aunt Susie's story at the beginning of the book. In Aunt Susie's story the child, Waithea, escapes from her mother; she undergoes transformation into a story even as her clothes metamorphose into butterflies. In "The Storyteller's Escape" the old storyteller is transformed into her story even as the "child who looked back" becomes the storyteller. The process of transformation and return through "looking back" parallels Leslie Silko's own relationship to Aunt Susie: Silko invents herself as storyteller and author in the process of "looking back" at and reinventing Aunt Susie and her story.

The pluralistic society we live in, locally and globally, requires the contextualizing of utterances—written and spoken, authored and received—to make sense of discourse across many ethnic, religious, linguistic, and political boundaries. Indeed, it is by explicitly addressing the question of contextualization across these frontiers, I believe, that *Storyteller* reaches out from local, family, and culture-specific grounding to encourage its audience to seek to recover and reposition the essential fictions by which we all live. "Storytelling brings us together," Leslie Silko says, "despite great distances between cultures, despite great distances in time" ("Language and Literature," 72).

## Storyteller

"Storyteller," an arctic allegory set in the forbidding reaches of the Yukon River, seems a strange choice as title story for *Storyteller*, a miscellany suffused with familiar scenes of Silko's beloved Southwest and the intimacy of a family album. The chilling remoteness of "Storyteller," on the other hand, the anonymity of its characters and its lack of connection with the autobiographical or mythical materials in the rest of the book, indicates a special role for this story. Silko herself has noted that this story has a particular significance within the body of her work: "Nowhere is landscape more crucial to the outcome than in my short story 'Storyteller' " ("Interior," 44). This comment emphasizes the necessity of seeing all her fiction in relation to landscape and place.

Every place is in some sense contested ground, and this is nowhere more so than in places where people of different values, cultures, and lifeways live within what is supposed to be shared physical and cognitive space. Mary Louise Pratt has introduced the term *contact zone* as a way "to refer to social spaces where cultures meet, clash, and grapple with each other, often in contexts of highly asymmetrical relations of power, such as colonialism, slavery, or their aftermaths."[20] Since the fifteenth century the Western Hemisphere has been such a contact zone, and Silko's writings meditate on the exigencies of American Indian life within such geographical, political, cultural, and psychological borderlands.

While Silko comments on how "Storyteller" elaborates the concept of relationship between people and place, even to the extent of seeing the landscape as an essential character in the story, this short story also introduces other critical themes that pervade all her writing. Language is an abiding preoccupation, and "Storyteller" takes up language in two senses: the language of individual and communal self-creation that is storytelling, and the language—and silence—that creates boundary, identity, and personal power within a multidimensional, polyglot contact zone.

The text traces the thoughts and memories of a Yupik woman as she waits in a jail in the arctic bush to be interrogated regarding the death of a storekeeper. This place is a sparsely populated, climatically rigorous world where newcomers are all "Gussucks," a Yupik word derived from "Cossacks" and reflecting the historical fact of Russian traders, explorers, and missionaries having been the first Europeans to move in on the region. The landscape is so crucial that it comes to have the force of a character; Silko observes in her own commentary on the story: "The Yupik woman knows the appetite of the frozen river. She realizes that the ice and the fog, the tundra and the snow seek constantly to be reunited with the living beings that skitter across it" ("Interior," 46).

The fatal impotence of those who understand neither the land nor their own desire leaves them literally overwhelmed. A thoughtless urge to gratify his sexual cravings sends the Gussuck storekeeper heedlessly across the ice in pursuit of a woman he has assaulted. She, however, has seen that the man is so enslaved to his lust that he cannot withstand her manipulation of it. The storekeeper's personal desire expresses the overwhelming cupidity of the whole Gussuck world, a perverse malignity of longing and frustration. At the moment of his attack the woman remembers that "[h]e hated the people because they had something of value ... something which the Gussucks could never have. They thought they could take it, suck it out of the earth or cut it from the mountains; but they were fools" (29).

The desire to take, to appropriate, to consume drives the colonial enterprise even as it impels the individuals caught up in the corporate project, and a naive overestimation of their power proves to be their undoing. The demise of one storekeeper swept away by the current rushing underneath the river ice is but a single moment in the fate of the whole project, a destiny inscribed in the tracings of the disappeared drilling rigs: "But the imprints and graves of their machines were still there, on the edge of the tundra above the river, where the summer mud had swallowed them before they ever left sight of the river" (22–23).

As Kathryn Shanley's analysis demonstrates, "Storyteller" reveals how the relationship between sexual, material, and psychological covetousness lies at the heart of the colonial enterprise.[21] An insatiable and perverse lust to possess and consume urges the Gussucks to this inhospitable place. As the old man has explained to the protagonist, the outsiders first came for the fur-bearing animals and the fish. Their appetites have depleted these resources, he tells her, and "[n]ow they come for oil deep in the earth. But this is the last time for them" (22). Compressed within these ominous words are 400 years of colonization through trade, religious conversion, and resource extraction, from the first visits of Russian sailing ships through the construction of the Alaska pipeline. The old man's prophetic utterance returns to the woman's memory as she looks out the window of her jail cell and sees the sun about to glaze over in an apocalyptic final freeze.

The protagonist, on the other hand, is not greedy for material goods or for power over others. Rather, it is curiosity, a hunger for knowledge, that drives her. A restless inquisitiveness sends her to find out what the boarding school is like, regardless of the old man's warnings; curiosity and something resembling boredom take her in the direction of the Gussuck drillers: "She wondered what they looked like underneath their quilted goose-down trousers; she wanted to know how they moved. They would be something different from the old man" (20). The same impulse sends her back to the red-haired oil driller with whom she has copulated, so she can find out the particulars of his pathetic fetishism. Curiosity about sex, or about Gussuck life in general, is only one expression, and not the most important one, of her desire and need. In contrast to the acquisitiveness and power hunger of the Gussucks she encounters, it is hunger for knowledge, closure, and a fullness of understanding that motivates the girl. Most of all she yearns for a satisfactory account of her parents' death, for completion of the story her grandmother has told her in tantalizing fragments. In the end, she herself enacts the completion of the story and then turns to recount her experience and her parents' as her own story, assuming the storyteller's place left vacant by the death of the old man.

"Storyteller"—as the title suggests—offers a meditation on storytelling that continues throughout the whole of the book, as well as throughout Silko's writings and lectures. The short story "Storyteller" contains many stories within it, but most are presented in attenuated, fragmentary form. At the heart of the central conflict of the plot are the stories of how the protagonist's parents met their death. A storekeeper had given one explanation, it seems, but the woman's grandmother believes that his story is a lie; the grandmother tells "the story as it must be told" of how she tried unsuccessfully to convey the truth to the authorities. But the girl senses that the grandmother's story is unfinished, the explanation incomplete, and she continues to search for "something red lying on the ground" (27) that will satisfy her craving for explanation and closure. There are also competing accounts of the death of the man who pursues the protagonist: one story, which the protagonist's attorney wants her to tell, and the counterstory that she insists is the only valid account, the story that "must be told as it is" (31).

Another story, alluded to only briefly, is the old man's warning of what will happen to the young girl if she goes to boarding school; also briefly mentioned is the story he tells her of what will happen if she joins him in bed, a story that she eventually discovers is a lie. At the end of "Storyteller," the villagers who have come to see the protagonist listen to her begin a story in words implying that this will be the tale we have just read, enclosing its events within a circle of storytelling. Woven fragmentarily throughout the narration of "Storyteller" is the old man's story of the hunter and the bear; it seems to be an ancient story that somehow—it is not clear how—must be implicated in the sordid contemporary events involving the woman, her family, and the Gussucks. There is, finally, the whole story composed of and reflecting on all these stories, the text of "Storyteller" itself. The threads that link these stories together are the recurring motifs of language and identity, power and desire.

Throughout "Storyteller" the narrator returns to the old man's story involving a hunter, a bear, and a cosmic, encroaching cold that will swallow both. It is almost as if this story has a life of its own, as if it were enacting the obliterating power of the impending annihilation that is its subject: the story virtually consumes the old man as the years go by, until little remains of him but his rustling voice and the continuing narration. The impersonal narrator of "Storyteller" strews hints and summaries and commentaries on this tale throughout the text of "Storyteller," but never actually tells it. For instance, at one point the narrator quickly summarizes what it has taken the old man months to tell: "After all the months the old man had been telling the story, the bear was within a hundred feet of the man; but the ice fog had closed in on them now and the man could only smell the sharp ammonia odor of the bear, and hear the edge of the snow crust crack under the giant paws" (26). Following this synopsis the narrator comments on style; the old man tells the story one night "describing each crystal of ice and the slightly different sounds they made under each paw; first the left and then the right paw, then the hind feet" (26). In short, "Storyteller" offers the reader considerable information about this story, but never a textual performance. The story's presence in the text occurs only in the narrator's tracings of its absence.

This absence of story—of the old man's story specifically—is related to "Storyteller" 's interrogation of a crucial aspect of language: its essential mendacity. The references to the old man's story, even as that same story is withheld from the reader, point to the limits of language and in particular the limitations of the written word. Any pretense to exact reproduction of the old man's story within the pages of the book *Storyteller* would be a kind of lie. In the hypothetical case of a text that purported to perform or recreate the old man's narration within "Storyteller," the result would be a text like the many redactions of traditional stories published by anthropologists, linguists, and other researchers. The distortions in these texts are many, from the erasure of contextual and performative elements to the insufficiency of translation. Representing such a distorted text as a story, or as this or that person's story, prevaricates to the extent that absences, distortions, and interferences are ignored or concealed; it is just such attempts at cultural appropriation, as Shanley points out, that are implicitly critiqued and rejected in "Storyteller." The old man's story can never be truly told in "Storyteller," because the pages of a book are the pages of a book and not the presence of the old man, his voice, his language, and his performance. Hence, it is the absence of the man's story that is the story "without any lies," and it is this absence, this centripetal inertia, that continually draws the story back into silence, that preserves the integrity of the old man's storytelling and makes it a figure for the protagonist's unflinching resolution to maintain her own integrity no matter the cost.

A refrain of horror and disgust at lying runs throughout "Storyteller." Yet at critical moments the content of the lie is withheld or ambiguous. Of the old man the protagonist remembers that "sometimes he lied. He had lied about what he would do with her if she came into his bed" (20). He lied, but what the lie was remains ambiguous and problematic. Had he promised her pleasure and then been unable to perform? Or had he cajoled her with promises of innocent caresses and then turned to molest her? Before going off to school she had discounted the old man's warnings because "[s]he knew what he wanted" (19), but did she know because of what he said or in spite of his words?

Such fragmentary and disrupted narration enacts the failure of communication characteristic of the contact zones that Pratt describes. Just as the colonial imbalance of power deforms sexuality, it nullifies, distorts, or precludes communication. "Intercourse"—whether verbal or sexual exchange between consenting equals—cannot happen. The grandmother in "Storyteller" is convinced that "the priest did nothing" about the murder of the girl's parents (25). She can tell the girl no more, she says, because "[t]he Gussuck storeman left the village right after that" (25). The story is unclear as to when, or whether, the storekeeper returns. Is the man who pursues the protagonist across the ice the same person who had told her parents that the canned heat he sold them was safe to drink?

It is plausible to read two storekeepers in the story, as Danielson does (Danielson, 335). On the other hand, Silko writes that the protagonist "lures the murderer onto the river's ice" ("Interior," 45), implying a single storekeeper. The story itself is ambiguous, and silent on the question of what happened to the (first) storekeeper after the grandmother's accusation. Where did he go when he "went away"? To a trial? To prison? To another job? He simply disappears. This is the silence that characterizes the colonial contact zone, the indifferent silence of the powerful in which the frustrated rancor of the powerless festers, in arctic wilderness or inner city. Whether trial, prison, or other features of Gussuck justice would have been satisfactory to the grandmother or her family is moot. The gap between the powerful and the powerless opens a void of unappeasable yearning for remedy.

A brooding fatalism hangs over this haunting fable of cruelty, misunderstanding, and revenge. The anonymous characters seem fated to act out some archaic, unfathomable arctic myth. A disorienting instability of time and space contributes to the sense of myth. The story proper covers only a few hours—perhaps not even that long—as the protagonist waits in jail to appear before a judge. The narration follows the woman's consciousness as she pictures in her mind the events that have conspired to bring her to this place. As is typical of mental processes and the fictional forms that imitate them, the protagonist's memories and thoughts move back and forth through time, from her present situation in the literal darkness of late winter to her life at the edge of the village with the grandmother and the old man, the deaths of her parents, her experience of boarding school, the death of her grandmother, the old man's story and the knowledge he passes on to her, and her encounters with the Gussuck men around the village.

It is impossible to extract from this disrupted narration a clear chronology of events in the woman's life, nor is there any indication of how much time passes between episodes. The reader has no way of knowing how long after her parents' death and the storekeeper's disappearance it was that the protagonist heard the grandmother's story of what happened, nor how long again before she went to the boarding school, although apparently she was much older than the other students. How much time passes between her return from boarding school and the events that finally bring her to the jail? Critics often refer to the protagonist as a "girl," but she could be a mature woman: several times the story refers to years passing.

All this ambiguity about chronology and sequence contributes to the mythic, allegorical texture of "Storyteller." The characters—the grandmother, the old man, the storeman (or men), the jailer, the dormitory matron, the village people, and the protagonist girl/woman—all have the archetypal anonymity of mythical personages. The girl, her grandmother, and the old man, like the supernaturals of the old stories, live at a distance from ordinary human interaction. They are marginalized and isolated at the edge of the village, treated with suspicion but respected by the villagers as central in some mysterious way to the community's continuing life. The old man "had not fished or hunted with the other men for many years, although he was not crippled or sick" (19); this is strange and otherworldly behavior in a precarious subsistence economy. The villagers come to visit him, as if approaching an oracle or a healer, to listen to his stories and leave their offerings in exchange.

Kenneth Lincoln has sought a specific mythical connection for Silko's story in the Greenland Eskimo myth of the Mistress of the Sea as related by Knud Rasmussen.[22] In "Storyteller" the grandmother's rage and physical suffering do call to mind the powerful, angry, mutilated girl in Rasmussen's retold legend. However, the Greenland story pays homage to the elephant seal as a principal of fecundity and regeneration, a sense entirely absent from the apocalyptic vision of "Storyteller": the watery raptures of the Greenland shamans, who dive deep into the sea in their sacred trances, are unthinkable in the unnamed village of "Storyteller," which lies "many miles upriver" from a town that is itself upriver from the Yukon delta (18). In Silko's story, those who enter arctic waters drown. The quality of myth also tends to efface the question of whether one or two storekeepers are present in the story. In the end the "facts" about the number of storekeepers become secondary to what the story has to say about the endemic and corrupting rapacity of colonialism.

"Truth" is less important than story. Only once do we find the word *truth* in "Storyteller"—when the protagonist recognizes that "what the old man said was true" (20)—but as with the absence of so much of the stories that are alluded to, the text does not contain what the old man said, and so that particular truth is withheld. What "Storyteller" offers is a fundamental opposition not between lying and truth, but between lying and story. For the protagonist there is only one story that is not a lie. Her intransigent insistence on her truth as the only truth, her story as the only story, corresponds with her equally rigid insistence on her own language. In boarding school, she understood language as her defense against encroachment on her selfhood, and she recalls now how "the dormitory matron pulled down her underpants and whipped her with a leather belt because she refused to speak English" (19).[23] The assault on her language, carried out as a physical assault on her body, prefigures the Gussuck men's sexual deviance and the Eskimo jailer's reliance on English. She insists absolutely on her own language. In this character's ruthless refusal to compromise, there is potential for the heroic, even the tragic.

The dramatic potential in the text is qualified, however, by its intense focus on a single point of view. For all the story's mythic resonance, it is thoroughly modern in its strict reliance on the narrative device of unified point of view. The natural world of the story comes filtered through the liminal consciousness of the protagonist, whose awareness fixates on the apparently imminent disintegration of the whole of nature: "She told herself it wasn't a good sign for the sky to be indistinguishable from the river ice, frozen solid and white against the earth. The tundra rose up behind the river but all the boundaries between the river and hills and sky were lost in the density of the pale ice" (18–19). The passage echoes the sense of disorientation and loss of boundaries that Silko herself recalls from her experience of living in the region: "Here the winter landscape can suddenly metamorphose into a seamless, blank white so solid that pilots in aircraft without electronic instruments lose their bearings and crash their planes into the frozen tundra, believing down to be up. Here on the Alaskan tundra, in mid-February, not all the space-age fabrics, electronics, or engines can ransom human beings from the restless, shifting forces of the winter sky and winter earth" ("Interior," 44–45). This is what the protagonist pictures in the apocalyptic vision she has in her jail cell: "That was how the cold would come: when the boundaries were gone the polar ice would range across the land into the sky" (27).

This monotone world lacking outline, perspective, and landmarks reflects the problematics of moral navigation in the story. The storeman pursues the woman to his death apparently because he wants to violate her, which she attributes to his jealousy of the oil drillers she has been free with. Yet self-defense is an issue never raised by the attorney, who only mentions accident and the view that "her mind is confused" (31). She herself does not relate her actions to self-defense. Nor does craving for retribution figure as her motive. The realization of her project is the story she begins to tell to the villagers, a story that, like the old man's story of the hunter and the bear, will both fulfill and consume her.

The woman of "Storyteller" is like the boy Paul in Conrad Aiken's "Silent Snow, Secret Snow."[24] Both Silko's and Aiken's stories trace what appears to be a dissolution of consciousness, manifested in the perception of a disintegration of boundaries in a snow-filled world. Rage and longing mark these characters and set them apart from the quotidian world; neither the worrying parents and fatuous doctor in Aiken's story nor the bureaucratic functionaries—priest, jailer, attorney, matron—in Silko's are of any consequence in their worlds of primal, abject desire. Desire, absolute and uncontingent, grounds and permeates "Storyteller." The absence, silence, and negation that constitute desire move the story—as inexorably as the headlong rush of the doomed storekeeper, or the pathetic machinery swallowed into the implacable bog, or the disappearing sun—into the void of the absolute.

In her uncompromising repudiation of the Gussuck world the protagonist bears a strange resemblance to that other model of passive aggression as the sign of personal integrity, Herman Melville's Bartleby the Scrivener.[25] Like Bartleby, who "prefers not to" do one thing and then another, until it seems that existence itself impinges too heavily on his sense of self, the Yupik woman steadfastly resists interaction with the world on any terms but her own. It is true that the ending of "Storyteller" finds the woman telling her story to the villagers who have come to hear it, suggesting continuity and perhaps regeneration; however, the example of the old man, whose place she has taken, and who ended his own days like Bartleby, communing with no one but himself, qualifies that suggestion.

For the protagonist of "Storyteller," truth is single and absolute, and the only way for her to maintain identity and integrity is to set impregnable boundaries around her language, her story, and herself, excluding all that would compromise her isolate vision. She hears her grandmother's voice telling her that "[t]here must not be any lies" (26), and "I killed him," she says of the storekeeper, "but I don't lie" (31). There is no room here for ambiguity, compromise, contestation, revision, qualification, or any alternative possibility: this is a frozen certitude, as rigid and as lethal as the frost that threatens to immobilize the sun. The protagonist of "Storyteller" is an icon of essentialism, and the story is an allegory on the essentialist position, an allegory that will be tested and contested in the remaining stories in *Storyteller*.

## Lullaby

One of Silko's most poignant stories is "Lullaby," the second of the short stories in *Storyteller*. "Lullaby" is cast in the mode of pastoral elegy. The setting is the area near a bar located close by Cebolleta Creek, a short distance from the village of Cebolleta. The particulars of the landscape are rendered with characteristic fidelity to an actual place. Ambrose Lucero, whose grandmother is buried in Cebolleta, writes: "One way to get to Cebolleta is to take the highway through Laguna, an ancient, hilly pueblo. . . . Just to the northwest down the highway, at the foot of the huge lava cliffs that border Mount Taylor, lies the moonscape of the largest uranium strip mine in the world . . . and right beyond there lies the new mining town of Cebolleta."[26] To get to the site of the story, according to Robert Nelson, "[t]ake the road past Paguate to Bibo and, just past Bibo, Seboyeta (or Cebolleta—I've seen it spelled both ways on maps). You'll pass the bar on your left and, just off the road on the right, is Cebolleta Creek, running north to south."[27] The contrast between the majesty of Mount Taylor—one of the most sacred places in Navajo and Pueblo geography and a home of powerful spirits—and the squalid reality of bar, town, and open pit mine contextualizes the reverie of an elderly Navajo woman whose thoughts we follow as recollections from her past eddy through her consciousness.

It is a snowy winter evening, and the protagonist is waiting for her husband to return from a bar where he is purchasing wine with their government check. As snow continues to fall and evening draws in she looks for him in the bar, then finds him on the street. As they trudge along the road toward their home, she suggests that they rest; they climb part way up a hill and shelter from the storm under some boulders, waiting, the story suggests, for death. During the short period of time, perhaps two or three hours, in which these banal events transpire, the narration follows her reverie as she recollects many of the details of the life that has been lost to her and comes to terms with loss and grief. This poetic meditation is the substance of the story.

The protagonist is named Ayah, and she has much to grieve for. Her thoughts go back to the death of her eldest son, Jimmie, killed years before while fighting for the United States government in an unspecified, distant war; it could have been the Second World War, the Korean War, or the war in Vietnam. She remembers burying two other children who died in infancy. Her most vivid recollections are of her two remaining children, Danny and Ella, and how they were taken away from her while very young—still learning to talk—in an effort, apparently, to cure them of tuberculosis. Removal became permanent estrangement, effected by the loss of their language; Ayah remembers their inability to communicate with her because they no longer understood Navajo by the time they were returned for a visit. The duplicity with which the abduction of her children was accomplished had engendered an anger toward her husband, Chato, that led to a long and bitter estrangement. Finally, as the story ends, Ayah appears to confront and accept the most fundamental loss, her own imminent death.

The story portrays Ayah as realizing stages of grief as formulated by psychologists: denial, anger, despair, and, finally, reconciliation and peace.[28] She remembers the sense of unreality, disbelief, and denial that accompanied the death of her eldest: "It wasn't like Jimmie had died. He just never came back" (44). She recollects and relives the anger at herself and at her husband, who has mediated the hostile colonial world to her: "She listened to Chato sullenly; she hated him when he told her it was the old woman who died in the winter, spitting blood; it was her old grandma who had given the children this disease" (46). Despair followed, first in the anguish of loss and then in long years of numbing resentment. Even after the passage of many years, that original pain persists in her memory: "It was worse than if they had died: to lose the children and to know that somewhere, in a place called Colorado, in a place full of sick and dying strangers, her children were without her. . . . She carried the pain in her belly and it was fed by everything she saw" (47). As Ayah rises to search for her husband in the bar, she realizes the depth of her alienation from this man: "for forty years she had smiled at him and cooked his food, but he remained a stranger" (48). The word *mourning* repeats like a melancholy refrain through the story as these memories emerge into her consciousness. On this day, however, each recollection carries with it a sense of understanding and—finally—of peace.

Implicit in these human deaths is the more abstract, but no less felt, loss of heritage, culture, and lifeway. There will be no children and grandchildren to teach and nurture in the way her mother and grand-mother had educated and cared for Ayah. Art, religion, language, natural history—all is being lost. Even the sacred compact with the earth seems broken, as suggested by the persistent drought the story refers to. Once the land had produced all that the people needed—wool and bright dyes for strong, waterproof blankets; leather for leggings and shoes; meat hung on the rafters to dry in the spacious, orderly hogan. Now, in their old age, Ayah and Chato find themselves reduced to a drab Army blanket, boots with holes in them, and a meager welfare check that buys rice, sugar, tinned peaches, and a few hours of oblivion from a bottle of wine. The harshness and emptiness of present life correspond to the coldness of the alien society that surrounds the Navajo world. Clinical efficiency rather than feeling or tradition rules in the white world into which her children Danny and Ella have disappeared. His former employer keeps Chato on to be exploited and then discarded like a bro-ken machine. The indifference and arrogance that rule such a cold milieu stand in harsh contrast to Ayah's traditional reverence for the natural world, family ties, and continuing life.

Ayah's world has been contaminated and damaged by these alien ele-ments, which have entered her life by way of a language she has learned to hate. She has lost everyone close to her, and she sees the English lan-guage, speakers of English, and even her own literacy in English as the means of that loss. Proud of knowing how to sign her name, she had unwittingly signed the papers that allowed her children to be taken from her, and seeing the damage her literacy has accomplished, she has blamed her husband all the years since then "because he had taught her to sign her name. Because it was like the old ones always told her about learning their language or any of their ways, it endangered you" (47). Chato is trilingual, speaking Navajo, Spanish, and English, which according to conventional wisdom should be an asset for him. In reality, his expertise only gains him access to the bar where he can drink with the Spanish-speaking patrons: "The bar owner didn't like Indians in there, especially Navajos, but he let Chato come in because he could talk Spanish like he was one of them" (48). There is a world of Indian/European history in the reference, as there is in Ayah's knowl-edge that when she finds him he is likely to be "passed out at the bot-tom of the wooden steps" and that "all the wine would be gone and most of the money too, from the pale blue check that came to them once a month in a government envelope" (48). Ayah's mistrust of and contempt for Chato's willingness to interact with the outsiders by using their language is confirmed by the inhuman treatment the couple receives when Chato's employer orders them off the ranch because they are no longer cost-effective. "All of Chato's fine-sounding English talk didn't change things" (47).

The bar becomes a contact zone, in Pratt's meaning of the term, as Ayah enters it in search of her husband and endures the stares of patrons whiling away the evening listening to "Spanish polka music playing on the jukebox" (48). She is conscious of their looking at her "like she was a spider crawling slowly across the room. They were afraid; she could feel the fear" (48). The image triggers another recollection, and as she returns her attention to the bar, she again senses the patrons' fear: "She felt satisfied that the men in the bar feared her" (49). The men's point of view is suppressed in the story, and the episode is a moment overdetermined by the conflicting codes and mutual misapprehensions of all the people in the bar. We do not know if the men compare this old woman to a spider, any more than they can know the complex individual that readers see emerge in the revelations of her story. Yet the fear that Ayah senses in them must result, she knows, from their apprehension of the spider—even if they do not "see" the spider as she does.

The spider, called Grandmother Spider or Spider Old Woman, is a revered figure of wisdom for all the peoples of the Southwest. She is the creator: some stories tell how she spins the world from her body, and in other stories she creates things by thinking of them and naming them. Hence her other name among the Keresan-speaking people: Thought-Woman or Thinking Woman. She is all-powerful, and she inspires abject fear and obedience. In many of the stories told about her, Spider Woman rescues her children from dangerous situations by giving them stern warning and good advice. She is benevolent but terribly powerful; death comes to her enemies and those who ignore or disobey her teachings. Gladys Reichard prefaces her summary of Navajo Spider Woman stories with the note that "Spider Woman plays a dual role; she is sometimes helpful to man and at others a danger so great that she has to be subdued. She is a symbol of the textile arts, having taught man weaving."[29]

Silko's reverence for Thought-Woman is evinced in the verse prologue to her novel *Ceremony*, which recognizes Thought-Woman as the muse of the novel: "Thought-Woman, the spider, / named things and / as she named them / they appeared. / She is sitting in her room / thinking of a story now / I'm telling you the story / she is thinking."[30] The brief passage in "Lullaby" is a moment of critical truth for the reader of the story: the informed reader will understand how it is that she knows the men ought to fear her, whereas those who remain outside Ayah's frame of reference, like the men in the bar, will think they see only a delusional old woman.

Navajo iconography and culture permeate "Lullaby." Navajos (and Apaches) are the southernmost of the Athabascan-speaking peoples, related to the Dene of southern Alaska and western Canada, and they apparently entered the Southwest about 1,000 years ago. From their interaction with the Plains peoples and the Pueblo peoples of that region they added agriculture to their hunting-based economy, and later, after the arrival of the Spanish, they became expert in metalworking and sheep and cattle raising. Their extraordinarily rich and complex religious ceremonies were developed in the context of their interaction with the Pueblo peoples, and many of their myths, in particular their emergence story of creation, reflect Pueblo influences.

Silko reflects nostalgically at several points in *Storyteller* on amiable relationships between Lagunas and Navajos, remembering gift exchanges and Laguna hospitality (187, 202), and she herself taught for a short time on the Navajo reservation. She also notes that, historically, relations between Navajos and many of their neighbors have not always been quite so harmonious, recalling the story of Juana, the elderly nursemaid to Silko's grandmother, who had been kidnapped by slave traders in her childhood (88–89). Silko's emphasis on the positive side of Navajo/Pueblo relations, especially as experienced in her family, reflects the implicit development through the series of short stories in *Storyteller* of a multitribal "Indian" identity forged in response and resistance to the colonial experience.

"Lullaby" expresses the blending of the spiritual and the aesthetic so often noted by students of Navajo culture. At the opening of the story, Ayah hears the wind sing a Yeibichei song. The term *Yeibichei* is often translated as "Holy People," and Yeibichei, or Yei People, are comparable to spirits; they are powerful beings who inhabit sacred mountains, springs, and other holy sites, and they also represent certain natural forces. Their connection to sacred places is more than merely residential, however; in English they are sometimes designated as the "inner form" of a particular place, suggesting something more like a soul: for instance, "in the underworlds Wind came to the Peoples living there from the mists of light existing in the cardinal directions and . . . these mists also contained inner forms likened to human forms which were the breathing means of the mountains situated in the four directions."[31] Animacy is a fundamental category in the grammars of Athabascan languages, and Navajo philosophy and worldview regard the universe as essentially animate, or as theologians might say, ensouled. Yei People are powerful creators and healers, and so they are called upon in ceremonies, especially rituals for healing the sick or injured. A Yeibichei song is a sacred song in a religious ritual, and the song that Ayah hears in the wind suggests that her story may be understood as a healing ritual.

The lyrics at the end of "Lullaby" echo the form of English translations of many Navajo sacred songs in a structure of verse and repetition as well as in imagery of earth mother and sky father, rainbow sister and wind brother.

> The earth is your mother,
>     she holds you.
> The sky is your father,
>     he protects you.
> Sleep,
> sleep.
> Rainbow is your sister,
>     she loves you.
> The winds are your brothers,
>     they sing to you.
> We are together always
> We are together always
> There never was a time
> when this
> was not so.
>
>               (51)

Earth and sky figure in some of the sandpaintings that form part of the great Navajo healing rituals called chants or chantway ceremonies. A sandpainting is "a symbolic picture [that] is made by strewing finely powdered dry pigments on a background on the floor of the hogan."[32] Two printed reproductions of sandpaintings show Mother Earth and Father Sky side by side. They have broad, roughly diamond-shaped bodies. On the body of Father Sky we see the sun, moon, and constellations, whereas from the center of Mother Earth's body emerge the four sacred plants: corn, beans, squash, and tobacco. An anthropomorphic rainbow encloses them on three sides.[33]

Both rainbow and wind are profoundly important in Navajo philosophy, and like other phenomena their various manifestations are personified in story, song, and image. A phenomenon resulting from the fusion of light and water, the rainbow is a powerful icon of integration and synthesis. In myths and stories the rainbow frequently figures as a bridge or pathway between earth and sky, permitting deities or people—or both together—to move between the natural world and the other world of the holy people. The rainbow can represent the road or path to long life, prosperity, and beauty—concepts central to the Navajo ideal. According to Reichard, "Rainbows in a sandpainting are a prayer. They are protective . . . and they may be given to a hero to keep him safe"; she also describes a rainbow "only a fingerlength long" and another that "could be folded and carried in a pouch or blanket fold, but through supernatural power became long enough for any purpose" (Reichard, 586–87). Other stories and myths feature the Rainbow People, who play an important part in the myths and sandpaintings of the Nightway chant.[34]

The idea of winds as "brothers" would be familiar to traditional Navajos. According to McNeley's extensive discussion, the concept of wind in Navajo philosophy is highly charged and complex. Wind is associated with life and breath on cosmic as well as personal levels and is indeed an intimate link between the individual and the universe: "Wind is conceived of as a single phenomenon, a deity formed as it were of component Winds which exist all about and within the living things of the world" (McNeley, 17). The wind that launched creation is part of the indwelling animating principle within each individual. Winds, moreover, "speak" to the person, instructing in appropriate, good, and safe behavior. "It is Wind conceptualized as Little Wind or Wind's Child that is thought to be sent to Earth Surface People as Messenger of the inner forms of various natural phenomena" (McNeley, 30); "the Navajo traditionalist conceives, then, that the Wind with which he is born and the Winds that are sent from the four directions to take care of him work together as constituent parts of Holy Wind to protect him from harmful outside influences. By this means he is shown the right way to behave and is warned of dangers" (McNeley, 40). Such a description of wind elucidates the lines of Ayah's lullaby: the wind "singing" to a person would be offering advice and comfort in the most sacred and healing way.

Finally, the emphasis on four through the placement of these corresponding pairs expresses the importance of the number four in Navajo numerology. The number four "is the number of stability and balance, of orientation in this world and the upper and lower ones, and of completion and wholeness" (Sandner, 210). Many commentators have noted recurrences of four in the emphasis given to the four cardinal directions, the four sacred mountains, the four parts of the day, and the four seasons of the year. "There are numerous other ramifications. Human life has four stages; each person who needs a ceremony should have it repeated four times in his lifetime" (Sandner, 210). For the person who recognizes the iconic patterning in Ayah's song, its few lines evoke a world of spiritual vitality, aesthetic sensitivity, and behavioral complexity.

"Lullaby" as pastoral elegy concludes with a return to the ancient healing song and a reconciliation on many levels. Concepts of return and circularity recur in Navajo thought and iconography. The hogan, the traditional Navajo home, is a roughly circular dwelling constructed as a deliberate microcosm of the round earth; its east-facing doorway admits the first light of the sun each day, just as Changing Woman, earth mother of the people, admitted the Sun to conceive the hero Enemy Slayer. The quartered circle, representing the earth and the cardinal directions, figures in many sandpainting designs as a symbol of harmony in the universe. Pathways and motion are also important. The ideal life is conceived as a journey along the correct, fruitful, beautiful road (the pollen path or rainbow path) which will take the individual back to the original—that is, the perfect—harmonious balance with the universe. Though Ayah's brief journey to the bar and along the road home appears outwardly to be rambling and dreary, inwardly it is leading her to a "sacred place" where she will experience healing. Following the implications of this reading, we may consider that the story offers its own healing ritual, hinting of the great traditional ceremonies that restore the individual and community to harmonious balance.

The tragedy and pathos as well as the beauty of Ayah's journey are precisely that it is made as a purely interior voyage; she has neither the extraordinary attention and care that a chantway ceremonial involves nor the possibility of communicating her healing with surrounding family and neighbors. She and Chato have only each other and the past. They have already completed part of the circle in having moved back to the old stone hogan in which Ayah was born and later gave birth to her children. The contrasting descriptions of the hogan bracket the many losses that this elegiac story recounts. Ayah's memory of the birth of her first child, with her mother attending her in the stone hogan, is bound up with the scent of bee flowers and young willow on a peaceful summer morning, but in her old age, with no young lives continuing to emerge from this birthing place, the stone structure seems little more than a hovel, an "old hogan with a dirt roof and rock walls" more evocative of death and burial than of birth and continuity (49).

As snow fills her footprints, Ayah makes inward observations about Chato's boots and her own, first comparing her worn rubbers to the beautiful elk and buckskin leggings and moccasins the people formerly had, then chuckling inwardly at Chato's worn and sock-stuffed boots "like little animals up to their ears in snow" (50). Animals also figure significantly in Navajo thought and iconography. After their introduction by European settlers, domestic animals—sheep, goats, horses, cattle—sustained the traditional way of life, and wild animals have always been a special kind of people, powerful and wise, in a universe in which all creatures are related as family. Navajo grandfather Chauncey Naboyah offers his insight into this universe, in the lyrical pastoral film titled *Seasons of a Navajo*, when he says that he would not know how to feel if he had no animals to live with and care for.[35]

Traditional thought, however, is not a sentimental romanticizing of nature. The natural world can be harsh: the hawk circling over Ayah and her children as they hide parallels the government authorities who will return inexorably to take the children away. Animals, like the Yeibichei, are neither good nor evil, friend nor enemy, but powerful beings who, when approached properly, may bring blessings. At the end of the story, Ayah sees the clouds as horses in the sky, figures of tremendous beauty and power, bringing strength and death at once: "The clouds moved east. They were massive and full, crowding together across the sky. She watched them with the feeling of horses—steely blue-gray horses startled across the sky. The powerful haunches pushed into the distances and the tail hairs streamed white mist behind them" (51).

These horses call to mind the great horses that Sun and Moon ride across the sky, especially the strong blue-black horse of Sun. In the Navajo tradition, the sun has four great horses, one for each of the cardinal directions, and the black is the horse of the North: "This northern cardinal horse represents the night sky and is called Sun's 'black jewel' horse in one Navajo myth. Though darkness can be associated with dreaded forces and places of danger, night is not necessarily considered an evil time."[36] In a painting by Navajo artist Adee Dodge titled *Space Stallion*, the horse is a "mighty midnight horse, which stands in the center of the sky on what appears to be the upper circle of the rainbow. . . . [He has] white ears, flowing white mane and tail, and a strong, sturdy body—all characteristics which emphasize the animal's prowess and stamina" (Clark, 26). The horse and skill in horse breeding are special gifts of Sun to his hero child, Enemy Slayer, also called Monster Slayer. However, the story says that Sun's gift was initially not welcomed, and as a consequence Enemy Slayer had to undertake a long and arduous quest to win back this great prize and bring about the emergence of the first horses among the Navajo people (Clark, 43–52). The description of the horses in Ayah's musings suggest that she also is persevering on a heroic journey. One by one she has encountered her monsters of despair and suffering and anger and has come to terms with them. Yet, unlike the quest of Enemy Slayer, her journey is a tragic one in the sense that she has no one to receive the hard-won blessings she has gained. Her wisdom will die with her.

The focus on Ayah's inner life contrasts the richness, nuance, and complexity of her emotions and imagination with the squalid appearance she and her husband offer to the outside world. Poverty and alcoholism are bitter realities whether in the inner city or on the "rez"; "bag lady" and "wino" are callous labels the story interrogates and also challenges the reader to question. N. Scott Momaday's poem "Plainview: 2" offers a comparable portrait of the poetic soul within a person whom many would label as a derelict; the poem opens with the lines "I saw an old Indian / At Saddle Mountain / He drank and dreamed of drinking / And a blue-black horse."[37] The poem continues with a litany repeating the injunction "Remember my horse" wheeling, blowing, standing, hurting, falling, an incantation in the manner of translations of Navajo sacred poems.

The pathos of "Lullaby" should also be seen against the photograph in *Storyteller* of Silko's beloved great-grandmother, Maria Anaya Marmon—Grandma A'mooh—reading from a picture book to two little girls, the author's sisters, Wendy and Gigi (33). The photo images the connection of grandmother to grandchild, contrasting with the ruptured continuity of lullabies that Ayah reflects on in "Lullaby." Another parallel is suggested in a second photograph of Grandma A'mooh (211): the elderly woman regards the reader with patience and serenity as she pauses in her crocheting of fine lace, and the picture calls to mind associations with Spider Woman, spinner of wisdom and stories. These portraits of aged women in scenes of domestic harmony and personal tranquility gloss Ayah's story not only in their contrast with the ravages of loss and decline Ayah has endured but also in their silence. By relating Ayah's thoughts and memories to the reader, "Lullaby" breaks Ayah's silence and reveals her ceremony. In a sense, then, the text of the story contains some of the wisdom Ayah should have been able to transmit to the younger generations of her family, and the reader of the story has the opportunity to stand in the place of those grandchildren.

## Yellow Woman

N. Scott Momaday has said many times that we are who we imagine ourselves to be, and that the greatest of gifts is to imagine oneself richly. "Yellow Woman," Silko's most well-known story, is about a young woman who imagines herself richly. The narrator, a young mother living a placid if boring existence with her family in an unnamed Pueblo village, elopes with a handsome, masterful stranger. The story takes place over the course of two days, from her awakening beside her lover after a night beside the river to the following evening when she returns to her home. She appears to be caught up in a liminal world between reality and dream or myth, and one of the pervasive themes in the story is its examination of liminal states of consciousness and its interrogation of notions of choice, control, and decision.

The narrator experiences the fulfillment of wishes familiar to readers of romantic novels, playing out in her brief interlude the fantasy of an exciting anonymous encounter, unburdened by guilt or consequences. The theme of the young wife seduced by a glamorous (seeming) man is of course a classic in literature of the Western world: Anna Karenina, Emma Bovary, and Hester Prynne spring easily to mind. "Yellow Woman" also suggests the folk tradition of the robber-bridegroom, a motif as old as the story of Paris carrying Helen off to Troy. Folktales of seduction and abduction often function as cautionary tales intended to reinforce community values and proper behavior in young women. "Yellow Woman" plays against these familiar themes, finding in the Pueblo myths of "Yellow Woman" a perspective to confront the moralizing and didactic assumptions that readers may bring to the text.

The story furnishes timely and paradoxical critical dilemmas. Readers who view "Yellow Woman" through a lens of conventional sexual propriety often object to the absence of guilt on the part of the narrator-protagonist for her marital infidelity and the story's suggestion that her attitude and behavior are reasonable. Even though she believes her husband is filing a missing persons report with the police, she seems not only content to abandon child and family but assumes that her adventure will be welcomed as a story to be retold: "I decided to tell them that some Navajo had kidnaped me, but I was sorry that old Grandpa wasn't alive to hear my story because it was the Yellow Woman stories he liked to tell best" (62).

On the other hand, readers claiming allegiance to feminist perspectives may be disturbed by the abduction motif and the implied violence of a powerful, seductive male. At two points in the story the narrator appears more captive than lover. First, when she has awakened him to say good-bye, he compels her to go with him: "I walked beside him, breathing hard because he walked fast, his hand around my wrist. I had stopped trying to pull away from him" (56). Later, when she moves to halt their lovemaking he tells her, "You will do what I say," and then he carries on (58). This emphasis on potential violence, even a suggestion of rape, corresponds with the cautionary function of seduction stories, which warn young women about the expected consequences of promiscuity. Yet, just as the young woman anticipates no adverse outcome to her infidelity, the story offers no criticism of this masterful, demanding male. The reader who expects censure either of adultery or of inegalitarian male attitudes will be disappointed.

The archetypal model that the young woman turns to in explaining her predicament to herself is the traditional Keres figure of Kochininako, or Yellow Woman. LaVonne Ruoff has discussed the parallels between "Yellow Woman" and traditional Keresan abduction stories as recorded early in the twentieth century by Franz Boas and John M. Gunn.[38] Furthermore, Robert Nelson points out that besides hearing many traditional stories told by family members, especially women elders, while she was growing up, Silko had access to two collections of Laguna narratives, Boas's *Keresan Texts* and Gunn's *Schat-Chen*, which were available in the Marmon household and in other homes in the community.[39] Silko has denied making much use of written sources, expressing her primary indebtedness to the stories told to her by family members, sometimes the same individuals who had served as consultants to ethnologists. In sum, Silko had an abundance of references and sources to draw from in creating the avatar of Yellow Woman in her story. In *Storyteller* she calls attention to the connection by framing "Yellow Woman" between a brief story fragment on what Whirlwind Man said to Kochininako and two redactions of traditional Yellow Woman stories titled "COTTONWOOD Part One: Story of Sun House" and "COTTONWOOD Part Two: Buffalo Story."

Who is Kochininako? In the two stories Silko titles "COTTONWOOD," as well as in the lurid tale of witchcraft called "Estoy-eh-muut and the Kunideeyahs," Kochininako is a strong-willed, independent woman who acts on her own imperatives regardless of social convention, leaving husband and family to mate with Sun in one story, with Buffalo Man in another, and with a witch in the third. In the first story her union with the sun is necessary for the continuance of the seasonal cycle; in the latter two she is sacrificed, to bring about an alliance with the buffalo people and to break the hold of a drought.

According to Boas, Yellow Woman is one of four sisters, the other three being Blue Woman, Red Woman, and White Woman. When they are referred to as a group they are all called "Yellow-Women," and Boas maintains that "generically the girl heroes of all stories are called Yellow-Woman" (Boas, 218). In Pueblo iconography the colors of the four sisters are associated with other elements of the natural world such as butterflies or the four cardinal directions; most importantly they represent the colors of maize, and the sisters personify the essence of corn, the all-important source of the people's subsistence. Silko includes a notation of the four colors in the narrator's careful enumeration of the colors of cactus flowers: "I saw every color that a cactus blossom can be; the white ones and the red ones were still buds, but the purple and the yellow were blossoms, open full and the most beautiful of all" (60).

Yellow Woman is frequently fickle and unpredictable, and she often displays traits of self-will uncharacteristic of an upstanding Pueblo person. These attributes, of course, are part of her nature as a mythical personage who represents an elemental force of nature and who is not held up as a role model for young ladies. Yellow Woman's identity as corn-woman renders her the expression of the Keresan peoples as farmers who identify themselves as "people of corn." The odd combinations of fickleness and nurturance, selfishness and self-sacrifice of this character in the traditional Yellow Woman stories become more coherent and understandable when she is seen as the expression of a community that depends on its yearly corn harvest for survival in a highly precarious environment.

No less mysterious and also fraught with multiple possibilities is the identity of the young woman's lover in "Yellow Woman." The protagonist proposes both ka'tsina and Navajo as possible identities for this charismatic stranger who calls himself Silva. In the pueblos, ka'tsinas are among the supernatural beings closely identified with natural elements, especially with clouds and rain; a ka'tsina can also be the spiritual essence or personification of an animal or a natural force.[40] For many years, ka'tsina ceremonies at Laguna and other Keresan pueblos have been closely guarded; women of the pueblo and all outsiders are excluded from many ceremonies.[41] Ruoff points out several potential ka'tsina identities for the man called Silva, but the narrator does not name any specific ka'tsina. She compares her experience to that of Yellow Woman who "went away with the spirit from the north" (56), and she and Silva ride northward high into the mountains to the lava and adobe house that, it is implied, is the place where Silva lives. At another point in the story she speculates on a possible human identity for her lover, and she wonders "about this man who could speak the Pueblo language so well but who lived on a mountain and rustled cattle. I decided that this man Silva must be Navajo, because Pueblo men didn't do things like that" (58).

The "COTTONWOOD" stories, which follow "Yellow Woman" in *Storyteller*, suggest another connection for Silva. "COTTONWOOD: Part One" tells how Yellow Woman journeyed away from her family and village and eventually encountered and mated with Sun. There are intimations that link the mysterious Silva with the sun. When the narrator steps outside the house after eating with her lover, she describes herself as alone in the sky: "I was standing in the sky with nothing around me but the wind," and her lover reiterates the cosmic perspective: "From here I can see the world" (57). The next day, after she finds her lover gone, she eats the food he has left behind: apricots that have been dried in the sun, their color and sweetness associated with the height of the summer season and the fullest presence of the sun. The narrator also remembers the stories about Yellow Woman in which the heroine gives birth to twins. Gunn retells a story in which Yellow Woman bears twins after having married and then escaped from a terrifying abductor who lives high on a cliffside, and another in which a young hero discovers that he is the son of Yellow Woman and Sun and seeks his father in Sun's mountaintop home (Gunn, 143–52; 161–65).

Yet one more parallel in legend and myth resonates in the person of this mysterious man. In many traditional stories about Yellow Woman her husband or suitor is a young man called Arrow-Boy or Arrow-Youth. The second of the "COTTONWOOD" stories in *Storyteller* tells how Arrow-Boy pursued Yellow Woman after she had gone to live with the buffalo people. As his name indicates, Arrow-Boy's métier is hunting, and he moves with ease among the game animals. Silva the cattle rustler is also a hunter, his prey being the bovine game that have displaced the earlier game animals within the hunting grounds belonging to the Pueblo peoples.

If it is not possible to assign a determinate identity to this mysterious figure, it is likewise impossible to discount or ignore any of the various identities that the story speculatively tries out for him. In this world of half myth, half dream, identity is fluid and metamorphic rather than fixed or static, simultaneously indeterminate and overdetermined. It is the possibilities the stranger raises that are important to the narrator and the story she is weaving, and it is the abundance of these possibilities that enriches her imagining.

As in Silko's other works, landscape and place are of great importance. "Yellow Woman" is not set within the orderly tilled fields and compact houses of the village. Rather, the protagonist has met her lover in a boundary area, along the river, and the two of them fulfill their tryst in a mountaintop retreat. Patricia Clark Smith and Paula Gunn Allen point out the significance of wilderness to Silko and other Native women writers. They compare "Yellow Woman" with traditional stories of human encounters with supernaturals and explain that identifying the masterful lover with the earth and with a particular geography is all-important: "The human protagonists usually engage willingly in literal sexual intercourse with the spirits who simultaneously walk the land and embody it. This act brings the land's power, spirit, and fecundity in touch with their own."[42] Silko does not name the pueblo that the narrator calls home, but the woman's description of the terrain and the places named indicates that their journey takes them through the volcanic foothills of Mount Taylor, which lies northwest of Laguna, and up into the heights of this most sacred of mountains to the Keresan peoples. As they start out for Marquez, a small town northeast of the mountain they have climbed from the south, she notes their pathway "on a narrow ridge that was steep on both sides like an animal spine" (60), and she looks out to see the land fall away into vast distances on either side; they are just east of the continental divide, the defining member that centers the landmass of the western continent. The protagonist's intercourse with the man called Silva involves her in a profound and centering union with both the immediate terrain and the earth itself.

While following the possibilities raised by the multiple layers of cultural content in the story, it is imperative to keep in mind that the entire event is portrayed as it is filtered through the consciousness of the first-person narrator. Much of the story's ambiguity and open-endedness results from this filtering. The protagonist's inner monologue weaves together different planes of reality: game or story; everyday prosaic existence; and magic, myth, or the supernatural.

Shortly after the story opens, the two characters allude to a role-playing framework for their tryst the previous evening. There are hints that the young woman initiated the game, as her lover reminds her that "[l]ast night you guessed my name, and you knew why I had come." In response she attempts to undo the game of role-playing and storytelling and move back to the everyday: "But I only said that you were him and that I was Yellow Woman—I'm not really her—I have my own name and I come from the pueblo on the other side of the mesa. Your name is Silva and you are a stranger I met by the river yesterday afternoon" (55). But she finds that, contrary to her expectations, the end of the previous day's role-playing game does not mean a sure return to the familiar everyday world. Instead, she is drawn into an experience of ambiguity and unpredictability that she continually attempts to interpret.

The narrator's uncertainty of perception through much of the story evolves from an initial indecision. At the opening of the story she awakens beside her lover and determines to return home; she then walks to the corral, leads out her horse, shuts the gate, and mounts the horse. At this point she "remembered him asleep in the red blanket" (54) and immediately undoes all her previous actions: she dismounts, tethers her horse, and walks back to rejoin her sleeping lover. It seems that the memory of her partner asleep in the red blanket can do what the actual sight of him earlier could not, that is, compel her to return, not to reconstruct the role-playing of lovers' games nor to rejoin the mundane world of her family, but as she obscures the tracings of their footprints by the river, to enter into a new and far more precarious reality.

From this point to the moment when the couple meets the rancher on the trail, the narrator is engaged in constant speculation, attempting to interpret the reality she has entered, including a questioning and redefining of her own identity. She tries out potential identities for her lover: he is just a man named Silva, he is a ka'tsina, a mountain spirit, he is "only a man—some man from nearby" (56), he is a trickster-seducer, he must be a Navajo cattle rustler even though he speaks "the Pueblo language" (58). More intriguing still is the narrator's uncertainty regarding her own identity. She is not Yellow Woman, she insists, because Yellow Woman's mythical world only existed in "time past and I live now and I've been to school and there are highways and pickup trucks" (56). She wonders whether the traditional stories are really about an actual woman like herself who discovered that she was Yellow Woman, and whether she may be on the verge of making a similar discovery as to her own identity. As the man called Silva pulls her along she imagines that someone else will appear on the scene to rescue her, not from abduction but from uncertainty about herself: "I will see someone, and then I will be certain that he is only a man—some man from nearby—and I will be sure that I am not Yellow Woman" (56). Amid these speculations she envisions the family she has left behind at home, imagining their interpretation of her absence as based on the same kidnapping motif that she is invoking. Her imagination attributes to Silva the initiation of their role-playing game, which earlier they both acknowledged had originated with her.

Matching her uncertainty about what kind of reality she finds herself in and the nature of her own character is the abundance of imaginative possibilities she can entertain as she goes about "imagining herself richly." The treatment of identity boundaries as fluid, provisional, even improvisational, parallels the interpenetration of different planes of reality—game or role-play, myth or dream, and quotidian material life—also familiar in classical texts like *A Midsummer Night's Dream*. "Identity" is not a fixed essence, and "reality" cannot be pinned down as some stable, preexistent entity.

The narrator's internal monologue of trying out provisional speculative identities corresponds with the role-playing that she and her lover engage in. Early in the story Silva reminds the narrator that they had, as it were, assumed the masks of Yellow Woman and her spirit lover and framed their tryst within the contours of the ancient myth. But, as Emory Sekaquaptewa reflects regarding the ka'tsina masks, such role-playing can actually be constitutive: "I am certain that the use of the mask in the kachina ceremony has more than just an aesthetic purpose. I feel that what happens to a man when he is performer is that if he understands the essence of the kachina, when he dons the mask he loses his identity and actually becomes what he is representing" (Sekaquaptewa, 39). Sekaquaptewa's observation suggests a reading of "Yellow Woman" that sees the lovers' game or role-playing become a gateway, a performative opening between the material and spiritual worlds.

Just such a turning point into a new reality occurs in "Yellow Woman" when the protagonist awakens in the mountaintop house where they have spent the second night of their encounter. Her mysterious lover is gone, and she even questions his reality, looking around for "some proof that he had been there" (58). Once again the protagonist determines to leave this man and return home. However, she stops to eat the sundried apricots. Here is a motif resonant from folktales worldwide, from Proserpine and the pomegranate to Pueblo witch-wife stories in which eating is a part of the initiation into witchcraft: the act of eating seals the individual's allegiance to an alternate mode of reality, whether the Greek land of the underworld or the perverted spiritual reality of witchcraft.[43] The narrator eats, she drowses, she calls into question the reality she has been defending: "I didn't believe that there were highways or railroads or cattle to steal" (59). When she wakes she relinquishes the last vestige of obligation to return home, rationalizing that her child and husband will be taken care of and that she will be transformed into myth, that "there will be a story about the day I disappeared while I was walking along the river" (59).

She has committed herself to the world of myth, story, and dream, the world that belongs to her lover as mountain spirit, and she sees herself become part of the tradition that lives in the stories about the adventurous and strong-minded Yellow Woman. Her story will enter the world of stories, and in so doing, it will vindicate her experience, validate her most important reality. There is a change in the demeanor of the protagonist and the relationship between the two lovers after she decides that going home "didn't seem important any more" (59). Now it is Silva who waits for her, and instead of making demands asks whether she will come with him. What had been a seduction, even an abduction, has come to look more like a partnership of equals.

Even as the narrator and her story have arrived at this new dynamic, their incipient community is disrupted by a hostile outsider; the world of "trucks and highways" comes to meet them in the person of a portly horseman, perhaps one of the Texans whose ranches Silva had showed her from the mountaintop. Drawing upon another myth tradition, we can see this couple as having created their own Garden of Eden uncontaminated by sin or guilt. The rancher intrudes upon that prelapsarian microcosm, bringing ugliness, hostility, and possible death.

Corresponding to the change in mood from idyll to dramatic confrontation is a radical change in the narrator's interpretive strategies. Whereas her sense of herself and, even more, of her lover has been tentative, questioning, and hypothetical through most of the story, she asserts univocal certitude regarding the unknown rancher's feelings, motives, and apparel. When Silva speaks to her she determines that the rancher is angry, and he is angry, she asserts, not on account of theft, destruction, trespassing, or any crime, but because of language. Language difference is multilayered. Silva, who "speaks the Pueblo language so well," uses that language to protect her from the rancher: "Go back up the mountain, Yellow Woman" (61); this is also the language that confirms her identification with the legendary Yellow Woman of adventure, risk, and daring. She then attributes the rancher's anger to his inability to understand their language: "The white man got angry when he heard Silva speak in a language he couldn't understand" (61). She goes on to reason that the man is unarmed, deducing this from a complicated analysis of his inner state of mind and an a priori expectation regarding his behavior: "The rancher must have been unarmed because he was very frightened and if he had a gun he would have pulled it out then" (61).

Certitude like this about events beyond knowing is characteristic of the unreliable narrator, and paradoxically moves this abrupt confrontation with the prosaic real world into a realm less certain than the dreamlike, almost magical, lovers' encounter. Everyday facts are now much more equivocal than imaginary constructs. The outcome of the confrontation remains ambiguous: "I think four shots were fired—I remember hearing four hollow explosions that reminded me of deer hunting. There could have been more shots after that, but I couldn't hear them. . . ." (61). Who or what was shot, or even if there really were gunshots, is part of the already receding liminal world the protagonist is leaving behind to return to the mundane milieu of husband, mother, grandmother, and the making of Jell-O.

A final turning point occurs in the story when the narrator literally turns around to look back to where she had left Silva and the rancher. After she hears the supposed gunshots, she chooses the downward path toward home, rather than the path Silva had told her to take "back up the mountain" (61), and she chooses it "because I thought it was safer" (61). "Safety" and "danger" are by this point in the story as ambiguous as all else: if her assumption is correct, that only Silva is armed, and if she really does hear shots, then from whom does she need to be safe? The answer to that question will have to wait for another story. Meanwhile, as the narrator prepares to enter her house, she is constructing yet another script for her adventure, a story that will, she assumes, satisfy the curiosity of the family that appears to be carrying on quite satisfactorily—as she had envisioned on the mountaintop—with their own everyday activities.

## Tony's Story

All of the short stories in *Storyteller* depict some version of Pratt's contact zone, the psychological/intellectual/physical borderland where different cultures lay claim to the same space. The ways in which colonizing projects have played out in such contact zones often show up in Silko's stories by way of small details: a bottle of perfume, the rusting hulk of a car, a drink of Kool-Aid. "Tony's Story" takes these conflicts as its central subject; the story asserts a stark and incisive critique of the power inequities of colonial structures.

"Tony's Story" opens on a scene of amiable multicultural synergy that mixes not only different religious traditions but sacred festival and secular carnival. It is the feast of San Lorenzo (Saint Lawrence), 11 August, and the pueblo is celebrating. People chat as they wait to buy hamburgers and soda pop, melons and chili, at refreshment stands. Some ride the Ferris wheel or merry-go-round. A group of men carries the statue of Saint Lawrence in slow procession around the village and back to its niche in the Catholic church. Inside the kiva, the sacred center of the Pueblo village, other men are preparing for the Corn Dance to be held the next day. Loud, boisterous talk and open imbibing of alcohol suggest that rules of behavior seem to be relaxed or infractions tolerated.

However, it soon becomes clear that these carnival festivities really mask endemic hostility and violence, and that lopsided power relationships remain rigid. The first of three violent encounters in the story occurs when a non-Indian police officer suddenly and without provocation attacks and seriously injures a young serviceman named Leon who has recently returned to the pueblo. Leon's friend Tony, the narrator of the story, witnesses the attack and is one of the men who accompanies Leon to the emergency room of an Albuquerque hospital. The entire incident takes place wordlessly; even when the tribal police ask the attacker what took place, "the big cop didn't answer" (124).

The policeman's behavior exhibits an irrational malevolence, a "motiveless malignity" that links this character with other literary types of pure evil; he reminds us of an Iago or a Claggart. The two young men at the center of the story, Leon and Tony, offer reason and faith, respectively, as ways of accounting for the reality of pure evil. As an ex-serviceman, familiar with the institutions and theories of the Western culture that has presumably produced the malevolent policeman, Leon should be able to deal with the officer: he is aware of "rights," he is familiar with procedures, he believes in the effectiveness of committees, meetings, and letters to higher authorities. Moreover, having been a soldier, he is willing, when persuasion and rhetoric fail, to enforce his rights with his .30–30. Logically, he should be better equipped for this conflict than the shy, fearful Tony, who believes that the officer is a witch and who wears an arrowhead amulet as protection. Nevertheless, it is Tony who understands the difference between crime and evil, between lawlessness and sin.

The story's meditation on the distinction between crime and sin is comparable to Melville's probing of the same theme in *Billy Budd*, and the parallel between the two stories is worth pursuing. Both are "inside narratives," as Melville subtitled *Billy Budd*, stories that offer an insider's view on a historical event and the way it is perceived. Both probe the psychological dimension of the public event, Melville through the narrator's reflection on the relationship of an act of involuntary manslaughter to a widespread mutiny, and Silko through the device of telling the story through the first-person narration of one of the principals. In *Billy Budd* Melville's narrator makes an explicit contrast between the "inside narrative"—supposedly a true or real account—and the erroneous "newspaper accounts" of the events aboard the *Indomitable*. Such a contrast remains unstated in the text of Silko's story but, as Lawrence J. Evers has shown, can be seen in comparison of the story with newspaper reports of the historical event on which "Tony's Story" was based.[44]

At the center of each story is a triad of characters emblematic of elementary principles the authors have set forth for examination. The clearest parallel is between the anonymous police officer in "Tony's Story" and the mysterious Claggart, who as master-at-arms of the *Indomitable*, acts as a police officer with ominous powers for "operating to the mysterious discomfort" of the sailors subject to his authority (Melville, 32). In "Tony's Story" the officer's irrational hatred of Indians is sui generis, just as Claggart's insane hostility to the young seaman Billy Budd has no perceptible source. The same evil that Melville calls "the mania of an evil nature . . . a depravity according to nature" is what Tony, in Silko's story, labels as witchcraft: unmotivated, irrational, and intractable evil (Melville, 40).

Coincidentally, in both men an ominous abnormality in the appearance of their eyes is a physical sign of their evil. Tony notes several times that the police officer's eyes are never visible behind his dark glasses. Although Tony has been warned not to, he strains unsuccessfully "to look beyond the silver frosted glasses" (126). The officer appears in the young man's dream as a character from the traditional tales of witches who use sacred paraphernalia and power to do evil: "He didn't have a human face—only little, round, white-rimmed eyes on a black ceremonial mask" (125). The disfigurement of Claggart's eyes at the moment of his slander of Billy Budd likewise signifies dehumanization: "those lights of human intelligence losing human expression, gelidly protruding like the alien eyes of certain uncatalogued creatures of the deep. The first mesmeric glance was one of serpent fascination; the last was as the hungry lurch of the torpedo-fish" (60).

The parallels extend to two other sets of characters. As a representative of rational man and belief in the power of societal institutions like law and government, the young soldier Leon is comparable to Captain Vere. The salient difference, and one fundamental to Silko's examination of colonial power structures in this story, is in the power assigned to each. Vere belongs to the ruling elite, and on board his ship he has absolute power. Leon, on the other hand, appears to lose whatever prestige his uniform may have gained for him in the larger society when he returns to the pueblo; however, he retains a faith (which appears naive within the context of this story) in his ability to call upon the institutions of United States law and government to protect him and his rights.

The faith of Leon in civil rights and legal remedies has a counterpart in Captain Vere's respect for the rational, orderly world of human law. In both stories, legal sanctions cannot prevail against an intellect or will that is able to subvert power and manipulate institutions. Law can deal with crime, and rational sanctions can punish transgressions of society's rules, but when confronted with sin, law has neither explanation nor remedy. The point is reiterated several times in *Billy Budd,* as when the narrator recommends the Hebrew prophets over doctors or scientists for understanding the "mysteries of iniquity" (Melville, 41). In a similar way, Leon's contempt for Tony's credulity and trust in an arrowhead amulet disturbs Tony, who perceives dangerous shortcomings in Leon's ready assumption that he can deal with the officer's "mystery of iniquity" through rational means. "I couldn't understand why Leon kept talking about 'rights,' because it wasn't 'rights' that he was after" (127).

The characters of Tony and Billy are the remaining members of each triad. Both Tony and Billy Budd are associated with non-Western, pre-Enlightenment culture. Leon criticizes Tony as naive and primitive, someone who has been "brainwashed" (127). Likewise, Melville portrays Budd as "Natural Man," comparing him to the sight of an African "Noble Savage": "a native African of the unadulterate blood of Ham," garishly handsome and beaming with "barbaric good humor" (Melville, 10). However, while Leon may regard him as primitive, Tony is no "noble savage" but rather a quiet, thoughtful young man who is an integral part of a highly evolved society. Tony's apprehension of the preternatural powers of the police officer are diametrically opposite to the naive trust of a Billy Budd.

Both Tony and Billy share a failure of language at a critical point in their respective stories, and that failure is linked to their incapacity to deal on equal terms with perversion of language. Each man appears to have very limited access to the language in which power is exercised: Billy Budd is illiterate and Tony—according to Leon—has limited English proficiency. When confronted with evil in power, these men are literally dumbfounded. At the respective critical moments, faced with the impossibility of reasonable communication, each acts instinctively and without premeditation. Billy's ability to communicate verbally having been literally paralyzed, he lashes out to land the single blow that kills his tormentor. Tony likewise acts spontaneously, as if in a dream or trance: "The shot sounded far away and I couldn't remember aiming. But he was motionless on the ground and the bone wand lay near his feet" (128).

In its treatment of the colonialism theme, "Tony's Story" can be read as a commentary on the issues raised in *Billy Budd*. In the military world of Melville's novel an absolute chasm between higher and lower classes parallels the power inequities of colonialism in "Tony's Story." Absolute power is invested in the ship's captain, and the elite officer class enjoys a share in power that is categorically unattainable to the ordinary seamen. Although crude and arbitrary, the system appears to have the virtues of intelligibility and unambiguity. However, it is vulnerable to the evil of a man like Claggart who can disrupt its transparency by manipulating the powerful and virtuous: a Claggart can coerce a Captain Vere to implicate himself in the very injustice he is charged with correcting. Such is the fundamental weakness of any system that tries to cloak power inequity in the trappings of reason and law.

In "Tony's Story," power inequity resides in distinctions of race and culture, rather than class, and maintains itself in the institutions of colonial regulation. The story depicts a typical colonial setup of ostensibly parallel governmental institutions: a tribal police force to enforce tribal laws while state police take care of their responsibility, a local pueblo governor theoretically independent of the state's governor, tribal prohibition statutes even stricter than state liquor regulations. The analogy breaks down, however, when it comes to the military: Leon has served in the United States Army, but there is no parallel Pueblo army. The absence is significant. Power is sham in puppet governments; they are powerless except as surrogates for the colonialist enterprise. In "Tony's

Story" tribal government is impotent: the elders are unable to call the officer to account for his actions; they can only write letters to some distant authority. The Pueblo tribal government portrayed in "Tony's Story" fits the description of British tribal rule in Africa: "indirect rule, established by the British in Africa, where the government recognized tribal entities and ruled through chiefs and tribal councils."[45]

The colonial enterprise in "Tony's Story" is arbitrary and apparently motiveless. The Pueblo village does not seem to be the site of resource extraction, indentured servitude, or sweatshop exploitation as the usual picture of a colonized community would show. Rather, this Native community functions within the colonialist scheme as waste dump, designated receptacle for whatever is classified as contaminated or undesirable to the colonizer. There is a long tradition of assigning such a role to colonized space, reaching back to British and French penal colonies in Australia, Georgia, or tropical islands suitable for the human outcasts of London and Manchester and Paris. The United States has continued the practice in its own policies. In recent history, during World War II, the federal government set up its concentration camps for Japanese Americans on Indian reservations, thus bringing together in space labeled as "empty" those people whose national origins or racial designation assigned them to marginalization and expendability. At the present time the perception of Indian communities as appropriate receptacles for waste is literally realized in the function of several as dump sites for nuclear and poisonous waste.

In "Tony's Story" it is the police officer who functions as the "hazardous material" consigned to the "exile" of this seemingly out-of-the-way village. The officer complains that he has been sent to this location because of some implicit character defect: "I don't like smart guys, Indian. It's because of you bastards that I'm here. They transferred me here because of Indians. They thought there wouldn't be as many for me here. But I find them" (126–27). Like many another dysfunctional bureaucratic operative, this man has been exiled to a location that might have been purposely selected for its apparent lack of resources to deal with his problems. Within the contact zone of "Tony's Story" the police officer remains the sole representative of the non-Indian world.

In the middle of the nineteenth century, George Copway, an Ojibwa historian, described the same situation on the Great Lakes frontier: "In their intercourse with the frontier settlers [Indians] meet the worst classes of pale faces. . . . This is not to be wondered at when it is generally known that the frontier settlers are made up of wild, adventurous spirits, willing to raise themselves by the downfall of the Indian race. These are traders, spirit-sellers, horse thieves, counterfeiters and scape-gallowses, who neither fear God nor regard the laws of man. . . . The Indians come in contact with such men, as representatives of the American people."[46] Whether drawn by the absence of legal restraints or sent involuntarily as punishment for transgression, the same type of people constitute the colonizing avant-garde: the lawless, the opportunistic, the deviant and dangerous. The malevolent, anonymous police officer of "Tony's Story" is one of these "scape-gallowses" who "neither fear God nor regard the laws of man." Someone, somewhere, had selected the Pueblo as a receptacle for this social and professional misfit.

Although the use of first-person narration throws emphasis on internal monologue and the questionable reliability of perception, "Tony's Story" is structurally the most dramatic of Silko's stories. After the initial stage setting and the introduction of the two protagonists, the story proceeds through three "acts," each centered on an exchange between Tony and Leon and the unnamed officer. The story's symmetry invites a moral reading in the terms of retributive justice: the officer's savage attack on Leon in their first confrontation eventually begets the brutality the policeman suffers in their third encounter. Between these violent encounters occurs the only verbal interchange between the officer and the two Pueblo men he has been harassing, and in it language is the signifier for the ignorance and misunderstanding that underlie and reinforce distortions of power. The officer asks a question that is at the least rude, and that may be a demand for privileged information to which he has no right: "What's your name?" The man's tone paralyzes Tony and renders him mute: "His voice was high-pitched and it distracted me from the meaning of the words" (126). This reaction to irrational attack resembles Billy Budd's mute struggle to articulate when confronted with Claggart's lie.

Leon invents a language deficit to ameliorate the situation: "He doesn't understand English so good" (126). The response is well suited to appease a powerful adversary in a colonial context: it reduces the individual characterized as language-impoverished to a condition of immaturity or even subhumanity and implicitly plays into the paternalistic colonial paradigm. Regardless of his assertion of rights and of being just as good as anybody else, Leon's statement offers an object lesson in the survival skills needed to negotiate the colonial experience. The explanation, of course, is false; the issue is not unfamiliarity with any specific language but the inadequacy of language itself. Tony's temporary loss of language, of *logos*, is a response to the fundamentally *illogical* bind he is in as a reasonable person subjected to the demands of an unreasonable but powerful interrogator. He cannot speak because there are literally no words appropriate to his situation.

In discussing the historical event on which "Tony's Story" is based, Evers points out the apparent inappropriateness of the young men's reactions when they take individual, unilateral action instead of referring their suspicions about the officer's witchcraft to tribal elders. Leon is the one who appeals to the tribal council, but on the basis of rights and legality rather than to seek a remedy for witchcraft. Tony, on the other hand, internalizes his anxieties and suspicions, rationalizing that "even to speak about it risked bringing it close to all of us; so I didn't say anything" (127). It may seem as if fear overcomes judgment. However, the story's implicit characterization of the tribal government as a surrogate for colonial governance leaves no body of elders in the story for Tony to consult on a matter as serious as witchcraft.

Silko's own comment on witchcraft and her depictions of it in her writings indicate that she sees belief in witchcraft as a product of societal stress: "When a community is, in the catch phrase, together, where things are fairly orderly, where the livestock and the food supply is good, where some widespread series of deaths of religious leaders hasn't hit, where everything is in good shape within the pueblo view, then there's not going to be any witchcraft."[47] Evers discusses the elements specific to Pueblo witchcraft as delineated in the story, and notes that Silko emphasizes the persistence of cultural belief (Evers, 252–56 passim). It is also important to see that she situates that belief within a particular set of political circumstances. It is not possible to account for the moral dilemma of a Captain Vere without considering the larger issues of the systemic injustice in war and empire; likewise, it is impossible to dismiss Tony as merely paranoid or just an unreliable narrator, or to read the story as validating traditional Pueblo beliefs regardless of the politics of colonial structures in the reservation system.

## Uncle Tony's Goat

"Uncle Tony's Goat" combines a comedy of manners and an initiation story in a seemingly transparent tale of pastoral nostalgia. Many years before, an uncle's large billy goat had knocked the narrator—then a seven-year-old child—to the ground and subsequently escaped into the hills. Notwithstanding the retrospective point of view, the lucid account lacks the self-consciousness of nostalgia or sentimentality. The un-named narrator serenely reconstructs a childhood perspective, and the sense of timelessness in personal memory coincides with the impression of a timeless, pastoral life within the whole story.

The narration suggests a verbal equivalent to the luminous placidity of a Dutch genre painting, as in this exchange: "When I was much older I asked my mother, 'What did he ever do with those knives and sling-shots he took away from us?' She was kneading bread on the kitchen table at the time and was probably busy thinking about the fire in the oven outside. 'I don't know,' she said' " (172). There is little overt sense of historical period or even much relationship to any outside, larger world. Time is the turning of the season, a September afternoon: "My uncle and my father were sitting on the bench outside the house when we walked by. It was September now, and the farming was almost over, except for bringing home the melons and a few pumpkins. They were mending ropes and bridles and feeling the afternoon sun" (172). Here, it seems, is a picture of the timeless, traditional, "authentic" Pueblo world that artists like Georgia O'Keefe and D. H. Lawrence sought in Taos and Santa Fe in the early twentieth century.

Central to the depiction of traditional Pueblo life in "Uncle Tony's Goat," and necessary for understanding the relationship between the narrator and Uncle Tony, is the important role that the maternal uncle plays within the Pueblo Indian family. The mother's brother, and espe-cially the mother's eldest brother, acts as the authoritative male and especially as disciplinarian in the traditional Pueblo family. "The mother's brother is thought of as a 'guardian' of his sister's children and has considerable authority over them."[48] At Uncle Tony's first appear-ance in the story the narrator alerts us to this important role: "He was old, getting some white hair—he was my mother's oldest brother, the one that scolded us when we told lies or broke things" (172).

Further moments in the story emphasize that Uncle Tony takes his duties seriously and carries them out rigorously. The narrator recalls that the worst scolding an older sister ever got came from their mother, whose harshest comment was "It's a good thing I saw you; what if your uncle had seen you?" (173), a warning that the other children, although very young, "understood very well" (173). At times the uncle's monitor-ing seems almost unreasonable, as when he confiscates the homemade slingshots and tin-can knives the children have been using for target practice on the wrecked car. Likewise, his warning that the children's arrows might be dangerous seems unwarranted as the arrows have not only missed their targets—the nanny goats and kids—they have not even stopped the animals' grazing. But it would be foolish to make such assumptions about Uncle Tony, as foolish as failing to reckon with the memory and intelligence of Uncle Tony's goat.

In the eyes of the narrator, Uncle Tony is no obsessive, puritanical disciplinarian. He is strong, virile, and accomplished. He personally manages an important family resource: "The goats were valuable. We got milk and meat from them. My uncle was careful to see that all the goats were treated properly" (172), and "Uncle Tony milked the goats and fed them" (173). The big billy goat of the title is in a class by himself: "This goat was big and black and important to my uncle Tony because he'd paid a lot to get him and because he wasn't an ordinary goat.... My uncle was the only person who could touch this goat" (173). The goat is aggressive, attacking anyone who comes too near, but he allows Tony to groom him, and Uncle Tony takes the opportunity to talk to this comrade every day. Most of all, the goat is sexually powerful, and his potency is a source of personal pride to Uncle Tony: "I think Uncle Tony was proud of the way the billy goat mounted the nannies, powerful and erect with the great black testicles swinging in rhythm between his hind legs" (173).

In classical comedy youth defeats age so that life can overcome death: the young and vigorous must displace the old and impotent. "Uncle Tony's Goat" can be read as a miniature rite of passage, a wry, nuanced comedy of manners that moves the narrator into a new position within a subtly altered family dynamic. Decoding the gestures, asides, and throwaway lines reveals the subtext of sexual contestation, reversal, and reconciliation that the story enacts.

When the children attack the female goats with their arrows, more is at stake than the animals' annoyance, as both narrator and goat are aware: "The billy goat never forgot the bows and arrows, even after the bows had cracked and split and the crooked, whittled arrows were all lost" (173). Never mind the inadequacy of their tools; the assault on the she-goats challenges the prerogatives of the children's uncle and his partner, the powerful, lusty goat. Uncle Tony has only to see the arrows to perceive what is coming, and he warns against a possible challenge to the current order of things: "You'd better not be shooting at things," he admonishes. "Something will get hurt. Maybe even one of you" (172).

The goat's violent attack is the turning point in the story. It permits a female authority to emerge, thus ameliorating a contestation of power that has been rendered in a phallic iconography of arrows and knives and that is clearly out of control by the time the seven-year-old lies bleeding in the dirt of the goat pen. The narrator implies a subtle shift in power and authority when he reports the mother's stern decree: " 'He ought to get rid of it,' she said. 'We can't have that goat knocking people down for no good reason' " (174–75). For all of Uncle Tony's severity, there seems no hope of saving the goat from sacrifice once the mother has spoken. Uncle Tony is not altogether the same commanding figure as he rides off to search for the goat while the narrator and the mother stand together to "watch his old roan gelding splash across the stream and labor up the steep path beyond the river" (175).

By the end of the story the contours of the classic comic design have been filled out. The (scape)goat has been released into the wilderness, taking along the burden of the narrator's guilt and the family's distress. The goat's escape satisfies everyone. Since the goat is not sacrificed, the narrator need feel no guilt. The mother does not have to worry anymore about unprovoked attacks and injuries to children. The social order has been restored, even invigorated, as the comedic formula dictates. Most important of all, Uncle Tony can relish the knowledge that his virile goat is living wild and free. Far from being a loss, the goat's escape actually releases this stern uncle into a new identity, and a rejuvenated persona as pleased, contented hunter emerges from the erstwhile rather cranky shepherd.

While subdued, the theme of hunting is pervasive, from the children's' arrow making to Uncle Tony's ride off into the hills in search of the errant goat. As Danielson notes in her structural analysis, a hunting motif winds throughout the poems, stories, and autobiographical pieces of *Storyteller* (Danielson, 338–45). Immediately following "Uncle Tony's Goat" there is a photograph of two little girls, Silko's sisters, holding the antlers of a deer carcass in the back of a pickup truck with a rifle resting on top. "Uncle Tony's Goat" reflects Silko's understanding of the symbiotic, even mystical, relationship between hunter and prey.

The oral traditions of the Lagunas, like those of other American Indian peoples, are replete with a sense of the intimate and reciprocal relationship of hunter and prey. The animal is seen as offering itself in gift and sacrifice for the sustenance of the people. In return, the people owe the animal respect and support in ritual and ceremony as well as in the observance of practices—such as not taking gravid females—that will support the increase and maintenance of the species. As Alfonso Ortiz points out, in the proscriptions against hunting animals in their mating season, one sees that the practical and the symbolic are insepa-rable aspects of the people's paramount project, survival and the con-tinuance of life: "Most important, the Tewa do not want to kill the females with young because this would jeopardize the future availability of game."[49] Hundreds of ceremonial songs have been written down and translated in which the hunter is represented as taking on the persona of the animal—usually a deer—in order to effect the animal's consent to be taken.

If "Uncle Tony's Goat" can be read as an allegory in which the goat is sent off into the wilderness, laden with the onus of the story's violent events, it also can be read as the transformation of the same goat out of the servility of domestication and into the freedom and nobility of the game animal. Hence Uncle Tony's satisfaction and even pride in the goat's escape: " 'There wasn't ever a goat like that one,' he said, 'but if that's the way he's going to act, O.K. then. That damn goat got pissed off too easy anyway.' He smiled at me and his voice was strong and happy when he said this" (176).

In a descriptive passage from his novel *House Made of Dawn,* N. Scott Momaday expresses this sense of the traditional hunter's awareness of being one among many natural predators in the Southwest's ecology: "Once there were wolves in the mountains, and the old hunters of the town remember them. It is said that they were many, and they came to the hunters' fires at night and sat around in the dark timber like old men wanting to smoke."[50] A few lines further on, Momaday also asserts the superiority of wild to domesticated animals: "The other, latecoming things—the beasts of burden and of trade, the horse and the sheep, the dog and the cat—these have an alien and inferior aspect, a poverty of vision and instinct, by which they are estranged from the wild land, and made tentative. They are born and die upon the land, but then they are gone away from it as if they had never been" (Momaday 1968, 57). Like a hunter in one of the old myths, Uncle Tony is more partner than owner of his great goat. When the goat abandons the cramped, dark shed and hies off to open country, Uncle Tony can likewise undergo transformation from proprietor of a domestic stud to comrade of a fellow creature of the wild; he can imagine his goat as unconfined as the wolves that, in Momaday's legend, come to sit by the campfires of humans.

In contrast to stories like "Storyteller" and "Tony's Story," "Uncle Tony's Goat" appears to keep an intrusive colonial entity firmly off-stage, with only passing mention of church and school. The story depicts a family living in close-knit harmony and cooperation in an uncluttered environment. The household lacks indoor plumbing and central heating; the mother bakes bread in an outdoor beehive oven; men manufacture bows and arrows; milking is done by hand. There is even a suggestion that the world of mechanization is on the way to defeat: a pickup truck had figured in the acquisition of the uncle's goat, but the only other vehicle mentioned is "an old wrecked car; its windows were all busted out" (172).

What Silko's story offers, however, is an opportunity to interrogate that picture of timeless serenity, and to question the essentialism of any search for total cultural authenticity or purity. The pastoral life itself, with its goats, horses, and pigs, developed after these domestic animals had been introduced by Spanish colonists into the Pueblo agricultural economy. Yeast bread and the beehive oven were likewise adapted into Pueblo culture after being introduced by the Spanish, and rusty coffee cans and pickle jars are of course items of recent manufacture. One of the subtexts woven into "Uncle Tony's Goat" is a depiction of the seamless blending of indigenous and imported usages, over time and governed by the structure of traditional indigenous life. The wrecked automobile in this story furnishes a pointed contrast to the wrecked machinery in the ruthless arctic world of "Storyteller"; in its slow decay the abandoned car is still useful for the target practice of children with slingshots.

In the context of Silko's ongoing preoccupation with encounters in the multicultural contact zone, "Uncle Tony's Goat" offers one of her most subversive readings of ideas of progress, assimilation, and inevitability. The everyday perception of culture contact, and of the idea of assimilation, postulates a one-way process, whereby native culture is assimilated—that is, erased—into the supposed progress of the colonizing entity. "Uncle Tony's Goat," however, offers the reverse process. The traditional household is intact and vibrant, having adapted the items it can use—Band-Aids, tin cans, water hydrants, pickup trucks. There is a church, picturesquely in the background, and a nun, Sister Julian, who never appears and who does not really matter. Likewise, the protagonist attends school, but it is clear that real education is being carried on at home in the family. A contemporary icon of progress and assimilation, the automobile, is represented by the "old wrecked car" (172). The major event of the story reverses the terms of "progress": in "Uncle Tony's Goat" real improvement is a passage from confinement to freedom, a transformation from domestication to wilderness.

## The Man to Send Rain Clouds

"The Man to Send Rain Clouds," like "Tony's Story," was written for a creative writing course while Silko was at the University of New Mexico.[51] The deceptively simple story describes the funeral rites for Teofilo, an old shepherd who is found a few days after he has expired under a large cottonwood tree; the story moves from discovery of the body by a man named Leon and his brother-in-law, Ken, on a windy March morning, to its interment that evening. In addition to Leon and Ken, the cast of characters comprises Louise and Teresa, evidently the men's wives, and Father Paul, the village priest.

LaVonne Ruoff has discussed Keresan elements in the burial customs described, such as tying a feather in the hair, painting the face of the deceased, and sprinkling pollen and corn (Ruoff, 170–71). In contrast to the other stories in *Storyteller*, the narrator here is detached and omniscient, moving only briefly into the perspectives of Leon and Father Paul. The narrative subordinates psychology, internal conflict, and character development to quiet, almost poetic description of the community's arrangements for Teofilo's passage into his new role. The story is very short, and the relationships in it are depicted with muted understatement; this lack of emphasis on the intrapersonal is itself an indicator of the non-Western perspective the story offers.

"The Man to Send Rain Clouds" resonates with a sense of the Pueblo people's intimacy with the rhythms of the natural world, and the story's integration into *Storyteller* clarifies these associations. His relatives discover old Teofilo beneath a large cottonwood tree, and the reference calls to mind the traditional tale Silko titles "COTTONWOOD Part One: Story of Sun House" in *Storyteller*. The "COTTONWOOD" story relates how Yellow Woman goes out in midwinter, racing against eternal night to draw forth and mate with the sun and cause the year to turn at the solstice. Yellow Woman must locate the sun by finding a great cottonwood tree in "a canyon of cloudy sky stone" (65). Silko ends her retelling with the lines "Cottonwood, / cottonwood. / So much depends / upon one in the great canyon" (67). In "The Man to Send Rain Clouds," much depends on a large cottonwood tree as well. The story opens with the line "They found him under a big cottonwood tree" and continues by

53

picturing how the "big cottonwood tree stood apart from a small grove of winterbare cottonwoods which grew in the wide, sandy arroyo" (182). The highlighting of the cottonwood tree sets the story within the context of the myths explaining the great cycles of the seasons and the place of humans within those cycles, and it prepares the reader to see old Teofilo as having an important part, through his death and the ceremonies attending the passage of his soul into the world of the ka'tsinas, in the ongoing cycles of nature.

The correlation of Teofilo's rites and the turn of the seasons continues in the reference to the sun "approaching the long mesa where it disappeared during the winter" as the family starts out to carry the body to its burial place (184). It is late March, near the vernal equinox: the sun is about to return to the village, remaining with the people for the days lengthening into summer and setting lower against the flat plain instead of behind the mesa each night. The astronomical sophistication of all the Pueblo peoples has received much attention. In Momaday's *House Made of Dawn* an old man of Jemez Pueblo remembers taking his grandchildren to stand where "they could see the black mesa looming on the first light, and he told them there was the house of the sun. . . . They must know the long journey of the sun on the black mesa, how it rode in the seasons and the years, and they must live according to the sun appearing" (Momaday, 197). In the last century an early ethnographer, Jesse Fewkes, noted the complex system that the Hopi used to calculate the time for seasonal ceremonies: "Astronomers or sun priests have given names to the different points on the horizon behind which the sun rises or sets corresponding to all the great festivals. . . . The eastern and western horizons are used as great solar clocks."[52] Teofilo's interment at sunset is also in keeping with the belief Fewkes notes regarding the Hopi that "the dead follow the sun to the west" and have their own village in the world of their clan ancestors (Fewkes, 491, 486).

Teofilo's role as he joins the ancestors, that of being a sender of rain clouds, is crucial to the ongoing survival of the traditional Pueblo community. The Rio Grande and Hopi peoples traditionally practiced dry farming augmented by irrigation in a challenging environment. It is impossible to overstate the importance of precipitation on the arid New Mexico plateau and indeed throughout the whole of the Southwest. An ecological report on the eastern pueblos notes that the major crops of corn, beans, and squash, as well as the subsistence of livestock and the people themselves, depend on late-summer rains and the recharging of underground aquifers from winter snowfall in the mountains. These sources of water are capricious: "Even with irrigation no farmer can predict whether or not his field is going to receive adequate moisture." As far back as the eighteenth century the notes of Fray Benavides, a Spanish priest who traveled in the region, record a famine that occurred as a result of drought.[53] Yearning for rain pervades the songs, myths, iconography, religious observances, and symbol systems of all the Pueblos. Hence the urgency Teofilo's kinsfolk feel to assure his ability to return the life-giving rain to the community. It is not merely symbolic or sentimental, but necessary to send him on his way with enough water so that, his thirst appeased, he will return as part of the rain clouds.

Teofilo's continuing importance and contribution to the community is an expression of the principle of reciprocity in traditional Pueblo life. The donations of food left by Teofilo's relatives and clansmen for the gravediggers' meal express the principle. The interrelationship between food exchange and ceremony has been noted as an example of the interrelationship of religion, economy, and social life: "The simplest acts of mutual assistance will be concluded by a shared meal or a gift of food; and formal gatherings of bilateral relatives or clansmen include a feast. . . . Critical events include birth ceremonies, initiations, marriage, death, and sickness. In the eastern Pueblos each of these nonperiodic events involves an exchange of food for services rendered" (Ford, 9). With his death Teofilo does not leave the community but remains a vital part of its system of gifts and exchanges, fulfilling his duty as a bringer of rain.

"The Man to Send Rain Clouds" interrogates the notion of the colonial contact zone as a place where power relations are always absolute and one-sided. The central conflict of the story is a dispute over who will conduct the funeral rites for old Teofilo: the people of the village or the Catholic priest, Father Paul. There is no question that the difference is resolved in favor of the villagers, who carry out the ceremony on their terms and even persuade the priest to assist them. In a kind of fatalistic resignation he agrees to bring the holy water to be sprinkled on old Teofilo's grave, even though he believes he is being manipulated for unspoken purposes.

There is a kind of pseudo-irony in the way Father Paul views his participation in the funeral observances. He suspects that the people are misleading him into taking part in "some perverse Indian trick—something they did in March to ensure a good harvest" instead of a funeral (185). But the funeral rites really are a fertility ritual, and fulfillment of the ceremonial requirements of the interment is in fact "something they do to ensure a good harvest." If there is any irony here, it is not that the priest mistakes what he sees, but that his habit of thinking in mutually exclusive binary categories (either funeral or fertility rite) precludes his ever being more than half right.

Father Paul's blindness extends to his failure to connect with the land as the members of the Indian community so matter-of-factly do. This failure, and the priest's dim recognition of it, manifests itself in his perplexity as he tries to "read" the drops of holy water. "He sprinkled the grave and the water disappeared almost before it touched the dim, cold sand; it reminded him of something—he tried to remember what it was, because he thought if he could remember he might understand this" (186). The clue is there for the reader, and for the priest if he could see: "the water fell through the light from sundown like August rain that fell while the sun was still shining, almost evaporating before it touched the wilted squash flowers" (186).

The blindness that estranges Father Paul from nature and the community speaks to a basic alienation of this lonely man. There is a pathos in his eagerness to sit down and chat with his visitors, but when they seek to engage him with their request he unconsciously reaches for "a glossy missionary magazine . . . full of lepers and pagans" (185). The story suggests that his lack of vision applies to more than these parishioners whom he finds so baffling: "The priest turned away from Leon and looked out the window at the patio full of shadows and the dining-room windows of the nuns' cloister across the patio. The curtains were heavy, and the light from within faintly penetrated; it was impossible to see the nuns inside eating supper" (184). His alienation is complete. Poor Father Paul is the only person in the story who has no communal feast to join.

It is possible to read "The Man to Send Rain Clouds" as a critique of single-minded quests for authenticity and the pursuit of cultural survival through avoidance of contamination. The contrasting example of such essentialism occurs in "Storyteller," in which we see the protagonist invest her identity in the avoidance of contamination, maintaining at all cost her exclusive monologue, "the story" that must be told "without lies"; her counterpart is the totally assimilated Eskimo jailer who wants to speak only English. These two characters represent the extremes of identity politics: his embrace of compromise—politics—results in the erasure of identity, whereas her fixation on identity renders politics meaningless. "The Man to Send Rain Clouds" offers, in contrast, a sense of culture not as a monologue whose purity must be maintained regardless of the cost, but as a dynamic process, a matter of strategic negotiations, respectful deliberation and consultation, a sensitivity to nuances of communication, and above all a sense of proportion regarding which things are matters of principle that must be maintained and which are secondary means that may be adjusted to suit the occasion.

The sense of cultural symbiosis evoked in this story recurs in the careful delineation of perceptions of time. During the day, time is marked off in different ways. Teofilo's body is found near daybreak, under a cottonwood tree that figures in myths about the return of the sun; his interment is completed as the sun sets behind a mesa said to be the house of the sun. Between these two events the people caring for the old man's remains take their noon meal marked by the ringing of the Angelus on "twin bells from the king of Spain" (184). Louise's thoughtfulness extends to including the priest's holy water; her quiet mention of it sends Ken and Leon to fetch Father Paul. Here is a community whose vision can embrace ancient myths, long-standing traditions, motor vehicles, Father Paul, and even the king of Spain.

# A Geronimo Story

"When I was a little girl there was a man right here in Bisbee who had seen Geronimo. 'Many's the time,' he would say, 'that I've seen Geronimo and his warriors riding along that ridge right there above the town.'" I was five years old, and a grown-up woman was telling me a story that had been told to her when she was a little girl by a man who was already old, about things that he had seen before she was born. I looked up at the escarpment rising steeply over the winding street and imagined that I could see the horsemen posed in silhouette against the turquoise sky, gazing enigmatically down on the town of Bisbee, Arizona. In my preliterate mind, those long-ago events stretched back an unknown distance into the far mists of time, yet the reality of Geronimo became as immediate as the stony mountainside rising from the narrow canyon street we stood on. A tiny thrill of danger and possibility passed through me. Now I had a real, personal connection with this powerful and dangerous man, Geronimo. He had been here, in this place, and surely if I tried hard enough, I too would be able to see him. This is my Geronimo story.

As with other historical figures who have undergone the transformation into myth, "Geronimo" lives far more in the stories told about him than in the historical record. A striking example of the strength of the myth is the preface to Angie Debo's exhaustive study of Geronimo and the history around him, in which the author opens his comprehensive examination of the historical record with his own Geronimo story remembered from childhood.[54] Silko's "A Geronimo Story" is aptly and precisely titled: no story can be *the* Geronimo story, because there is no single story; rather, this is *a* Geronimo story, one of many.

Unique among Silko's stories, "A Geronimo Story" is set in the last century, sometime in the 1880s when Geronimo and his band were clinging to their independence in the rocky fastnesses of the southern Arizona and northern Mexico mountains, desperately pursued by soldiers, vigilantes, and bounty hunters. The narrator, a man named Andy, recounts a trip he took when he was about 12 years old; he had ridden with his uncle Siteye and other members of the Laguna Regulars—scouts for the United States Army—with a Captain Pratt, ostensibly to assist a certain Major Littlecock in locating the legendary Apache chieftain Geronimo. Retrospective distance, however, shapes only a few key passages, and most of the story is closely focused through the viewpoint of the adolescent boy. "A Geronimo Story" is a deconstructionist parable in which the absence of Geronimo becomes the pretext for a deer hunt, and one of the subtexts is the permeability as well as the toughness of cultural and linguistic boundaries. The story celebrates hunting, storytelling, and the common human grounding of difference.

In "A Geronimo Story," as in the other stories in *Storyteller,* language protects identity and assists survival. However, in "A Geronimo Story" it is a white man, Captain Pratt, who invokes the protective value of language. When Major Littlecock makes a sexual slur, in English, against the Laguna men, Siteye responds in kind, in Laguna. The bilingual Captain Pratt then deflects the escalating hostility by claiming ignorance of language: "I'm sorry, Major, but I don't speak the Laguna language very well" (221). Everyone—Pratt, Littlecock, and the Laguna men—knows that Pratt is lying, but the hapless Littlecock has no choice but to accept the obvious prevarication. The relation of language to truth is tenuous and secondary throughout the whole episode. Littlecock's insinuation that the Laguna men will threaten or disgust the white women of Pie Town, and Siteye's assertion that Littlecock prefers horses as sexual partners, are strategic moves in the constant power negotiation that distinguishes the contact zone. In a deft and paradoxical maneuver, Pratt positions himself on the side of the Lagunas by denying knowledge of their language; it is a trickster's gambit that achieves what confrontation or outrage could not.

Above all, "A Geronimo Story" insists that "language" is more than lexicon, orthography, or grammar. Littlecock possesses remarkable but useless linguistic versatility. He pompously lectures Pratt on how it "is very useful to speak the Indian languages fluently," and he has "mastered Crow and Arapaho, and . . . [is] fluent in Sioux dialects" (221). Notwithstanding these accomplishments, he cannot grasp the information the Laguna scouts try to communicate to him about Geronimo's real whereabouts, even though both Siteye and the captain "told him in good English" (220). It is tempting to seek a literary/historical allegory in the passage. Some of the earliest work on the preservation of American Indian languages was undertaken by army officers who had learned the languages of the people they were in the process of conquering, and the pretentious major may be an allusion to them.

The salvage ethnographers and linguists who replaced the soldiers may be another target of the satire. The project of salvage ethnography was undertaken to preserve in text as much as possible of languages that were being deliberately wiped out in a gigantic effort of ethnic cleansing, accomplished through genocide on the frontier and boarding-school education in centers of American civilization. Hence, the ethnographer/linguist's aim in compiling written texts of vanishing languages was to produce books that nobody would be able to read. In "A Geronimo Story" the character of Littlecock fuses soldier and scholar in a personification of obtuseness that may serve as a cautionary exemplum for the reader who tries to comprehend a story, a language, or a culture, but who brings only utilitarian values and a cold intellectualism to the matter.

The sexual innuendo in the major's name reflects the comic mood of this tale. The name suits the man, with its suggestion of a physical equivalent for his meanness of mind and character. It also reminds us of Andy's recollection of his uncle Siteye, who is "big like an elk who is fast and strong" and who refuses to allow the pettiness of racial friction to deflect him and his men from more important concerns, even as he also refuses to ignore or defer to slander and insult (212). The sexual discord and suspicion that is at the heart of racism underlies Littlecock's demeaning assumption that the Laguna men will offend the women of Pie Town; his uniform renders him representative of a racist society whose mandates he carries out. Littlecock's insult and the men's response to it are part of Andy's initiation into the conflicting mores of the contact zone in which he lives. The adult Andy, recollecting Littlecock's attitude, connects it with his memory of encountering the ugly term "[s]quaw man" applied to Captain Pratt (215).

The allusion to the pejorative "squaw man" is one of the most specifically biographical references in Silko's novels and stories. The fictional character of Captain Pratt derives from Leslie Silko's great-grandfather Robert G. Marmon, who appears in three different photographs in *Storyteller*. The book opens with a picture of Marmon, his young wife—Leslie's beloved Grandma A'mooh—and their infant son, Leslie's grandfather Henry. Robert G. Marmon's image closes the text as well, in a later photograph showing him surrounded by sons, son-in-law, and two grandsons who are the author's father and uncle. A third photograph, placed immediately following "A Geronimo Story" shows "The Laguna Regulars in 1928, 43 years after they rode in the Apache Wars" (272). In the picture Robert G. Marmon stands with a dozen other elderly men under a great oak tree. The reader may feel invited to pick out an Andy, a Siteye, a Mariano, or a George from the row of men calmly gazing at the camera. Even before the publication of *Storyteller*, Silko had associated her fictional characters with the Laguna Regulars of her great-grandfather's time by using the title "The Laguna Regulars and Geronimo" for a taped reading of the story that she made in 1977.[55]

The stories about Captain Pratt that Andy hears in "A Geronimo Story" echo details that Leslie Silko retells from family anecdotes about her great-grandfather. In *Storyteller* (16–17) and later in an essay titled "Fences against Freedom" she reveals that Robert Marmon "endured the epithet 'Squaw Man' " (*Beauty*, 104), and she retells the family story of how he refused to enter an Albuquerque hotel after the owner had denied entry to his sons (*Beauty*, 104–5). The outrage at injustice, exploitation, and cruelty that pervades "Fences against Freedom" and its companion piece, "The Border Patrol State," also in *Beauty*, continually engages Silko's attention and is the foundation for her monumental novel, *Almanac of the Dead*.

In "A Geronimo Story" the Laguna men understand the uses of language in power negotiations, as is clear from their own critique of the comments they make at the expense of Major Littlecock and the white community: "Anybody can act violently—there is nothing to it; but not every person is able to destroy his enemy with words" (222). The statement is redolent with irony, not least because the enemy is supposed to be Geronimo, not the American soldiers. The men know, however, that it is the Littlecocks of the world—of whatever race or color—that constitute the real and dangerous enemy. Lies, jokes, and insults are valuable tools in the verbal repertoire of combatants in the contact zone. So are curses, even when dispensed in a joking manner, as Siteye does when he says, "I am only sorry that the Apaches aren't around here. . . . I can't think of a better place to wipe out. If we see them tomorrow we'll tell them to come here first" to destroy the town that has offered its presumed protectors such a peculiar welcome, compounded of food and insult (221). The comment on destroying enemies with language also reverberates against Siteye's story of the massacre near the Mexican border. The massacre might have been easy, and the gruesome event wiped out the enemy in that place. But the whole white world remains, prepared to replace an unlimited number of storemen, ranchers, corrupt police officers, soldiers, and Pie Towns. If the Indians' enemies are to be destroyed, some other means besides armed conflict will be required.

The comic perspective of "A Geronimo Story" offers a view of the contact zone in which boundaries can be flexible, elastic, a permeable interfacing of differences. There is room for accommodation and compromise. Laguna men ride with U.S. troops but retain their autonomy and independence. Siteye admires Captain Pratt for—of all things—his devotion to afternoon tea: "I admire him for that. Not like a white man at all; he has plenty of time for some tea" (215). It is worth noting as well, however, that the historical context of "A Geronimo Story" provides openings and possibilities that the rigid colonial structures of "Tony's Story" preclude: the New Mexico Territory of the 1880s is the site of a genuine contestation of power, and unlike the impotent tribal authorities of "Tony's Story," the Laguna Regulars are a genuine, functioning military force representing an autonomous community. The character of Captain Pratt has a special role in this unique contact zone. Captain Pratt is white, and like the storekeeper, priest, and construction workers in "Storyteller" and the sadistic policeman of "Tony's Story" he is a potential enemy. Paradoxically, words do destroy him—as enemy—when he accepts the Laguna language, in its deep structure as well as its surface manifestations.

Silko's choice of Pratt as the name for this complex and mediating figure points to that paradox. The name may follow a cue in family history, recalling the "George H. Pradt (or Pratt)" who, according to Ruoff, accompanied the Marmon brothers to Laguna in the 1800s (Ruoff, 168). However, there is a much more well-known Pratt whose actions Silko's story glosses. Captain Richard Pratt, founding headmaster in 1879 of the Carlisle Indian boarding school, coined the infamous motto "Kill the Indian and Save the Man" to sum up the Indian education program's goal of eradicating Native cultures.[56] Silko's Captain Pratt, by contrast, has become humanized, "not like a white man at all," through his education in Laguna language and custom.

Language vanquishes other enemies as well. Geronimo, another putative enemy, is present only in the tracings he leaves—his abandoned campsites (if they are his) and the stories told about him. Pursued by soldiers and scouts, he retreats forever in an infinite regress of language and story. Poor Littlecock, like an old soldier bereft of enemies, can only fade away: "His face had a troubled, dissatisfied look; maybe he was wishing for the Sioux country. . . . If he hadn't killed them all, he could still be up there chasing Sioux" (223). This is the paradox of hunting and storytelling (and reading): success is defeat, for the object is to search—not find.

Among the eight stories of *Storyteller,* the three that call attention to their metafictive quality through inclusion of "story" in their titles form a thematic triad. "Storyteller" and "Tony's Story" emphasize a univocal, rigidly defended, singular point of view, and examine the consequences of such a perspective; ambiguity and unreliability characterize the narration. "A Geronimo Story," by contrast, offers a transparently reliable narrator even as it choruses with many voices, many stories, many perspectives.

Several stories embedded in "A Geronimo Story," ranging from ancient myth to family anecdote, resonate with the major theme of Andy's initiation. The Navajo myth of the origin of the lava beds, the story of how Andy got his first horse, a story about the massacre of a white settlement, and Siteye's story of his encounter with a snake are some of the accounts that figure in Andy's journey.

As he narrates his story, Andy recalls how riding along the "dark stone ocean" of the Malpais lava beds had reminded him that Navajo tradition portrayed the volcanic eruption as a battle between a dangerous giant and the Hero Twins who originated Navajo culture; the lava is "a great pool of blood" remaining from the slain giant (217). Andy's digression on the acquisition of his first horse makes another Navajo connection: his mother had traded a fine new sewing machine to a Navajo for the expensive red-gold stallion. Siteye tells an anecdote that echoes the myth in yet another way, as an account of the traces of a violent and bloody encounter: on a previous expedition the Laguna Regulars and United States soldiers had come upon the bodies of a whole settlement of white men, women, and children who had been massacred by "Geronimo or some Apache" (215). The three stories—the acquisition of the horse, the volcanic eruption, and the massacred village—stand out in Andy's memory as significant markers in the journey toward manhood that he recounts.

Violent struggle, instruction and discipline, and visionary experience characterize the classical rite of passage story. "A Geronimo Story" opens the possibility of violence as part of Andy's initiation into manhood, for the Laguna Regulars are part of a military force setting out to engage an enemy. That possibility is modified by the inference from the three embedded stories; they imply that although violence is always a possibility in human encounters, especially those that take place in these contact zones of differing values and lifeways, negotiation and a judicious redistribution of resources can also be realized.

Linda Krumholz describes "A Geronimo Story" as "an initiation ritual for Andy, as he learns new places and the unspoken relations between Laguna and white men."[57] Even more important, however, is the process of discipline and education in fundamental Laguna values, a process that precedes "relations between white and Laguna" and offers the strategies that can be used to maintain autonomy. Certainly Siteye proposes a lesson in autonomy when he notes the Laguna men's refusal to bury the massacre victims. Nevertheless, flexibility and cooperation remain primary values in this story. The amicable relations between Navajos and Lagunas suggest a paradigm for harmony between Lagunas and Apaches that will be invisible to Littlecock and his forces. Andy's nostalgic recollections of Navajo horse traders also offer another hint of Marmon family history in this story. In an essay titled "Hunger Stalked the Tribal People" (*Beauty*, 97–98), Silko describes how her ancestors established friendly relations between Navajos and Lagunas, and the consequent tradition of friendship and exchange of gifts between the two peoples.

In "A Geronimo Story" Siteye adds yet another dimension of story and memory to the Malpais when he explains that this barren and dangerous territory had been a place of refuge for their Laguna ancestors: "In little caves they left pottery jars full of food and water. These were places to come to when somebody was after you" (217). Siteye's knowledge resonates ironically against his later comment on the foolishness of the army officer who insists that he knows where Geronimo is:

"We aren't hunting deer," he [Siteye] said, "we're hunting people. With deer I can say, 'Well, I guess I'll go to Pie Town and hunt deer,' and I can probably find some around here. But with people you must say, 'I want to find these people—I wonder where they might be.' " (220)

Tracking people requires an act of sympathetic imagination, the ability to put oneself in the place of another human being and to see through that person's eyes; it is an ability that must begin with recognition of common humanity. Siteye's information about the hidden caches in the volcanic caves suggests a parallel between Lagunas of ancient days hiding out (possibly from raiding Apaches) and Geronimo's beleaguered company seeking sanctuary in mountain hiding places. Being able "to understand this world / differently," something Silko's great-grandfather Marmon had learned (256), is beyond the capacity of the officious Major Littlecock. This is the reason why he will never find Geronimo. Siteye's statement is also prophetic: the men do end up finding some deer around Pie Town and return after a successful hunt.

Andy's text enacts the exacting attention to the particulars of the landscape that constitutes a crucial aspect of the initiation journey. His task is to learn the way, in many senses of that word, and "the way," "the journey," is a meaningful phrase at several points in the story. Initially Andy does not understand why they are going where Geronimo is not, although Siteye reveals the real meaning of the project: "It will be a beautiful journey for you. The mountains and the rivers. You've never seen them before" (214). By the end of the story the young man understands his mentor's words. Andy's narration plots the journey with scrupulous geographical exactitude. The first leg takes the men from the village of Laguna, south across the San Jose River, and west and south through the Acoma reservation to the edge of volcanic badlands, in Spanish the *mal pais* and today the Malpais National Monument. The second day finds them continuing southward along the eastern edge of the lava beds overlooking the Acoma plain, until they begin to climb into the Zuni Mountains for the second night's camp. In the morning they continue southward, crossing the continental divide and descending into the settlement called Pie Town, equidistant from the villages of Datil to the east and Quemado to the west. (All three of these sites are now located on U.S. Route 60, which leads to the west into the White Mountains and a present-day Apache reservation.)

The second day's ride concentrates on the instruction that Siteye gives Andy and on the youth's continued induction into Laguna manhood by way of learning his relationship with the land. Andy recalls first how his father and Siteye had taught him "to remember the way" (218).

After reviewing the details of geology, flora, and climate that must be noted and remembered, he says, "I closed my eyes and tested my vision of the trail we had traveled so far. I could see the way in my head, and I had a feeling for it too" (218). The practice has utilitarian value: just such a method has enabled the mature Siteye to reconstitute their route in his mind, although he had made the trip only once years before as a child; he can even map it out in improvised drawings scratched in the mud. However, more important than the instrumental utility of tracking skills is the deep and personal relationship Andy is forging with the land itself. Andy engages in a process of incorporating the landscape into his being: as he visualizes the details of the landscape it becomes a vital part of his inner life, of his feelings.

Another story at this point in the text complements and augments the learning process. Siteye tells of an incident from his childhood. He had lost his way home, but was able to find the trail back by following a rattlesnake he had carefully observed previously. The anecdote is replete with important lessons. Siteye's careful study of him had rendered the snake familiar. However, although Siteye had "a feeling for" the snake, just as Andy has a feeling for the land, the creature was neither pet nor friend. Nevertheless, if treated with the proper deference, the snake could be an important source of knowledge. Siteye had been successful in finding the path home because he had learned how to maintain an appropriate relationship with the terrain and its creatures. He had been properly incorporated within the life of the land. Such a relationship with the land is neither sentimental nor exploitative, neither the purely emotional absorption of romantic attachment nor the objectifying gaze of aesthete, scientist, or capitalist. "Incorporation" as I mean the term here signifies the complementary operations of entering into the processes of the land on its terms, and of internalizing the land within one's being, as Andy does in his process of visualization.

The result of such an undertaking is a contemplative attitude that permits the measured reflection and judicious balance that Andy admires in Siteye's storytelling. The idea of a beautiful journey connects the physical journey through this remarkable terrain, the educational initiation process that Andy undertakes under the mentorship of Siteye, and the understanding of story and text that the metafictional level of this Geronimo story proposes. A key element in valuing the beauty of a story is appreciation of rhythm, pace, and time. Andy particularly relishes Siteye's sense of pace and timing as well as his diction and delivery, all elements of his fine storytelling style: "It was beautiful to hear Siteye talk; his words were careful and thoughtful, but they followed each other smoothly to tell a good story. He would pause to let you get a feeling for the words; and even silence was alive in his stories" (215). This aesthetic appreciation of Siteye's stories complements the other lessons Andy learns about the value of language as a strategic instrument in power negotiations.

An appreciation for the amplitude of time emerges as an important value in "A Geronimo Story." The story opens on a scene of haste, confusion, and urgency as Andy heads for the corral full of agitated horses to saddle his own and his uncle's mounts before their journey. Then, the end of Andy's narration places the men in a contemplative stillness as they sit on their horses and gaze over at their home village "for a long time remembering the way, the beauty of our journey" (223). A generous sense of time belongs to the man who is mature, a full human being. It is not merely Captain Pratt's tea drinking that Siteye admires, but that "he has plenty of time" for his brew (215).

This leisurely sense of time and the satisfaction of adjusting one's life and story rhythms to it contrasts sharply with the conflicted apprehension of time in "Storyteller." The Yupik protagonist of "Storyteller" "told herself that it wasn't a good sign" (17) to see the sun "frozen, caught in the middle of the sky" (18); this is a nihilistic vision of the disappearance of time and the end of life, movement, and journey. The enervating frost that brings machines to a standstill and confines human beings permeates "Storyteller," a tale driven by centripetal energy that fragments and devours the many stories that leave only traces in the text. Andy, on the other hand, as the narrator of his Geronimo story, not surprisingly renders his story in accordance with the aesthetics he has outlined in it. His narration is deliberate, copious, replete with detail: he has plenty of time to describe the exact color of his horse, his mother's sewing machine, a Pie Town woman who walks with a limp.

The stern and absolute resistance in "Storyteller" to any impingement on one's language and identity also complements and contrasts with the polyglot assurance of "A Geronimo Story." The rigid certitude and unconditional rejection of compromise, the disdain for any truth but her own, that mark the protagonist of "Storyteller" stand in pointed contradiction to the adroit manipulation of language that Andy respects and even admires in "A Geronimo Story." Nowhere is the contrast between the stories more evident than in the climactic event of each, the encounter of protagonist and river. In the context of Andy's initiatory journey, the visionary moment occurs when he stops to drink from a mountain stream: "Cold water—a snow stream. I closed my eyes and I drank it. 'Precious and rare,' I said to myself, 'water that I have not tasted, water that I may never taste again' " (223). Andy's virtual if not physical immersion places him "in the moment," as the phrase is, and lifts him out of time for that epiphanic instant. The revivifying, Heraclitean stream he savors offers a powerful counterstatement to the engulfing Alaskan river of "Storyteller," which sweeps away anyone not armed with strong, icy, psychological and physical barriers. The two stories, as suggested earlier, offer complementary visions. Neither position suffices alone: an inflexible devotion to truth at all costs is ultimately self-consuming, but disregard of fact or truth results in cynicism. "A Geronimo Story" offers a different view of language and identity, one in which the instrumentality of language is governed not by a monological sense of truth that seeks only the one "true" story, but rather by a sense of beauty: appropriateness, humaneness, generosity, decorum, respect. The linguistic versatility of a Littlecock may be real, it may be accurate, and in that narrow sense it may be true, but allegiance to a rigid monologue in whatever language he uses disempowers him as a human being. The creative and sustaining capacity of language, "A Geronimo Story" suggests, lies in its potential for beauty. The beauty of Siteye's storytelling, its decorum, appropriateness, thoughtfulness, and care inhere in the character of the person who can be both firm and flexible as the needs of life demand.

The open-ended inclusiveness of "A Geronimo Story" is exemplary of Silko's understanding of traditional Laguna concepts of story and text. Writing about the appearance of a huge stone snake in the vicinity of the uranium mine at Laguna, and "attempts to confine the meaning of the snake to an official story suitable for general consumption," Silko explains that the "Laguna Pueblos go on producing their own rich and continuously developing body of oral and occasionally written stories that reject any decisive conclusion in favor of ever-increasing possibilities."[58] Her protagonist Andy is part of that process, as she is herself.

## Coyote Holds a Full House in His Hand

"He knew he could be a lawyer because he was so good at making up stories to justify why things happened the way they did" (259). So muses the protagonist of "Coyote Holds a Full House in His Hand," last

67

of the eight short stories in *Storyteller*. He is a gray-haired Laguna man "over thirty" who lives in the house of his late mother; she had called him "Sonny Boy" and had indulged his every wish despite her other children's disapproval (257, 258). Although his story is told entirely from his own point of view, who Sonny Boy really is and what happens to him remain enigmatic. Is he an avatar of the powerful, appetite-driven trickster, Coyote, and does he have a rollicking sexual adventure? Or is he a pathetic voyeur whose most daring exploit amounts to no more than feeling up a roomful of middle-aged housewives? The question itself is at the heart of his story, which centers on how reality is constructed through the process of interpretation. Like the first-person narratives "Yellow Woman" and "Tony's Story," and like "Storyteller" and "Lullaby," this narrative so closely filtered through a single central consciousness is as much "about" what happens in the mind as it is about the sequence of events it purports to depict.

Silko's emphasis on the story as a study of the processes of consciousness becomes evident when we compare the *Storyteller* printing to the text as it was first published in *TriQuarterly*.[59] As we know from her letters to James Wright, Silko was assembling *Storyteller* during 1979, closely attending to the texts and photographs that were growing into the book. On 14 October 1979 she wrote to Wright that the book was at the publishers, presumably complete, and then six days later sent him the manuscript of "Coyote Holds a Full House in His Hand" (*Letters*, 90). *TriQuarterly* printed the story a few months after that, only shortly before it reappeared in *Storyteller*. Wright liked the story's comedy but felt that something had eluded him: "I know something about Coyote, but not enough. Still, I'm sure I grasped the story. It is fine" (*Letters*, 93). Silko queried in response: "I'm not sure, Jim, if I understand the difficulty you found with the story. I hope we can talk about it" (*Letters*, 95). The exchange indicates that Silko was concerned with the clarity of the text and readers' grasp of its meaning. The *TriQuarterly* printing suggests an editorial hand intervening toward standard English in matters such as sequence of verb tenses and hyphenation, whereas *Storyteller* is an idiosyncratic work that Silko maintained close control over. For all these reasons I believe the *Storyteller* text better reflects Silko's intentions, with a single exception as noted later. My comparison of the two texts also suggests that Silko's choices, in particular with regard to punctuation, operate to emphasize the delineation of mental processes and make the story a study of how events are constructed through processes of interpretation and storytelling.

Most of the differences between the two versions are matters of comma punctuation, and they consistently point to a more fluid, almost stream-of-consciousness mode in the *Storyteller* text. Here, for instance, is the protagonist pondering his mother's pampering despite the family's misgivings: "But she always stood up for him in front of the others, even if she did complain privately at times to her nieces, who then scolded him about the bills from the record club and the correspondence school" (*TriQuarterly,* 168). The same sentence in *Storyteller* reads, "But she always stood up for him in front of the others even if she did complain privately at times to her nieces who then scolded him about the bills from the record club and the correspondence school" (258–59). The differences are consistent throughout the two texts, the *Storyteller* version always tending to effect a continuous, uninterrupted stream of image and association.

In a few places more extensive discrepancies occur. Close comparison of a passage showing significant alterations reinforces the sense of the *Storyteller* text as representing a state of mind; changes are italicized in both passages:

> *TriQuarterly:* Hopi men were famous for their fast hands and the way they could go on all night. *But* some of the jokes hinted that he himself was as lazy at lovemaking as he was with his shovel during spring ditch cleaning, and that he *would take a girlfriend* to the deep sand along the river so he could lie on the bottom while *she* worked on top. Later on, some of the *old* men took him aside and *said he shouldn't* feel bad about Mildred, and told him about women they'd lost to Hopis when they were all working on the railroad together in Winslow. Women *believed the* stories about Hopi men, they told him, because women *liked* the sound of those stories, and *the women didn't* care if *it was* the Hopi men who *were* making up the stories in the first place. (169)

> *Storyteller:* Hopi men were famous for their fast hands and the way they could go on all night. Some of the jokes hinted that he himself was as lazy at lovemaking as he was with his shovel during Spring ditch cleaning and that he *took his girlfriends* to the deep sand along the river so he could lie on the bottom while *they* worked on top. *But* later on, some of the *older* men took him aside and *told him not to* feel bad about Mildred and told him about women they'd lost to Hopis when they were all working on the railroad together in Winslow. Women *believe those* stories about Hopi men, they told him, because women *like* the sound of those stories, and *they don't* care if *it's* the Hopi men who *are* making up the stories in the first place. (259)

In two places the absence of pauses indicated by commas gives the *Storyteller* version the sensation of unsorted spontaneous sequences of thought. It is this effect that Wright seems to be noting when he comments that the story is "rapidly and cleanly written" (*Letters*, 92), even though Silko had mentioned it as having gone through "4 or 5" drafts (*Letters*, 90); the effortlessness of the thought process represented in the text is assumed to pertain to the writing process producing the text. The use of present tense for the reported credulity of the women also conveys the sense of immediacy and a leveling of time distinctions that is associated with the rendering of stream of consciousness.

The other notable difference between the two passages is the emphasis in the *Storyteller* text on the plural partners in stories about Sonny Boy's sexual endeavors. The ribald scenario does not emerge from his memory of any actual encounters but comes out of the jokes that he knows people are telling about him. His meditation implies worlds of stories, in which multiple jokes about his sexual exploits generate the concoction of multiple partners, both jokes and partners alike being the creation of the teller/interpreters' imaginations; his introspective construction of reality recapitulates the Laguna men's communal invention of Laguna women via the women's ready acceptance of stories fabricated by Hopi men. In discussing the story with Wright, Silko underscores this idea of multiple stories creating a reality of their own: "My interest is in what allows us to laugh at stories which are not altogether funny in and of themselves, but become funny when people begin to recall and tell other stories about related incidents" (*Letters*, 95). The comment denotes a communal activity, not quite public in an urban sense but certainly not private, a live performance in speech, gesture, and expression. Wright had also inferred a quality of oral storytelling in "Coyote Holds," he reported: "Come to think of it, I felt as much like a listener as a reader" (*Letters*, 93).

Although the story lacks the voice of a first-person raconteur, the diction that renders the protagonist's central consciousness suggests internal monologue. The passage relating the protagonist's analysis of the village postmistress is exemplary of Silko's rendering of local diction and also emphasizes the ambiguity inherent in the protagonist's interpretation of events.

> The Mexican woman thought Pueblo men were great lovers—he knew this because he heard her say so to another Mexican woman one day while he was finishing his strawberry soda on the other side of the dry

goods section. In the summer he spent a good number of hours there watching her because she wore sleeveless blouses that revealed her fat upper arms, full and round, and the tender underarm creases curving to her breasts. They had not noticed he was still there leaning on the counter behind a pile of overalls; ". . . the size of a horse" was all that he had heard, but he knew what she was talking about. They were all like that, those Mexican women. That was all they talked about when they were alone. "As big as a horse"—he knew that much Spanish and more too, but she had never treated him nice, not even when he brought her the heart-shaped box of candy, carried it on the bus all the way from Albuquerque. He didn't think it was being older than her because she was over thirty herself—it was because she didn't approve of men who drank. That was the last thing he did before he left town; he did it because he had to, because liquor was illegal on the reservation. So the last thing he did was have a few drinks to carry home with him the same way other people stocked up on lamb nipples or extra matches. She must have smelled it on his breath when he handed her the candy because she didn't say anything and she left the box under the counter by the old newspapers and balls of string. The cellophane was never opened and the fine gray dust that covered everything in the store finally settled on the pink satin bow. The postmaster was jealous of the letters that were coming, but she was the one who had sent him into the arms of Mrs. Sekakaku. (257–58)

As in the rest of "Coyote Holds" this paragraph is notable for its length, as it meanders from his memory of eavesdropping on a conversation in Spanish while loitering in the general store to generalizations about all Mexican women to recollections of the box of candy to rationalizations regarding his drinking to observations on last-minute provision purchases to the supposed jealousy of the postmistress.

Sketching out the protagonist's interpretive strategies as he analyzes the postmistress may serve as a cautionary model for the reader approaching the whole story—and for the reader approaching American Indian literature generally. Indeed, Sonny Boy listening to the Mexican women gossip is not too unlike the reader encountering native texts in translation, except that he has the advantage of understanding a little Spanish. He hears a single phrase, which is repeated in altered wording: first, "the size of a horse" and then, "As big as a horse." The postmistress's actual words in Spanish are absent, as are the originals for most "original" American Indian texts in translation. It is impossible to know what the postlady "really said," and the limited point of view presents only Sonny Boy's interpretation, shaped to the outlines of his fantasy needs. Similar temptations have beguiled many a critic into wonderfully fantastic readings of native texts in translation in the absence of any knowledge of the originals or their context.

Sonny Boy's imagination weaves the five-word phrase into a baroque portrait of the lust of all Mexican women and the jealousy of this particular lady. Finally, he ends with the splendid failure of logic that accuses her of being both indifferent to him and also jealous of his other romantic prospects. The vignette sketches for the reader a strategy for construing the story as a whole: Mrs. Sekakaku and all the Hopi women, the protagonist's brothers, Mildred, the villagers who tell stories about him, the older men—all are, like the postmistress, as much creations of his interpretive requirements as they are characters who actually interact with him.

The story's title invites the reader to see Sonny Boy in the context of the traditional trickster figure of southwestern cultures. Silko's narrative strategy of linking this self-conscious, ineffective voyeur with the vigorous, conniving Coyote suggests ironic possibilities for reading the character against the myth. It is true that Sonny Boy shares both the sexual and alimentary appetites of the mythical Coyote, and particularly an obsession with fat. It is true, also, that he makes a trickster's wager and eventually does hold a "full house" in his hand, both in the flesh and in the snapshot he comes away with.

Unlike Coyote, however, Sonny Boy is fundamentally a romantic. He woos his prospective sweethearts with the swain's offerings of candy, flowers, perfume, and love letters; he takes his pleasure in anticipation and deferral. The success of his impromptu ceremony is important precisely because of its uniqueness, and he is at pains to preserve its displacement of the anticipated night with Mrs. Sekakaku, abandoning her well before any of the Hopi men can come around to make inquiries and without satisfying her awakened desires. It is the extraordinariness of the protagonist's Coyote achievement—a sharp contrast with the usual run of his life—that constitutes the meaning of this story. To identify the character himself with Coyote, then, would be to miss the point of this important adventure; "something in his life was about to change because of this trip", and the event becomes important because it is different, and not because it is typical of his life (260).

The cellophane-wrapped candy gathering dust under the post office counter figures the series of substitutions, displacements, and deferrals that constitute the protagonist's adventure. Indeed, for all his preoccupation with libidinous fulfillment, most of his gratification occurs in the purely imaginary love life of the voyeur and the fantasizer, whether the object of his interest is the Laguna postmistress, Mrs. Sekakaku's niece, or the little girl playing jacks among the Hopi clan mothers. His actual pursuit of happiness involves a high degree of self-textualization. In his amorous letters to Mrs. Sekakaku he essays a conventionally romantic strategy: "He said he wished he could see the beautiful Hopi mesas with snow on them" (258). The ruse is consistent with Sonny Boy's approach to the rest of his life, in which he opts to encounter the world in a series of textualized displacements. Unable to finish school after first running away and subsequently injuring himself, he determines on correspondence school. Although he imagines himself successful in the spirited, confrontational discourse of the courtroom trial, he gets no closer than eavesdropping on a trial from outside an open courtroom window. The most poignant of these maneuvers is his habit of carrying snapshots with him so that "he could tell people about himself while they looked at the photos in the plastic pages of his wallet" (260). The photographs, it turns out, are designed to suggest connections nonexistent in his real life, pictures that strangers take of him "outside the fancy bars and restaurants in the Heights" of Albuquerque neighborhoods, where "he didn't think Indians were welcome" (261). Even the climax of his encounter with the Hopi women, in which tactile gratification finally replaces voyeurism, is described at first in terms of distancing and displacement: "He closed his eyes so he could feel them better—the folds of skin and flesh above the knee, little crevices and creases like a hawk feels canyons and arroyos while he is soaring" (264).

Not surprisingly in a story alluding to the exploits of Coyote, sexual gratification is often figured in animal associations, here beginning with the inferences on horses in his post office reverie. The drollest as well as the most highly developed of these animal tropes is Mrs. Sekakaku's little dog. As in "Storyteller," the way in which a dog is connected with sexuality is key to the story's atmosphere and tone. An icon of the rage and depravity that pervade the tragic world of "Storyteller" is the impotent oil driller's pathetic talisman, a picture of "a woman with a big dog on top of her" (24); furthermore, for all his sense of his superiority to the Gussucks who keep dogs in their houses, the old man links himself and the protagonist to the village dogs: "Once the old man had seen her tease the dogs and he shook his head. 'So that's the kind of woman you are,' he said, 'in the wintertime the two of us are no different from those dogs' " (21). Standing in vivid contrast is the comic air of "Coyote Holds," simultaneously bemused and priapic, summed up in the vignette with Mrs. Sekakaku's dog.

At first the little pet is absurdly menacing and the joke is on Sonny Boy: "It sounded like a small dog but it also sounded very upset and little dogs were the first ones to bite." However, he soon recovers his Coyote-inspired confidence: "So he turned and at first he thought it was a big rat crawling out the door of Mrs. Sekakaku's bread oven but it was a small gray wire-haired dog that wouldn't step out any further. Only lonely widows let their dogs sleep in the bread oven although they always pretend otherwise and scold the dogs whenever relatives or guests come. It must have known it was about to be replaced because it almost choked on its own barking. 'Not much longer little doggy,' he was saying softly while he knocked on the door" (261). Mrs. Sekakaku supports the protagonist's interpretation of the dog as his sexual rival when she signals her invitation to him after the ceremony at Aunt Mamie's house by kicking the dog and blocking up the oven with an orange crate.

A combination of compassion and humor underlies Silko's treatment, in this and other writings, of a brutal side of American Indian life. Discussion of substance abuse, especially alcoholism, often meets resistance among Indian people; this reaction is not surprising in view of the prevalence of ugly stereotypes and racist attitudes. Silko has confronted substance abuse in her novels *Ceremony* and *Almanac of the Dead* with graphic delineation of its destructiveness. The approach in her short fiction is more subdued but no less pointed. Certainly the devastation brought about by alcohol underlies the tragedy of "Storyteller," in which two people are so desperate for wine that they consume canned heat. Both "Lullaby" and "Coyote Holds" offer portraits of alcoholics. In "Lullaby" Chato and Ayah take what comfort they can for their losses in the bottles of wine purchased with their government checks. In "Coyote Holds," Sonny Boy's telltale breath, his liver problems, and his naive embrace of alcohol as a necessity of life are classic markers of the alcoholic.

Early in her career, in a foreword to a portfolio of drawings by Indian artist Aaron Yava, Silko asserted a need to address such grim realities of Indian life: "I care as much as any Indian people, about the 'Indian self-image' and 'Indian Pride.' But we have been taught to value truth above all else; and these scenes are true, and they must not be hidden. To hide them, is in a sense, denying that these Indian people exist, denying that our cousins and uncles exist because they could be my cousins and uncles."[60] The portraits of Chato, Ayah, and Sonny Boy recuperate the complicated inner lives of individuals whose complexity and humanity too often become erased under labels like "bag lady" or "drunk." In contrast to the elegiac sense of loss in "Lullaby," comedy is foremost in "Coyote Holds," even though, as Silko notes, such stories may not be intrinsically funny (*Letters*, 95).

In the comic spirit of Coyote stories, "Coyote Holds" can be construed as a joking version of ceremonial myth. The narrative does follow the outline characteristic of the origin myths for ceremonies: the protagonist is exiled or must leave the community to pursue a dangerous mission, he (or she) is guided by powerful spiritual mentors, engages in a struggle or is subject to a challenging discipline, learns a ritual, and eventually comes back to share with the community the knowledge and power that has been gained. In Sonny Boy's case the male bonding ritual he anticipates on his return to Laguna (coupled with the possible danger of remaining on Second Mesa) overrides the prospect of climactic fulfillment in a night with Mrs. Sekakaku. "He had something important to tell the old men" (*TriQuarterly*, 174). Here indeed is the triumph of storytelling: for Sonny Boy, at any rate, it is a pleasure superior to sex. This is the only place where the *TriQuarterly* variant makes more sense than the *Storyteller* text, which reads, "to tell the old man" (265). There is no individual "old man" in the story who would be the auditor for Sonny Boy's report; rather, the protagonist appears to be returning to the older men who had earlier comforted him with their stories about Laguna women lost to the legendary prowess of Hopi lovers, carrying with him a story of his own and photographic evidence of his triumph. Like the legendary heroes, he is returning to the community with new and important ritual knowledge. Something—not everything, but something—has indeed changed in his life.

It should also be noted that the joking aspect of the story is neither disrespectful nor vitiating of ceremonial power or its importance. Clowning and humor, often ribald or grotesque, are well integrated into some of the most sacred American Indian traditions. This aspect of the story is also noted in Silko's comments to Wright: "This happens a lot at Laguna with stories about funerals, and I know in other places, humor's link with the most grave and serious moments has always been acknowledged" (*Letters*, 95).

Finally, this last of the texts in *Storyteller* completes the meditation woven throughout the book on language as a medium of identity and reality-construction. For Sonny Boy, English is the language of dream and desire, of his daydream career as an attorney and his amatory correspondence with Mrs. Sekakaku, facilitated by the United States postal service. A moment of doubt when "he thought his understanding of the English language must be failing" gently recedes as he reinterprets the situation in Mrs. Sekakaku's living room and, tricksterlike, reshapes himself as medicine man in order to seize the opportunity to impress these redoubtable Hopi ladies (261). We have come full circle from the inflexible protagonist of "Storyteller," who denies all languages but her own and for whom all stories but her own are lies, to the complaisance of Sonny Boy, for whom difference in language is virtually meaningless, as he hears all stories end up being the same story, whether told in English, Spanish, or Laguna. The differences between these protagonists could not seem more polar, yet they share a realization of the necessity and power of story and the act of storytelling. It only seems paradoxical that both "Storyteller" and "Coyote Holds a Full House in His Hand" end on a note of regeneration, with both protagonists preparing to share their stories with audiences eager to welcome these new additions to the communities' riches of knowledge and understanding.

# Uncollected Stories

Besides the eight stories collected in *Storyteller*, there are few examples of Silko's short fiction in print. Her first anthologized fiction appeared in *Come to Power*, which printed "A Geronimo Story" and a one-page vignette titled "Laughing and Laughing."[61] Subsequently "Laughing and Laughing" reappeared, substantially revised, in *Storyteller* as part of a series of tales of seduction and adultery. In 1974 Kenneth Rosen edited the first anthology of short fiction by American Indian writers, *The Man to Send Rain Clouds*, comprising 19 stories by six writers, all from the Southwest. In addition to five of Silko's stories later included in *Storyteller*, *The Man to Send Rain Clouds* contains two other brief texts that have not been reprinted: a very short piece titled "Bravura" and a fragment called "*from* Humaweepi, the Warrior Priest."[62] One other story not reprinted elsewhere, "Private Property" appears in *Earth Power Coming*, a collection of short stories edited by Silko's friend and fellow poet of the neighboring pueblo of Acoma, Simon Ortiz.[63]

"Laughing and Laughing" offers a good illustration of Silko's sense of the plasticity of the oral tradition and her continual experiments in working the dynamics of oral storytelling into the more static form of writing. The opening sentence reads "There was this man from Mesita," evoking both a seemingly casual raconteur and a conventional opening formula. The tale continues with the inclusion of improvisational phrases typical of oral storytelling: "Anyway, the story goes . . . ," "I don't know," "I guess," "maybe," all repeated through the first half of the single paragraph that constitutes the text. By the time we reach the middle of the narration the story has acquired its own momentum, and the qualifying phrases disappear. The tale ends with another framing formula from oral conventions: "So that's what happened, and everybody was laughing and laughing when they heard about it at Laguna, Paguate and Seama—we were all laughing about something that happened at Mesita."

In *Storyteller* the same story is reconstituted in an untitled piece beginning "His wife had caught them together" (89); it appears in a series of six untitled texts and three photographs that include family history, regional history, Laguna legend, and personal memories. The series of stories is like a conversation among several voices. Compared with the earlier version titled "Laughing and Laughing," however, the *Storyteller* piece beginning "His wife had caught them" is relatively formal and self-consciously writerly. No first-person pronoun introduces the narrator into the text, and the improvisational phrases and references to audience reaction have been excised. The piece is typeset with ragged right margin, which suggests pause indications for oral performance. This version also contains a second episode in which a man discovers a couple copulating in a barn, complementing the plot of "Laughing and Laughing," in which a woman and her sisters discover her husband with his lover in a cornfield.[64] This story of the hapless adulterer surfaces one more time in Silko's work, in "Private Property," discussed later in this chapter.

The metamorphoses and accretions in the different versions of "Laughing and Laughing," besides offering diverting opportunities for comparative interpretations, interrogate the whole notion of written prose fiction. "Laughing and Laughing" counts as a piece of short fiction in Rosen's anthology because it has a title and appears in a collection of poems and short fiction. In *Storyteller*, a narration of the same set of events, which lacks a title but is actually more formal in presentation and diction, is not considered a short story. Rather, the *Storyteller* presentation merges the story into a written enactment of the ongoing stream of discourse that constitutes "oral tradition." This formal experimentation and playful subversion of rigid genre boundaries is part of Silko's attempt to compose a written text that realizes some of the functions of the oral storyteller.

"Bravura," like "Humaweepi," is a youthful effort; in fact, in an interview Silko identified it as the first story she wrote in college (Perry, 322). The story contrasts a "new age" fan of native people with an actual Indian person, the narrator; both are apparently university students. The title character, known only as Bravura, is "a poet" who sets himself up in an abandoned church near an unspecified Indian village in the Southwest. Not surprisingly, the clueless Bravura inflates both his importance and his misunderstanding. He pompously declaims, "A poet doesn't belong in the university—he belongs with the people and the land" ("Bravura," 150), but he takes inane offense at children's jokes about his beard; he happily overpays his rent-gouging landlord but grudges a shopkeeper 40 cents for a soft drink.

The satire is heavy handed, suggesting that the author has not yet found a way of rendering a humorless buffoon like Bravura as his own parody. The delineation of the narrator is likewise problematic. What Bravura preaches, his anonymous classmate practices. The narrator moves without self-consciousness between cultural worlds: he displays traditional understanding of the community, landscape, and environment but is happy to drink a Coke as well. The deliberate and sometimes obtrusive contrast between the two characters suggests that the narrator's voice provides the moral center of the story. Thus, the ethnic slur is especially jarring when the narrator characterizes his avaricious neighbor as "the old Jew Mexican" ("Bravura," 152). The story suggests a community in which similar stereotypes are a common shorthand for analyzing behavior when the narrator relates of the same person that "Dan's relatives referred to him as the stingy old Mexican" ("Bravura," 151). The lack of ironic distance from this narrator is disturbing. The story is very slight, a little allegorical piece not equipped for the complexity of character development that the narrator's gaffe implies. The piece is interesting, however, as an early example of the ambiguity and potential for unreliability that pervades Silko's handling of first-person narration in very sophisticated tales like "Yellow Woman" and "Tony's Story."

Per Seyersted quotes Silko as saying that she had written a text of "about 50 pages, aimed at sixth graders, about young people being against strip mining" (Seyersted, 23). An excerpt from this effort appears under the title "*from* Humaweepi, the Warrior Priest," in *The Man to Send Rain Clouds.* As Ruoff points out, this story delineates how continuity of tradition is maintained through ritual initiation and storytelling. The first section depicts Humaweepi's apprenticeship with an old man who inducts him into intimate knowledge of and identification with the natural world: the old man shows the youth how to gather edible plants and where he can sleep without bedding, also advising him to walk in yucca sandals or no shoes at all. All the episodes in the story reinforce the idea of learning from nature through imitation and identification, and the old man stresses at several points that "[h]uman beings are special . . . which means they can do anything," such as sleeping on the ground, walking barefoot through snow, or foraging for food ("Humaweepi," 162). The significant element of the old man's teaching, paradoxically, is that it emphasizes the uniqueness of human beings within nature. Other creatures do not learn the behavior and acquire the skills or abilities of species different from their own; only humans are able to realize the kind of comprehensive accomplishments the old man describes.

In this brief exploration of Humaweepi's education, we see Silko trying out a motif she will return to several times in her fiction. The theme of a young man's initiation into the wisdom of his community finds a sophisticated expression in the comedy of manners "Uncle Tony's Goat," in the nuanced and steady journey toward maturity of "A Geronimo Story," and finally in the intricately orchestrated process of healing and insight undertaken by the protagonist in *Ceremony*.

In "Private Property" Silko experiments with a new mode for exploring the theme of community through storytelling. The story is notable for its departure from the strict unity of point of view in her other short fiction. One of Silko's most successful efforts at comedy, "Private Property" is reminiscent of Faulkner's "Spotted Horses" in theme and approach. Both stories display a sense of the oral storytelling voice, the modulation of narrative exaggeration, and the obtuseness and pettiness accompanying the insight and wisdom of close-knit communities.

"Private Property" weaves its narrative through varying points of view: these include an omniscient intrusive authorial voice that opens the text with a synopsis of a traditional legend, the cranky musings of the elderly widowed sisters-in-law Etta and Reyna, the disparate perspectives of Reyna's niece Juanita, Juanita's sister Ruthie, and Ruthie's husband, and, throughout the story, a communal voice that almost takes on its own character, the "they say" of clan and village gossip. Sometimes point of view shifts with a marked division in the typeset text, and sometimes one perspective segues into another in midparagraph.

The narrative weaves in and out through time as well. Loosely constructed around the events of a morning in which a trio of horses breaks through a fence, the story sifts through Etta's recollections of her orphan childhood, her life at boarding school, and her job with a former teacher after the death of her husband; it brings in the village joke about how Juanita's uncle Joe died twice, and it juxtaposes the joke with Juanita's own memory of her uncle; it fills us in on how Cheromiah got his horses, and it reaches into the magic time of legend and myth. The sense of an indeterminate collective storytelling voice contributes to the defeat of chronology as present and remembered events become part of a fluid, many-centered story-in-progress.

Threaded through the narrative is a continuing critique of the concept of "private property." Ostensibly, the story offers "sharing" as a core Pueblo value, as in the maxim that Reyna and Etta have heard from their late mother-in-law: "The old lady said to share and love one another. She said we only make use of these things as long as we are here. We don't own them. Nobody owns anything" ("Private," 25). Etta disagrees. She enjoys privacy, her water-greedy hollyhocks, and her big yard, and she means to protect them. These are values that Etta has learned from living in the world of white people, first at boarding school, then with her husband in an Arizona town, and after that as companion to her boarding-school teacher: "The years away taught her differently. The yard is hers. They can't take it just because she had lived away from the village all those years" ("Private," 27).

However, the lines between "sharing" and "owning" are not simply drawn along the axis of cultural divide. Juanita believes she is the only one left carrying out the traditional duty of caring for elders, yet she worries that relatives who feed her pig will come back at butchering time to claim a part of it. Those same relatives, in turn, poke fun at Juanita's assumption that her uncle has died by attributing her mistake to her haste to collect her inheritance. "Somebody is always fighting over something" in the village, in Etta's view ("Private," 27). In her own life, Etta has received warmth and affection from her white teacher, in sharp contrast to the harsh criticism of the clanswoman who was her foster mother.

The real oppositional force to the village community's joking, bickering, and backbiting about sharing versus property rights is the instinct and vitality embodied in Cheromiah's horses and played out in Ruthie's husband's infidelity. A gift from his father-in-law, "the horses belong to Cheromiah, but the horses don't know that. 'Nobody told them,' that's what people say and then they laugh" ("Private," 23). What Ruthie's husband sees after his lover has been driven out of the cornfield is Cheromiah's horses breaking down Etta's fence, running free from one more attempt to catch and corral them.

The story of Ruthie's husband is Silko's completest elaboration of the tale originally printed as "Laughing and Laughing" and reworked in *Storyteller*. In "Private Property" the story ends with the husband's point of view as, having returned to his hoeing, he glimpses Cheromiah stalking his horses. The significant departure from earlier versions is the elaboration of the characters of the wronged wife and her sister, aunts, and clanswomen. The story has followed the threads of their lives that have brought them to this point, and they do not stand in silent accusation, as in "Laughing and Laughing," but raise a great noise: "They gesture with their arms and yell. . . . They are scolding the rest of the village over husband-stealing and corn that is sickly. Reyna raps on the fence post with her cane. Juanita calls him a pig. Ruthie cries because the beans won't grow" ("Private," 29). Apparently, sharing does not apply to spouses, and the vigor of the corn and beans is not improved by lack of restraint or the breaking of marriage vows.

The character of Etta is the most intriguing and enigmatic. She is clearly associated with the legendary child described in the opening: she is an orphan, she lives "among the ashes," she goes out in a kind of exile to grapple with challenges. According to the intrusive narrator's commentary on the legend, "the child's reliability as a narrator is believed to be perfect," suggesting an authoritative voice for this character ("Private," 21). The child is the hero of the legend, successfully defending the community against monster, drought, and famine. Etta has gone out into exile and adventure as the traditional hero does, but the knowledge she has returned with—property rights and real-estate values—is neither welcome nor apparently appropriate to the community. As Etta mutters over the drawbacks of village life, her internal monologue is more reminiscent of the fence-loving neighbor of Robert Frost's "Mending Wall": "She is thinking about the row of tamarisk trees she will plant along the fence so people cannot see her yard or house. She does not want to spend her retirement with everyone in the village minding her business the way they always have. . . . The village people don't understand fences," and on and on it goes ("Private," 27). The traditional legend has no more capacity to govern the story than Ruthie has to rein in her husband or Cheromiah to corral his horses or Etta to control her garden. The legend of the orphan child may itself be of ambiguous origin: it seems to be a variant of the Cinderella story, a tale which was apparently one of several introduced into Pueblo storytelling matter by a nineteenth-century anthropologist. Such ambiguous origins only add to the richness of indeterminacy in the story.

The lack of closure in theme as well as in narrative structure mark "Private Property" as another interrogation of the storytelling process, with the emphasis on process. The story is only secondarily about the virtues of sharing over the defects of private property—or vice versa. It is about the continuing contestation and dialogue regarding these things that constitute the life of the community. Etta, despite her old foster mother's accusations that she was ruined by the white school, is not an outcast, she is part of the village, as much as Juanita, Reyna, Cheromiah, Ruthie, Ruthie's husband, Ruthie's husband's lover, and the unconfined horses. The story subverts the binary fences between "private property" and "sharing" in all their manifestations. Who is "right" is impossible to determine and does not matter anyway. The vital matter is the ongoing dialogue carried out in bickering, gossip, communal meal preparation, scolding, neighborly greeting, and of course storytelling—the continual debate.

# Notes to Part 1

1. Leslie Marmon Silko, "Slim Man Canyon," in *The Remembered Earth: An Anthology of Contemporary Native American Literature*, ed. Geary Hobson (Albuquerque: University of New Mexico Press, 1981), 208; hereafter cited in text as *Remembered Earth*.

2. Leslie Marmon Silko, "Interior and Exterior Landscapes," in *Yellow Woman and a Beauty of the Spirit: Essays on Native American Life Today* (New York: Simon and Schuster, 1996), 37, 42–43; the essay is hereafter cited in text as "Interior," and the book as *Beauty*.

3. Joe S. Sando, *The Pueblo Indians* (San Francisco: The Indian Historian Press, 1976), 35; hereafter cited in text.

4. Leslie Marmon Silko, *Storyteller* (New York: Arcade, 1981); hereafter cited in text by page number.

5. Arnold Krupat, *The Voice in the Margin: Native American Literature and the Canon* (Berkeley: University of California Press, 1989), 134–201; Linda Danielson, "*Storyteller*: Grandmother Spider's Web," *Journal of the Southwest* 30.3 (Autumn 1988): 325–55; hereafter cited in text.

6. For a revisionist look at the concept of "marginality," see Barbara Babcock, " 'A Tolerated Margin of Mess': The Trickster and His Tales Reconsidered," in *Critical Essays on Native American Literature*, ed. Andrew Wiget (Boston: G. K. Hall, 1985), 153–84.

7. Leslie Marmon Silko, "An Old-Time Indian Attack Conducted in Two Parts," in *Remembered Earth*, 211–15; hereafter cited in text as "Attack."

8. Michel Foucault, "What Is an Author?" in *Textual Strategies: Perspectives in Post-Structuralist Criticism*, ed. Josue V. Arari (Ithaca, N.Y.: Cornell University Press, 1979), 141–60.

9. Leslie Marmon Silko, "Language and Literature from a Pueblo Indian Perspective," in *Beauty*, 50; hereafter cited in text as "Language and Literature."

10. Andrew Wiget, "Telling the Tale: A Performance Analysis of a Hopi Coyote Story," in *Recovering the Word: Essays on Native American Literature,* ed. Brian Swann and Arnold Krupat (Berkeley: University of California Press, 1987), 299.

11. *Keres* designates a language belonging to the Keresan group of languages including those spoken at Laguna, Acoma, and other New Mexico pueblos; the word has also been spelled *Queres,* according to Spanish orthography.

12. Among many printed versions of this tale are Tristram P. Coffin's example in *Indian Tales of North America* ([Philadelphia: American Folklore Society, 1961], 145–46), which he titles "The Bungling Host" according to the Aarne-Thompson motif index, and Sam Blowsnake's four variations in *The Trickster,* ed. Paul Radin (New York: Schocken, 1978), 41–49. T. C. S. Langen defines *version* and *collection* as a theoretical basis for understanding the relationship of individual instances of a given tale (versions) to a set of core elements (collection) in "Estoy-eh-muut and the Morphologists," *Studies in American Indian Literatures,* 2d ser., 1.1 (Summer 1989): 1–12. Silko wrestles with the same issue in one of her letters to poet James Wright: "There actually is 'the story' which people hear and tell, with different details, according to how their family or village tells it. But there is also another sense of the story, and that is 'the story' of a particular telling"; see *The Delicacy and Strength of Lace: Letters between Leslie Marmon Silko and James Wright,* ed. Anne Wright (St. Paul, Minn.: Graywolf Press, 1985), 86; hereafter cited in text as *Letters.*

13. See Barbara Babcock, "At Home No Womens Are Storytellers: Potteries, Stories, and Politics in Cochiti Pueblo," *Journal of the Southwest* 30 (1988): 356–89.

14. Robert A. Nelson notes another connection between story, place, and personal history: while making a film version of one of the Laguna stories, Silko built a stone cottage at the foot of Dripping Springs mesa; the structure has since fallen into ruin ("A Laguna Woman," unpublished paper).

15. The entire letter and also the reference to "exuberance" in another letter are reprinted in *Letters,* 6–9, 22.

16. Gerald Vizenor, *Earthdivers: Tribal Narratives on Mixed Descent* (Minneapolis: University of Minnesota Press, 1981), xxi.

17. Emory Sekaquaptewa writes in "Hopi Indian Ceremonies" that "[t]o the non-Indian, 'Indian' may have some validity. But it does not derive from a particular Indian culture. It is something that has been concocted by the non-Indian. . . . It is a stereotype, and not an accurate reflection of our empirical reality. . . . In terms of bringing awareness of the Indian to the non-Indian, it serves well. Once the non-Indian becomes aware of the existence of Indians and the richness of their cultures, then he is ready to become interested in a specific tribe of Indians. If this is what is happening, then it is a good thing"; in *Seeing with a Native Eye: Essays on Native American Religion,* ed. Walter Holden Capps (New York: Harper & Row, 1976), 41; hereafter cited in text. For a detailed

analysis of the concept of "the Indian," see Robert F. Berkhofer Jr., *The White Man's Indian: Images of the American Indian from Columbus to the Present* (New York: Random House, 1978).

18. Leslie Marmon Silko, "Old and New Autobiographical Notes," in *Beauty*, 196–200.

19. Kenneth Roemer, "The Heuristic Powers of Indian Literatures: What Native Authorship Does to Mainstream Texts," *SAIL—Studies in American Indian Literatures*, 2d ser., 3.2 (Fall 1991): 8–21.

20. Mary Louise Pratt, "Arts of the Contact Zone" *Profession 91* (New York: MLA, 1991), 34.

21. Kate Shanley Vangen, "The Devil's Domain: Leslie Silko's 'Story-teller,' " in *Coyote Was Here: Essays on Contemporary Native American Literary and Political Mobilization*, ed. Bo Scholer (Aarhus, Denmark: SEKLOS, University of Aarhus, 1984) 116–23; reprinted in this volume.

22. Kenneth Lincoln, *Native American Renaissance* (Berkeley: University of California Press, 1983), 224–32.

23. Numerous autobiographies and investigative reports have documented the Dickensian character of United States and Canadian boarding schools for Native children. Official policy was to destroy family and tribal ties, thus extinguishing Indian identity. The autobiographies of Basil Johnston and Helen Sekaquaptewa, for example, offer poignant accounts of this experience; see Basil Johnston, *Indian School Days* (Norman: University of Oklahoma Press, 1989), and *Me and Mine: The Life Story of Helen Sekaquaptewa*, transcribed and ed. Louise Udall (Tucson: University of Arizona Press, 1969).

24. Conrad Aiken, "Silent Snow, Secret Snow," in *The Collected Short Stories of Conrad Aiken* (Cleveland: The World Publishing Company, 1960), 216–35.

25. Herman Melville, "Bartleby the Scrivener," in *Billy Budd and Other Tales* (New York: Penguin, 1979), 108–143; book hereafter cited in text as Melville.

26. Ambrose Lucero, "For the People: Leslie Silko's *Storyteller*," *Minority Voices: An Interdisciplinary Journal of Literature and the Arts* 5.1–2 (1981): 1.

27. Personal communication: e-mail conversation, October 1996.

28. Elizabeth Kübler-Ross, *On Death and Dying* (New York: Macmillan, 1969). Also see *Death: Current Perspectives*, ed. Edwin S. Shneidman (Palo Alto, Calif.: Mayfield, 1976).

29. Gladys A. Reichard, *Navajo Religion: A Study of Symbolism* (Princeton: Princeton University Press, 1974), 467–68; hereafter cited in text. For a brief history and description of the Navajos, see Clyde Kluckhohn and Dorothea Leighton, *The Navaho* (Garden City, N.Y.: Doubleday & Co., 1962).

30. *Ceremony* (New York: Viking, 1977). For anthropological notes on Spider Grandmother in Keresan traditions see especially Elsie Clews Parsons, *Pueblo Indian Religion*, 2 vols. (Chicago: University of Chicago Press, 1989); and Franz Boas, *Keresan Texts*, pt. 1 (New York: The American Ethnological Society, 1928); hereafter cited in text.

31. James K. McNeley, *Holy Wind in Navajo Philosophy* (Tucson: University of Arizona Press, 1982), 18; hereafter cited in text. Also see Leland Wyman and Berard Haile, O.F.M., *Blessingway* (Tucson: University of Arizona Press, 1970).

32. Leland C. Wyman, *Navaho Sandpainting: The Huckel Collection* (Colorado Springs, Colo.: Taylor Museum of The Colorado Springs Fine Arts Center, 1971), 15.

33. Donald Sandner, M.D., *Navaho Symbols of Healing* (New York: Harcourt Brace Jovanovich, 1979), plate facing p. 132; hereafter cited in text; David Villaseñor, *Tapestries in Sand: The Spirit of Indian Sandpainting* (Healdsburg, Calif.: Naturegraph, 1966), 34.

34. For discussion of rainbow as pathway and bridge see John Bierhorst, ed., *Four Masterworks of American Indian Literature* (New York: Farrar, Straus and Giroux, 1974), 326, 337–38; for the story of the Rainbow People in the Nightway see James C. Faris, *The Nightway: A History and a History of Documentation of a Navajo Ceremonial* (Albuquerque: University of New Mexico Press, 1990), 182–227 passim.

35. *Seasons of a Navajo*, (Phoenix, Ariz.: Peace River Films for KAET, 1985).

36. LaVerne Harell Clark, *They Sang for Horses: The Impact of the Horse on Navajo and Apache Folklore* (Tucson: University Arizona Press, 1966), 26; hereafter cited in text.

37. N. Scott Momaday, *In the Presence of the Sun: Stories and Poems, 1961–1991* (New York: St. Martin's Press, 1992), 9.

38. A. LaVonne Brown Ruoff, "Ritual and Renewal: Keres Traditions in the Short Fiction of Leslie Silko," in *American Women Short Story Writers: A Collection of Essays*, ed. Julie Brown (New York: Garland, 1995), 167–89; hereafter cited in text; reprinted in this volume.

39. Robert M. Nelson, "He Said / She Said: Writing Oral Tradition in John Gunn's 'Ko-pot Ka-nat' and Leslie Silko's *Storyteller*," *SAIL—Studies in American Indian Literatures*, 2d ser., 5.1 (Spring 1993): 44. Also see John M. Gunn, *Schat-Chen: History Traditions and Naratives* [sic] *of the Queres Indians of Laguna and Acoma* (Albuquerque: Albright & Anderson, 1917); hereafter cited in text.

40. Other spellings of this word include *katsina, kachina, katcina*; I use the spelling of the text being quoted.

41. Edward P. Dozier, *The Pueblo Indians of North America* (New York: Holt, Rinehart and Winston, 1970), 155–57; John Upton Terrell, *Pueblos, Gods and Spaniards* (New York: The Dial Press, 1973), 93–94.

42. Patricia Clark Smith with Paula Gunn Allen, "Earthy Relations, Carnal Knowledge: Southwestern American Indian Women Writers and Landscape," in *The Desert Is No Lady: Southwestern Landscapes in Women's Writing and Art*, ed. Vera Norwood and Janice Monk (New Haven: Yale University Press, 1987), 178.

43. For a discussion of this motif in versions of a Pueblo story see my article, "The Witch Lady Story: Narrative Art in a Hopi Tale," in *Native American*

*Literatures,* ed. Laura Coltelli (Pisa, Italy: SEU—Servizio Editoriale Universitario, 1992), 3–25.

44. Lawrence J. Evers, "The Killing of a New Mexican State Trooper: Ways of Telling an Historical Event," in *Critical Essays on Native American Literature,* ed. Andrew Wiget (Boston: G. K. Hall, 1985), 246–61; hereafter cited in text; discussion of "Tony's Story" reprinted in this volume.

45. Brian M. Fagan, *Clash of Cultures* (New York: W. H. Freeman & Co., 1984), 280.

46. George Copway / Kah-ge-ga-gah-bowh, *Indian Life and Indian History by an Indian Author* (Boston: Albert Colby and Co., 1860), 241.

47. "A Conversation with Leslie Marmon Silko," *Sun Tracks: An American Indian Literary Magazine* 3.1 (Fall 1976): 32; reprinted in this volume.

48. Fred Eggan, *Social Organization of the Western Pueblos* (Chicago: University of Chicago Press, 1950), 264.

49. Alfonso Ortiz, *The Tewa World: Space, Time, Being and Becoming in a Pueblo Society* (Chicago: University of Chicago Press, 1969), 113.

50. N. Scott Momaday, *House Made of Dawn* (New York: Harper & Row, 1968), 56; hereafter cited in text.

51. Donna Perry, ed. "Leslie Marmon Silko," in *Back Talk: Women Writers Speak Out: Interviews by Donna Perry* (New Brunswick, N.J.: Rutgers University Press, 1993), 322; hereafter cited in text.

52. Jesse Walter Fewkes, "Ancestor Worship of the Hopi Indians," in *Annual Report of the Smithsonian Institution* (Washington, D.C.: Smithsonian Institution, United States Government Printing Office, 1921), 491; hereafter cited in text. I am going to anticipate here objections to my use of non-Laguna or non-Keresan sources to explain Pueblo elements in Silko's fiction, especially in view of commentary that inappropriately extracts significance derived from one culture to interpreting texts from another. Silko herself uses the more generic "Pueblo" as often as the specific "Laguna" when she talks about traditional customs and attitudes, and she has never restricted her writing to Keresan material, as "Storyteller" and "Lullaby" demonstrate. Furthermore, she has the same access as any other educated person to published sources and, like Momaday, has apparently relied on translations of Navajo texts from Bureau of American Ethnography (BAE) publications and other sources for the flavor of Navajo thought. The material I cite from Ortiz, Fewkes, and Ford is not limited to information on specific historical events or tribal practices but is the clearest articulation I can find of customs and attitudes common among the Pueblos.

53. Richard I. Ford, "An Ecological Perspective on the Eastern Pueblos," in *New Perspectives on the Pueblos,* ed. Alfonso Ortiz (Albuquerque: University of New Mexico Press, 1972), 4, 5; hereafter cited in text.

54. Angie Debo, *Geronimo: The Man, His Time, His Place* (Norman: University of Oklahoma Press, 1976), ix.

55. Per Seyersted, *Leslie Marmon Silko,* Western Writers Series No. 45 (Boise: Boise State University, 1980), 48; hereafter cited in text.

56. Judith Nies, *Native American History: A Chronology of the Vast Achievements of a Culture and Their Links to World Events* (New York: Ballantine Books, 1996), 291.

57. Linda Krumholz, " 'To Understand This World Differently': Reading and Subversion in Leslie Marmon Silko's *Storyteller," ARIEL: A Review of International English Literature,* 25.1 (January 1994): 107.

58. Leslie Marmon Silko, "Fifth World: The Return of Ma ah shra true ee," in *Beauty,* 133.

59. Leslie Marmon Silko, "Coyote Holds a Full House in His Hand," *TriQuarterly* 48 (Spring 1980): 166–174; hereafter cited in text as *TriQuarterly.*

60. Leslie Marmon Silko, foreword to *Border Towns of the Navajo Nation,* by Aaron Yava (Alamo, Calif.: Holmgangers Press, 1975), np.

61. Leslie Marmon Silko, "Laughing and Laughing," in *Come to Power: Eleven Contemporary American Indian Poets,* ed. Dick Lourie (Trumansburg, N.Y.: The Crossing Press, 1974), 99.

62. Leslie Marmon Silko, "Bravura" and "*from* Humaweepi, the Warrior Priest," both in *The Man to Send Rain Clouds: Contemporary Stories by American Indians,* ed. Kenneth Rosen (New York: Vintage, 1975) 149–54, 161–68; hereafter cited in text as "Bravura" and "Humaweepi."

63. Leslie Marmon Silko, "Private Property," in *Earth Power Coming: Short Fiction in Native American Literature,* ed. Simon J. Ortiz (Tsaile, Ariz.: Navajo Community College Press, 1983), 21–30; hereafter cited in text as "Private."

64. Further complicating these intertextual relationships is yet another mutation of the second part of the *Storyteller* version, which Silko performs in the video *Running on the Edge of the Rainbow,* in the Words and Place Videocassette Series (New York: Clearwater Publishing Co., 1982). The performance differs from the written text in several places, notably in not naming the principals and in elaborating in tall-tale fashion on the obesity of the woman partner.

THE WRITER

# Introduction

From the beginning of her career, Silko has articulated a strongly developed theory of her writing, its backgrounds, and the dynamic of written and oral verbal arts that she sees in her writing and in the life of her birth community of Laguna, New Mexico. Throughout her own writing and in the interviews she has granted she outlines a unique dual education that prepared her for the work she has undertaken. On the one hand, she received the sort of conventional education in primary, secondary, and postsecondary institutions that anyone schooled in America shares. However, the identity assigned to her as "marginal" in two senses—mixed-blood within Pueblo society and "Indian" in the Anglo or "American" world—and the response of others to that identity, complicated that educational experience for her. The origins of Silko's social activism and outrage at injustice can be traced to experiences of discrimination and cruelty that she, like so many other Indian children, encountered and observed at Indian schools, and she carries with her a deeply felt anger and sadness for the mistreatment of Indian children. Nevertheless, she acknowledges the benefit this schooling provided by introducing her to subjects, like Norse mythology, that have enriched her thinking and writing.

Parallel with her institutional schooling, Silko also benefited from the tutelage of elders in her family, especially the aunts, grandmothers, and great-grandmothers who lived nearby in the large extended family of Marmons around Laguna. In her essays, speeches, and interviews she expresses her sense of having received a unique education in Pueblo traditions from these women, who had also been educated in dual traditions and were deeply learned in their ancestral lore as well as literate and scholarly.

It is clear that Silko values this heritage tremendously and has given much thought to how best to carry on the obligation of keeping alive and transmitting its wisdom. Her interviews and essays return again and again to a highly sophisticated, evolving analysis of the dynamics of oral tradition in the construction of community, and the experimentalism of her fiction is often allied with efforts to recuperate some of that dynamism on the written page.

The interviews chosen for reprinting here were conducted early in her career and are less accessible than much of her other theoretical work. It is evident that even as a young writer she has developed a sense of authority and sureness about her material: she is well educated in the traditions that ground her writing and confident of the modes that she believes are valid for her to both transmit and transmute those traditions. The ideas introduced in these early theoretical discussions continue in her later lectures, interviews, and published essays.

# Interview with Lawrence Evers and Denny Carr

*Q.* How long has your family, the Marmon family, been in this house?

*S.* Well, this house we're in now is the old Santa Fe depot. I guess Grandpa Marmon bought it off the Santa Fe railroad when they changed the tracks. The railroad used to come right by here, and it went all the way around the village. In fact, there's a funny story that Harvey Paymella was spreading around the University of New Mexico. I wrote a poem about it. It's not a very good poem, I think, but it explains Harvey's Hopi theory on Laguna population. Harvey was saying that this is what the Hopis say. The fact that the Santa Fe railroad used to come so close to the village, right around it, the fact that there was a train that came by every morning about four a.m. and blew its whistle and woke everybody up, well, that explains why there are so many Lagunas around today. Disregarding Harvey and his scandalous Hopi population theory, the fact that the railroad came through here was very important. It had a great impact on the pueblo.

*Q.* The coyote poem we were talking about (*"Toe'osh:* A Laguna Coyote Story," *Carriers of the Dream Wheel* (Harper & Row, 1975), p. 223), does the Marmon family come into that poem?

*S.* "Some white men came to Acoma and Laguna and they fought over Acoma land and Laguna women, and even now some of their descendants are howling in the hills." Well, I don't know how the rest of the Marmons feel about that line. Also, it isn't just the Marmons. I would have to include the Gunns, Paula's family, and the Pratts. John Gunn and Walter Marmon, my great-grandfather's brother, came to Laguna after the Civil War. In fact, I have seen John Gunn's blue uniform, Civil War uniform. I tried the coat on, I wore it. They came to this part of the country as government surveyors. My great-grandfather came out a lit-

"A Conversation with Leslie Marmon Silko," reprinted from *Sun Tracks* 3.1 (1976): 28–33, by permission of Lawrence J. Evers.

tle while later after Walter was established. He began to write a memoir of his years here. I think it would have been very interesting, but he never finished it. He came out here in the late 1870's and died about 1935. As far as I know he was just to the part about coming as far as Albuquerque when he died. He got there by train, and then rode on horseback to Laguna. When he got here his legs and his behind were so blistered that he walked the last twenty miles because he couldn't bear to be on the horse. That's as far as he got. So what I know of him comes from what my grandmother mentions or my dad.

They had a contract with the government, and they were the ones who laid out the bench markers which are all around here to this day. Climbing around in the hills you'll find a really old corner, brass bench marker, and that's one of the ones that either Walter or Robert put in. My great-grandfather married a woman from Paguate. They had two children, and then she died. Then he married my great-grandmother, her younger sister. They had nine or ten kids one of which was my grandpa. I guess he taught school over at Acoma for a while.

One anthropologist has written about the Marmons and the impact they had at Acoma pueblo. His account emphasizes the fact that they were Presbyterians. I think maybe he gets the Marmons confused with old man Gorman who cleared out right around the time the Marmons came in. They bought the Gorman mission. It's true they were Presbyterians. My great-grandmother had been sent to school at Carlisle, Pennsylvania, and she was a very strong Presbyterian. Anyway, it's funny that the anthropologist thought it was so disruptive. When you look around here now and see how many people show up at the Presbyterian church. My grandfather and his brothers and sister never practiced that religion at all. I think maybe the ethnologist was only dreaming or wishing. Maybe he was a latent Presbyterian himself. Anyhow that's some of the background. My great-grandfather was a governor here at Laguna one year. I imagine that caused quite a stir.

*Q.* The river seems to be important to you in your writing. Is it important here at Laguna?
*S.* Well, look here where all the Marmon houses are here by the river, down in below the village. They put us in this place. I always thought there was something symbolic about that, sort of putting us on the fringe of things. The river's really close by. It's just a short walk from here, and I was always attracted to it as a kid. I loved the river very much, but I knew it was a small river, and I didn't make any great

demands on it. It's just a great place to go and play in the mud and splash around. There are willows and tamarack, and there are always stories. You just hear them. The river's the one place where things can happen that can't in the middle of the village, obviously. I guess from the very beginning there was always the idea that the river was kind of a special place where all sorts of things could go on. I got stuck in the sand down there once, and my Grandma pulled me out and switched me. But I kept going back, even when I was twelve, thirteen, fourteen, except by then my idea of the possibilities for the river had grown. They included not only catching minnows and little frogs, but I began to realize the possibilities which the people have forever realized. The river was a place to meet boyfriends and lovers and so forth. I used to wander around down there and try to imagine walking around the bend and just happening to stumble upon some beautiful man. Later on I realized that these kinds of things that I was doing when I was fifteen are exactly the kinds of things out of which stories like the Yellow Woman story, I finally put the two together: the adolescent longings and the old stories, that plus the stories around Laguna at the time about people who did, in fact, just in recent times, use the river as a meeting place. The river was a sort of focal point bringing all those together. The stories about places give one the ideas or materials, at least, for fantasies and dreams or expectations. All of your expectations and your feelings about the place are developed by what people say about it. And you are better prepared in turn for the stories that people tell and have always told about the place.

It goes back to the function of the stories, these gossip stories. No, I don't look upon them as gossip. The connotation is all wrong. These stories about goings-on, about what people are up to, give identity to a place. There's things about the river you can see with your own eyes, of course, but the whole feeling of the place, the whole identity of it was established for me by the stories I'd heard, all the stories: the early stories, the goings-on, and the warning stories about the old man who lost a team of horses in the quicksand at a certain point on the river. That's how you know, that's how you belong, that's how you know you belong, if the stories incorporate you into them. There have to be stories. It's stories that make this a community. People tell those stories about you and your family or about others and they begin to create your identity. In a sense, you are told who you are, or you know who you are by the stories that are told about you. I see now that the ideas and dreams and fears and wonderful and terrible things that I expected might happen around the river were just part of an identity that the stories had made for it. By going to the river, I was stepping into that identity. And I think it happens for other individuals, families, and clans. That's why stories are told by clans.

Stories were important in this way for us Marmons because we are a mixed breed family. People in the main part of the village were our clanspeople because the clan system was still maintained although not in the same form it would have been if we were full blood. The process went on, but it changed slightly for us. The way it changed was that there began to be stories about my great-grandfather, positive stories about what he did with the Laguna scouts for the Apaches. But then after World War One it changed. Soon after that there came to be stories about these mixed blood people, half-breeds. Not only Marmons but Gunns and Pratts too. An identity was being made or evolved in the stories the Lagunas told about these people who had gone outside Laguna, but at the same time of the outsiders who had come in. Part of it was that the stories were always about the wild, roguish, crazy sorts of things they did. Maybe greedy and bad, there were both positive and negative things. But the identity was made for our families, and we're a big bunch of people now. So that happened.

In a sense it made it easier for me than for somebody like Simon Ortiz who doesn't have that kind of separate identity. A very different set of possibilities are open to him because he is a full blood Acoma man whose father is very involved in the religious things. There's a whole different set of stories and expectations for him that sometimes can constrict him. I don't say that negatively, of course, it's just different. I have great latitude by contrast.

*Q*. Many contemporary poets are remaking or "rescuing" songs and stories from old BAE reports, and their efforts are often thought of as the Native American oral tradition. You seem to be working from a more vital source, from what you hear now, rumor, gossip, and the like.

*S*. Yes, that's probably the basis for my acquaintance with language. For a long time I was sort of self-conscious about not knowing the Laguna language better than I do. I had that in that one poem about my Grandfather. I always had the feeling that he died too soon. And I was given to feel—by some of those poets—that to be a worthy human being if you were coming from a pueblo, you should know the stories just the way the anthropologists reported them. Yet I was never tempted to go to those things and do what they did. There were some things that I heard and some things that I knew, and I thought, well, you know, you've just got to stick with it, with what you've heard, with what you have. I figured that anybody could go to the anthropologists' reports and look at them. I have looked at them myself, but I've never sat down with them and said I'm going to make a poem or a story out of this. The more I think about it, I realize I don't have to because from the time I was little I heard quite a bit. I heard it in what would be passed off now as rumor or gossip. I could hear through all that. I could hear something else, that there was a kind of continuum that was really there despite Elsie Clews Parsons. In 1930, you know, she wrote off Laguna as a lost cause. She said it had no kiva, that it was dead. I think she wrote that somewhere. And the same went for the "oral tradition."

I guess somewhere along the line I must have been hearing, and you still can. It's like last year at Laguna Feast they had a trash fight. There were some Navajos down at the trash pile, and they had a fight. It's called a trash pile fight. Every year at Laguna Feast there are these incidents. I always loved stories about them so much that the things in the anthropological reports looked dead and alien. I couldn't do anything with them anyway, even though theoretically they came from here. So I leave those things to those people that are so impoverished that they have to go resurrect them.

I also know the attitudes of people around here to those reports. You don't know how accurate they are. I started writing a story about ethnologists just continually milking their informants, kind of reversing that. When I started to write, I started to laugh. I never did get past the first meeting. This Charlie Coyote type starting to size up the anthropologist, he's talking about someone else who's been in the kitchen all this time pretending not to understand what was going on. After he leaves they start discussing, "What'd you tell him that for? Those are outrageous lies." I've always been real leery of the kinds of things that the ethnologists picked up, another reason not to fool around with it.

*Q.* The kinds of things you do pick up, how do you give them form? How does a Leslie Silko poem develop?
*S.* I just go at it. Somehow it just starts to come together. With the coyote story ["*Toe'osh:* A Laguna Coyote Story"], I wrote it after I came back from a writers conference in Wisconsin. At first, it started out to be something just about Simon Ortiz and about the conference back there. And then . . . then, somewhere I started to think about the coyote thing because Simon had read one of his coyote poems. He'd been talking

about *Toe'osh*. Then all of a sudden I did this big switch. I started thinking that all these years there have been all these things. One was this
Navajo story that the students told me about when I was teaching at
Navajo Community College. I started remembering all these other
things. It was like suddenly seeing that there are other kinds of coyote
stories than just the ones in the BAE. Then I knew exactly how these
things had to be said. I figured out what kind of coyote stories they were
going to be. They were going to be like that one about the Lagunas, the
politicians, and the turkeys. Once you see those connections, then it's
easy. It's getting around to where you can see that's the hard part.

*Q.* Earlier you mentioned a talk you had with one of your neighbors this
morning about that poem. Would you talk about her reaction again?
*S.* Well Nora was talking about the part about the coyote chain, that old
story. I guess she was excited to recognize it. It's very, very sketchy the
way I've got it, as little as I could say and still get across what happens.

*Q.* Would you read that part?
*S.* O.K. This is part seven of the poem.

> They were after the picnic food
> that the special dancers left
> down below the cliff.
> And *Toe'osh* and his cousins hung themselves
> down over the cliff
> holding each other's tail in their mouth
>     making a coyote chain
> until someone in the middle farted
> and the guy behind him opened his
> mouth to say "What Stinks?" and they
> all went tumbling down, like that.

So this morning I guess Nora's grandchildren ran across that story in
*Carriers of the Dream Wheel*. She said that she had her grandchildren read
the poem to her, those things, and then that got her started. It brought
up that story. Then my fantasy of what was probably said was "well, the
way the story really goes is like this . . ." Then I think she went ahead
and told them that and said how, when she was young, how many of
those stories she'd heard. She was talking about an old man and her dad
and how they would sit around the stove. Then, jokingly, before they
began, say, "The storyteller cannot begin. The storyteller cannot tell

stories unless there's some parched corn or pinons at the least." So someone would have to jump up and get this for the storyteller before he would begin. Otherwise he wouldn't. So she was recalling that this morning. She said that there were one or two stories that would take almost the whole evening just to complete and by that I would imagine from like five or six all the way to I don't know what time. People around here aren't too strict about when you go to bed. You just sort of go when you want to, so it could have been like eleven at night.

So the younger kids came across this poem and in reaction she said let me tell you the whole story. One of my frustrations in writing, you know, is that unless you're involved in this, in these stories, in this place, you as a reader may not get it. I have to constantly fight against putting in detail and things that would be too tedious for the "outsider." At the same time I have to have some sort of internal integrity there in the piece. But I'm satisfied with that. What I was doing in that coyote piece wasn't to retell it just the way it would be told by someone like Nora here. I hope the young kids have or develop a taste for the longer versions too. This one's really a funny one. Coyote comes over to the edge of this mesa and peeks over and he sees these dancers. The way my aunt describes it, the dancers are from a dance society that no longer exists, it's completely died out, so they were very special. And they had laid out all the food that they were going to eat after they got done dancing or practicing dancing, or whatever. Whatever they were doing down there was kind of mysterious. So the story is kind of cinemagraphic, the opening scene is like the opening scene of a movie. Coyote is peeking over the edge, and there are all these nice things down there, and the dancers are laying them out not knowing that Coyote is peeking over. You get the sense that Coyote's all alone. Then he kind of goes "mmmm, wow. It looks good, but it's way down there." I guess it's on a mesa where it's miles to go around and get down. So finally he has an idea. He runs back from the edge, and he starts calling, "ooooh, ooooh," you know, calling all his cousins. And they gather, and he says, "I've got this idea. Look. Look down there." And they all look, and they're excited, but they say, "Well, how are we gonna get it?" And he says, "Ah, that's why I've called you. I have this brilliant idea, and this is how it's going to work." Some of them are kind of doubtful, and they say, "Wow, this is really high, and if anything were to happen . . ." "No, no, don't worry." And then, you get the coyote chain, so that in the longer version it's really funny because when it finally happens, when one farts and they all fall down, it's even better because Coyote's been reassuring all the others, telling them there's not a thing to worry about that everything's gonna go fine. I've thought about this a lot. The one thing he hadn't taken into consideration happens. So the longer version is really a lot of fun. It's a good story.

*Q.* Working from these longer versions, then, does condensing become a problem for you in your work?
*S.* I guess the problem with condensing comes from the fact that the people around here have a lot of time, or they make time, to talk. So the people really appreciate hearing a good story, and a good story was a story that would last long enough at least. It was one that has all kinds of details and gestures. When you tell certain things, you might be expected to act out these facial expressions and gestures and so forth. So the Laguna stories whether they're the very old time ones like coyote stories or whether they're something that happened at the last Laguna fiesta, there has always been a problem condensing them for the outsider, for the non-Laguna. One of the things I recall reading in one of the anthropologist's books was the Lagunas had a seemingly inexhaustible capacity for cataloguing and listing and also hearing the reciting ceremonial detail. There's the same sort of inexhaustible capacity for describing places and directions. In describing places and directions, there are stories that identify the place. These kinds of things make condensing a problem. It all depends on how much you want to make your stories acceptable to communities outside this one. I condense, but I try to be very careful to preserve the essential quality that stories have that makes them stories. If that is cut, then you've ruined the whole thing.

*Q.* What about witch stories, you use some in your novel and other places, where do they fit into contemporary Laguna oral tradition?
*S.* It wasn't until I went out to Chinle that I ever heard witch stories, because people here don't consider it to be a polite subject for conversation. I agree with Simon, although I always have to qualify with the fact that I was growing up down here at the foot of the village and up at the mill, that there's just not a whole lot of that that goes on anyway. Simon has said, too, that when a community is, in the catch phrase, together, where things are fairly orderly, where the livestock and the food supply is good, where some widespread series of deaths of religious leaders hasn't hit, where everything is in good shape within the pueblo view, then there's not going to be any witchcraft. It goes against the def-

inition of witchcraft. Witchcraft is happening when the livestock are skinny. Simon has said, and my sense is pretty much the same, that there's not much of that that happens around here. It can almost be said with pride. The occurrences are rare, and when they do occur they were handled by everybody. It wasn't like just one person dealing with it.

The whole Navajo thing seems different to me. First of all, witchcraft activity is incessant. It seems to touch almost everybody, and the means by which the Navajo seem to be attempting to deal with it were a little bit more like on an individual family basis. Tremendously expensive ceremonies and payments of money to medicine men seem to be necessary, whereas when the pueblo people worked these things out, you would have some kind of community thing not so much focused on the sick one. Navajos get so specific. This kind of sandpainting for this particular patient. Navajo perception of witchery seems much more widespread and involved. What I'm getting around to saying is I never heard many of those stories here, except for the classic. I heard that one and that says just about everything you need to know about witches. I heard that one, but that's the only one. I *never, never,* while I was growing up, ever heard anybody say so and so's sick or so and so died because of witchcraft. But the whole time I was in Chinle and Lukachuchai, it was so and so's got a rash on his hands because he did this, and so and so wrecked her car, and that was obviously because so and so caused it. The stories are all over there, you can't avoid them. If I hadn't gone up there, I probably never would have gotten into witchcraft in my writing.

Once I got into it, I began to try to understand how witchcraft fits into the whole scheme of things. That's when I got more interested in witchcraft as it *might* have occurred around here. I develop some of that in the novel.

*Q.* Does the Black Corn story appear in the novel?
*S.* The Black Corn story is there. I have the whole story at the beginning now, but we're going to cut it. But it comes into the novel at various points, I will still have some fairly direct references to it. It's there in so far as everything Arrow Boy sees in the Black Corn story, the main character in my novel sees, but in a different form. Arrow Boy in the story sees them in their cave. And part of the curse and prophecy thing is there, the jumping through the hoop three times. Towards the end, everything Tayo sees is what Arrow Boy saw, but in a different century and a different form. It's there, it almost has to be. There's just no way around it. The reason I first put the Arrow Boy story in the beginning

was to clue people in who might not know. It was an afterthought, so I'm pulling it out again. I think it works without that whole thing in there, that's the way I wrote in the first place.

In the novel, I've tried to go beyond any specific kind of Laguna witchery or Navajo witchery which is why that one story is so important, that sort of curse-prophecy thing. I try to begin to see witchery as a sort of metaphor for the destroyers or the counter force, that force which counters vitality and birth. The counter force is destruction and death. It's one of the things that Ben Barney and I have worked out. We have tried to get away from talking about good and evil. Part of it is a kind of affectation. We're trying to affect the old, old, old way of looking at the world, but I think a lot of it is still implied. It's just that in recent years we've gotten into the habit of talking about black and white and good and bad. But back when, it was force or counter force. It may seem corny, but it is the idea of balance, an idea that the world was created this way. In the novel it's the struggle between the force and the counter force. I try to take it beyond any particular culture or continent because that's such a bullshit thing. It's all Whitey's fault, that's too simplistic, mindless. In fact Tayo is warned in the novel that *they* try to encourage people to blame just certain groups, to focus in on just certain people and blame them for everything. Then you can't see what the counter people or the counter forces are really doing. I think that's important, and I wanted to get that in. So, what I'm trying to say is that ultimately I go way beyond any kind of local experience I might have had.

Q. There's a passage in the novel, isn't there, that begins something like, "white people created witches," but then somebody says, "that's too simple, white people are only tools which the witchery manipulates. They invented white people."
S. It's sort of outrageous. Another name for the counter forces are the manipulators. That comes out in the old story, which I'm sure is in Parsons, about one of the many times when our mother got pissed off at the people. It was the magician who came down from the north. I have that story in the novel. The magician was showing the people all kinds of tricks, how to do this and that and the other. He'd make water come out of the north wall, he'd touch a log and it would jump up and become a mountain lion, and the people's eyes were getting real big. And the twin brothers who were caretakers of the corn mother altar got excited. Everyone was standing around watching this guy. He was going through

a whole routine, and everybody got all excited and involved in this magic, and they forgot to take care of the altar. At one point the magician says, "You guys want some of this magic?" And the twins say, "Yeah, yeah, boy we could really use that for the fields. We could do anything. We wouldn't have to work anymore. This is fantastic. We'll take some." And they got all involved, and in the meantime the corn mother gets very angry, and she says, "Well, if they're so happy with that, then I'll just leave them with it. Go ahead and see how far it takes you." The whole point being that they've become manipulators. They create nothing. They merely take what is around, whatever it is, whether it's a simple sleight of hand or some of the magician's tricks or whether we're talking about using races of people or philosophies or technologies. What should emerge is that the manipulators, the white people, according to this awful story I made up, will be manipulated. The whole point of the novel is that they're trying to manipulate everybody. One of the big battles Tayo begins to have to deal with is to keep the end of the story right. They're trying to manipulate him into doing something that would change the way the story has to go. It goes back into the ceremony thing that started long ago, and, of course, it goes on and on. So they're manipulators. They cannot originate things. That's why they jump into animal skins, and that's why I had that note that live animals were horrified of them.

*Q.* So the oral tradition is anything but dead and buried in dusty reports at Laguna.

*S.* Yeah, we're going stronger than ever. Even just the good old adultery stories are better than ever and much more intricate because not everyone has in-door plumbing, so that you no longer have that excuse to go out, which was a pretty good one. It's just like what I was saying earlier about the Laguna Feast stories. They just go on and on and on. There's no end to it. The feast changes, but the stories keep right on going with very few differences. The way I end my novel, one of the endings, is to have the old woman say something like "I'm getting too old to even get excited about the goings-on around here anymore. It doesn't even excite me anymore." She said, "It's all beginning to sound like I've heard all those stories before, only some of the names are different." At which point she goes to sleep. That's one of the endings of the novel, probably not the one we'll keep, but that sense of a continuity is just there. You can hear it all around.

# Two Interviews with Per Seyersted

## 1: Laguna, New Mexico, January 7, 1976

*Per Seyersted:* You went to school in Albuquerque, didn't you?

*Leslie Marmon Silko:* Right. Four years I went here to the day school, just across the road here, and then I finished up school in Albuquerque.

*PS:* Did you feel it as difficult to be outside the Laguna environment?

*LMS:* Well, I've never encountered any kinds of vicious racial confrontations. I suppose it was more feeling very strange, everything about Albuquerque and the kids I was going to school with, and that whole setting was very strange, kind of alien, and I moved through it as best I could, which I think most of the people from the Pueblos and from the reservations do even now. We move through the city, we talk with the people, but there's an extreme amount of tension that one feels and it can only be described as strangeness. We were fortunate that our parents sent us to small schools, not to public schools, and at the Catholic schools of course they were very strict about any sort of teasing and things like that, so we were pretty secure there. But I can remember one fall after hunting season we'd all done well and we got deer and my dad's aunt over at Paguate dried the meat and made jerky out of it. I can remember in the eighth grade taking my lunch to school. I hated to get up in the morning to make my lunch and I would take a large handful of dry meat and stuff it into my paper lunchbag and then maybe put in a candy bar and an orange and that was my lunch. This was a girls' school; my classmates on either side of me kind of jumped up and kind of scooted back, and they said, "What's *that?* It looks terrible," and I said, "Will you want to taste some of it?" and they said, "No!" Fortunately I was old enough, or maybe secure enough, not to feel . . . or at least I wasn't conscious of feeling ashamed of having brought that. It also had

"Two Interviews with Leslie Marmon Silko," reprinted from *American Studies in Scandinavia* 13 (1981): 17–33, by permission of the editors.

to do with my attitude which was I was always . . . I made the most of being different, and so I can remember laughing at them and telling them, you know, actually taking a piece of meat—and these are eighth grade, ninth grade girls—and either sort of shoving a piece of meat, of this dry meat toward them and watching them jump as if it were a snake or something. I mean, I took that attitude that *they* were the ones that were silly and not myself that thus . . . So it was that I was aware of encountering, but it was that kind of conflict more than it was any kind of brutal or vicious kind of . . . it was more subtle.

*PS:* Compared to many other people who are not "in the mainstream of the American life," wouldn't you say that you have had a great security, a great strength in the fact that you are solidly based in your own culture, and that as you said, you feel the *others* were stranger?

*LMS:* Yeah, just maybe I think of it more in terms of even just the place. A lot of these hills and mesas I showed you this morning: there's a sense of familiarity almost like certain places being a parent or relative, in other words, being related to the land in a familiar way, and there's a kind of security there which I always feel. You know, when I was going to the university, during the school term I lived in Albuquerque, but as soon as we would leave Albuquerque and gradually drive back into this area, a feeling comes just of being in a place. Not to mention that I have always felt . . . when the people here like the sacristan that we met up at the church . . . you know, I remember Joe from the time I was so little that I wasn't in school, and he remembers me, and there's also, of course, then, that kind of security. There again I . . . when that security is tied in with people . . . of course, people pass away, eventually . . . that's the beauty of the land, you know, that these things . . . and this is why it is important to me: my father tells me stories that his father told him about certain places, and it is as if when one goes back to these places that all of those past things that happened in that place, in a sense, their presence is still there, and so you don't lose it, even though human beings may pass away and old age comes and so forth. And there's a sense of having even with one's relatives back through the years . . . that somehow they are still there, they are still a presence. So, yes, then you have this, and it never fails. I was afraid when I came back from Alaska that maybe somehow it wouldn't feel that way anymore. Two years in Alaska was the longest I have ever been away from this part of the country. It was magical. I came back and maybe I felt it more strongly than I ever had.

*PS:* You have chosen to write about a number of male characters, haven't you?

*LMS:* Yeah. I guess it goes back to the fact that when I was growing up I never thought of myself as having any sort of gender one way or the other. I mean, certainly I was aware that I was a girl, but if you've noticed my grandmother, she is in and out and she is seventy-four—when she was growing up she was a Model A mechanic, and even now, my uncle has a coin-operated laundry here and she fixes those machines and she carries heavy things. So she was there when I was growing up, and my father had three daughters, I was the oldest, and my father made no connections between the fact that we were daughters and not sons. He took me deer-hunting when I was seven years old, and then when I was a little girl I can remember when the crews would come to plaster the house, that they were women. The people who plaster the houses here traditionally have always been women, men do not plaster houses. So in all my surroundings I never . . . I mean, I realized I was a girl, but I never saw that one's experiences or one's activities had to—either in my own family or just around me—I never made the connection that because of one's sex one would be limited to certain kinds of experiences. I had a horse when I was eight years old, and as I got older I would go up north to the ranch—this is an area I write about a lot—and I would help them gather cattle and drive cattle.

*PS:* So because of your own experience and because of the manners and customs of the Laguna pueblos . . .

*LMS:* Right—

*PS:* It simply was natural to you to have seen many aspects of what otherwise mostly men do . . .

*LMS:* Right. And not to think that, not to feel that, in terms of the consciousness that I . . . that there was something that one must exclusively be forced to stay within one consciousness.

*PS:* How do you look upon black aesthetics, the fact that some blacks feel that only blacks should write for blacks, only blacks can judge anything written about the blacks. Is there any such feeling among Native American writers, and do you share it?

*LMS:* I think it depends on whether the . . . if the non-Indian writer wants to attempt to create a consciousness and pass off this consciousness as an Indian consciousness. I think there is an area where I would tend to say that that's on very uncertain, unsteady ground, that sooner or later in one's imagery and one's handling of that consciousness this non-Indian writer is going to get herself or himself into trouble. I think that the most important thing that any writer, any writer should remember in writing about any other person or group or culture is for the writer to remember where he or she has come from, and to always remember one's own experiences, and to be true . . . or at least not to forget that the eyes that you've seen these people and these things with and the words that you use and the feelings you are putting into the work are *yours*, and they are coming from your origin, they are coming from your ancestors, and so that to always remember, then, always keep that one thing straight, a perspective, *then* if one is honest one does not pretend to be the expert upon blacks, or the resident expert on upper middle class college professors or whatever, we keep this perspective. I think that's most important. Oliver LaFarge was a pioneer, he was the first, perhaps, to discover the difficulties when one attempts to take on the consciousness of a person worlds away from one's own culture. He would have done much better to have done a novel about the Eastern person, the white person who cared very much for the native American people, but who was Harvard educated, an ethnologist. Then he could have given us the different kinds of emotional things of the conflicts which he must have gone through, because I know that at that time, that the Navajos didn't always embrace him with open arms. But we don't get this, and as a writer I feel that that's the important thing. I think that's where the center lies.

*PS:* Yes. Unless you are a commercial writer.

*LMS:* Right. I guess, when I talk about writing I am always thinking about writing from the heart. And one must write from one's heart. And that seems to me so much more valuable for everybody, and as a native American people we could learn so much from an honest account from a person like LaFarge which we do not have, we could learn a lot about how *he* felt. We know how *we* feel, or the people they knew how they felt to have him around.

*PS:* You mentioned your father and your grandfather and all they have told you. Don't you feel that you have quite a store of material at the back of your head that you can call back at your leisure and in time bring to something, that you have a great *donnée* of material that you can use when it suits you?

*LS:* Oh, right, precisely. I think of even my technical skill as a storyteller as a birthright. I recently went up to Laguna-Acoma highschool and spent all day with English classes. I said to them: "You know, they talk about different geographical areas and different groups of people having a resource, like they have uranium, they have gold, they have timber as a resource. This area is very interesting," I said, "doesn't it seem interesting to you that Simon Ortiz would come from Acomita, and I would

107

be at Laguna, and then there's this one other guy, Robert Fernando, who one day just out of the blue sat down and wrote a fine short story." I said, "Don't you think there's something suspicious about this," I said, "because I do. Certain areas and certain people have another kind of 'resource,' " and I said, "I think we all have it, we are very fortunate, we are lucky. Our greatest natural resource is stories and storytelling. We have an endless, continuing, ongoing supply of stories." And I said to them, "All of you have this and you should not forget it, and you shouldn't look upon Simon and myself as some kind of accident." I think it is something that many people here already possess, it is a part of the way of life, storytelling is. When you meet somebody around Laguna, you take a lot of time, you say, "Hello, how are you? Say, did you hear about what happened the other night?" And then you take the time to start at the very beginning of what happened the other night. "My goodness, it started at noon the day before," and then you go into this very detailed telling, including the dialogue, of what so and so said to so and so. Well, this is something that the people have always done, this is something you hear from the time you are a little child. It's you talk about having a sense of the story and of recounting the story, just what elements need to be there and which don't. The people, all the people that I've ever known and continue to know have given this to me.

*PS:* Yes. But still, you wouldn't say that just anyone here could write a story like "The Man to Send Rain Clouds"—you have gained something from what you have read, too, haven't you?

*LS:* Oh, right, I've . . .

*PS:* —some sense of technique, at least

*LS:* Yeah. I did a lot of reading when I was a child. There, again, I think, indirectly having developed this great appreciation for stories, I loved to read; and I loved the fact that you could go to books and inside of books were more stories, and stories from other places, and people around here have a tremendous appetite for stories and they don't even care where they came from. And so, yes, I did a lot of reading.

*PS:* What did you mostly read?

*LMS:* When I was thirteen or fourteen, I was very much interested in American authors, John Steinbeck and William Faulkner, and oh, Edgar Allan Poe. Possibly, again, what one reads is determined by the kinds of books that one finds. I can remember encountering Shakespeare in highschool and not liking Shakespeare very much, and then falling in love with him in college. Well, the first kinds of things I've read I can remember are Faulkner and Steinbeck and Poe. I don't know how much this most recent story I've written [Silko was here referring to "Escape Story"], the structure and all sorts of things turning in upon themselves, whether Borges, the Argentine, I'd love to read him, I became fascinated with him, maybe some of my most recent experiments and things were indirectly from him. Also Flannery O'Connor—I use her all the time in my classes, and I tell my students, "Look, look what she's done." The students'd say, "Oh, she just writes about the same old area and countryside." "Well," I said, "Yes, that's true. I understand as a person, especially as she was ill in her later years she really didn't move around very much," and I said, "and that in a sense is one of her greatest achievements, just to take these same sorts of things again and again and again to make these magnificent stories, you know."

*PS:* Yes. Do you use much invention or do you have so much inherited that you do not need to go much beyond that?

*LMS:* Well, you know, I never know how much I imagine and how much is actually what I have heard and have forgotten and it comes back. Sometimes it can be rather frightening. Some other things I can't account for: One of the stories I wrote, the Tony story, the killing of the State policeman. OK, my father talked about it, and I heard other people talk about this incident that took place. I sat down and wrote this story, and in the story I took it from a very specific point of view, Tony's point of view, and I thought at the time that I was inventing this whole thing with the witch. Well, Larry Evers at the University of Arizona got very intrigued with the fact that Simon had written about the State police killing and *I* had, and so Larry started to do research into the old trial records and so forth, and he found that the man, the accused not only told the psychiatrist he thought the state policeman was a witch—it was also used as a defense in court in the trial. Now, I tell you, when it was happening I was four years old, I couldn't have read it in the paper. I didn't know very much about it. Anyway, Larry sent me the letter and I kind of got almost physically ill to read that what I thought had been my imagination turned out to be true. But I started to go back over the details of the killing, and I can remember my dad—you know how my dad talks, you've been talking to him—he told me about the killing of the policeman and he said, "They put the cop's body in the car and they set that car on fire, and later on when the people went and found the remains (and then this is my dad, the way he likes to talk) all that was left of that cop would fit into a shoebox," you know. I go back now, and what I must have known, and what must have clued me in a kind of subconscious way was that you burn witches' remains, and see, that was one part of the story that I had heard and it had been impressed upon me by dad—they had burned the state policeman's body. That was the clue, the key. But I never know, I never know until much later, and then people will come to me and say, "How did you know this," or "Where did you hear that?" And, then they will tell me something, you know, and they'll say, "This actually happened." And all I can think is that maybe as a little child I listened awfully closely or something, maybe I was always listening, I don't know.

*PS:* How far back do you remember?

*LMS:* I sometimes remember things when I was two or three, but the trouble is, living with people like my people here are, just the way my dad is always telling things, you lose sense of whether you really are remembering it or whether you just heard it. One's own history and experiences are being recounted constantly . . . you hear it so much, you don't know whether you are really remembering it at that moment when you were two years old, or whether you just remember them telling you about it.

*PS:* How do you feel about the American Indian Movement?

*LMS:* I feel that they're on one road that runs parallel to the road that I travel. I've seen the kinds of things that they talk about, I've been up in South Dakota and North Dakota, I've friends up there. In other words, I can sympathize and understand what they are saying. But there's no subtlety to their view. They oversimplify the world. They oversimplify things, and I'm bored with the oversimplification. They'll say, "This person here, so and so, he is in jail now, the reason he is in jail is because he did something while he was drinking, and the evil system has him in jail, the corrupt white system has him in jail and he is going to rot there." OK, I know a lot about the American justice system and that part is true. Once you're thrown in jail, unless you have lots of money for a fancy attorney, that's where you're going to stay. OK, that part is true. But what they miss is all of the personal subtleties and the unique experiences and aspects of this individual's life which have brought this person to this place in time. It is much more important to explore all of the possible depths and all of the possible details of a person's life and to range through time—back to a time before this person was born. This is how you begin to understand why these things happen. I feel it is more effective to write a story like "Lullaby" than to rant and rave. I think it is more effective in reaching people. A.I.M. is simply another political group, and I find them too similar to other American political groups.

*PS:* How do you feel about the Bicentennial—do you have feelings about it?

*LS:* Oh, I do, definitely, I have all kinds of things to say—I think it's one reason I'm very anxious to try to get the novel out during 1976. I just want to make sure that during this year when all of this sort of celebrating is going on, that Americans can be reminded that there are different ways to look at the past 200 years. I just want to make sure that beside all of the rhapsodizing about Paul Revere and George Washington and Benjamin Franklin that Americans are reminded that this great land, this powerful nation they are celebrating was established on stolen land. It was the resources, the metals, and minerals, it was the water, it was the coal, that enabled those people who came to America to build this nation. In this Bicentennial year we should remember, we should remember that it was on this stolen land that this country was settled and begun. In Anglo-Saxon law, in common law, when something is stolen, no matter how many times the stolen property changes hands, in common law, that piece of property still belongs to the original owner. It doesn't matter whether the people take the stolen article in good faith. The property remains stolen. As long as this fact is acknowledged, then I'll be satisfied, and they can celebrate all they have done with this stolen land and the stolen resources and they can pat themselves on the back for the achievement.

*PS:* What Native American writers do you like?

*LMS:* It's probably better to tell you what I *don't* like rather than what I do like as I like almost all of the . . . Also, there are so few of them. What I don't like: Well, again, I hesitate to go on about what I don't like. Let me just say that I see things, then, in poetry sometimes that seem to me a bit precious, or somehow it seems that the writers are bowing to expectations—that is, they feel that they are expected, because they are Native Americans, to write in a special way.

*PS:* In subject matter and attitudes more than in technique?

*LMS:* Well, even now in technique. I think it is probably the white writers more than any who have actually dictated what they think "Indian writing" should be. People like Rothenberg and of course Gary Snyder perfected the "white shamanism" movement. The attitude of the white shaman is that he knows more about Indians than the Indians know. It has happened with Indian graphic art and painting. The people who buy the paintings tell the Indian artist, "Don't do that, that's abstract— Indians ought to only do realistic sorts of paintings," and, "Oh, don't

111

paint that, that's a picture of a drunken man passed out on the street of Gallup. That won't sell in our gallery, you know." In other words, white patrons have very much controlled and molded it. I can see it happening with the writing—publishers using Jerome Rothenberg's chants as a standard for judging poetry that Native Americans may write because Rothenberg appeals to the romanticized notion of what Native American literature is.

*PS:* Do Native American writers as of today feel any pressure from publishers as to what to write, how to write?

*LMS:* I don't think we are aware of any pressure yet. If there is going to be any pressure in the future, probably not a pressure to be angry as with the blacks, but perhaps more of this pressure to fall into some of these preconceived . . . having people like, not Rothenberg specifically or someone like that, saying, "Why are you writing about 1952 GMC pick up trucks and Ripple wine?" you know, "Why aren't you writing about . . ." In other words, if there is any pressure it might be a Carlos Castaneda–Don Juan backlash, where Indian writers might be expected to always write about ethereal, mystical sorts of things when in fact those may not be the feelings they experienced at all.

# 2: Oslo, September 12, 1978

*PS:* What time is "The Man to Send Rain Clouds" set—is it very recent?

*LMS:* Yes, it is very recent. It's perhaps in the middle 1960s. It's a quite recent story. The reason I am so sure of this is because it's based upon something vaguely similar that actually happened.

*PS:* Yes, I believe you had some special inspiration for this story?

*LMS:* Well, it's like most of the inspirations for my stories. One weekend I drove to Laguna from Albuquerque, as I often did to visit home while I was in undergraduate school. When I would get to Laguna I would hear all the news, all the stories of things that had been happening that week, that month, since I had had my last visit. And one particular weekend I went home, and they said, "Did you hear that old man Sorsino died?" and I said, "Oh, oh no, I didn't know that," and they said, "Yes, they found him out at sheep pen. He'd been dead for a day or so, and the sheep were scattered all over by the time they got there." And then my Grandmother said, "And the Catholic priest was very angry," and I said, "What about?" "Well," she said, "they buried the old man without telling the priest. They just did the traditional ceremonies and had a traditional funeral and they didn't tell the priest, and the priest was very upset." And I said, "Oh. Well." And that was all, and I didn't think more of it because visits, if you know Laguna and the way the people tell stories, that was only one of many things I heard that weekend. And I went back to Albuquerque where I was attending the University of New Mexico, and that semester I was taking a creative writing class, and one of my professors, the following week told us we had to write a short story. And I thought, "Well, I'll just write about poor old man Sorsino." So I wrote about him imagining how it must have been when they found him, and also I tried to imagine the Catholic priest and his feelings. So that's how this story came.

*PS:* In *Ceremony,* you make a very interesting combination of the fact that your pueblo or the pueblo close to it, Acoma, is very old, as age goes in America, together with the fact that close to Laguna you have had the various uranium and atomic installations.

*LMS:* That's something that for a long time I suppose I didn't really appreciate, the irony. The Pueblo people have always concentrated upon making things grow, and appreciating things that are alive and natural, because life is so precious in the desert. The irony is that so close to us, in Los Alamos, New Mexico, scientists began the scientific and technological activity which created the potential end to our whole planet, the whole human race. The first atomic bomb was exploded in New Mexico, very close by us. To me it is very striking that this happened so close to the Pueblo people, but I suppose it is just one of those accidents of history.

*PS:* Have you by any chance read Frank Waters' book where he makes that connection between the old and the new culture?

*LMS:* No, I never have. I think it was easier for me to make the connection, because as a child, people still talked about that day when the bomb was exploded. It was done early in the morning before sunrise, and people at Laguna, some of the old people that got up before sunrise, as was their practice, remembered that the whole sky in the southeast lit up, and it was a remarkable sort of thing and people remember it. So I think that's where I made the connection.

*PS:* I understand that when you came to visit us now, Norway wasn't entirely unknown to you.

*LMS:* When I was just a schoolgirl, I had a teacher in the fifth grade, and she was of Scandinavian background. Very early, she read us some of these Scandinavian or Norse tales, and so I learned about Tor and Odin and Loke, and all the wonderful stories of Vulcan, and she read those

113

stories to us, and as a little girl, coming from Laguna, I love stories, we have a great appreciation for stories. And I thought these stories were quite wonderful, and so after she read to us—she only read us a few—I asked her where I could get the book, because it was a large book, and I read the whole book, and—well, tonight we were talking about this— the most sad thing for me is that at the end of this book of Norse tales is a chapter which in the book I read was called "Twilight of the Gods," and I had to read that all these gods would die and that this time ended, and it was very upsetting. It was tragic for me, because at Laguna, we believe that those times did not truly end, but that things only change, and so I was quite horrified to read that for some other people in this other place, that there was this twilight of the gods. So I, years ago, already loved these characteristic deities from the Norse country.

*PS:* Wouldn't you say, coming from Laguna, from these old Pueblos, that storytelling is not only a way of life, it is also as a sort of continuation of past life in that community, and therefore important to you also for that reason?

*LMS:* Oh yes, very much so. In fact, one of the older women—we called her Aunt Susy—who told me a lot of the stories, and who in some sense trained me, if that's what you want to call it, helped me to love the stories and learn them—she always said when she told the stories that there was an old custom, long ago, where the storyteller would say to one of the persons in the room, "Go open the door, go open the door so that they can come in," and it was as if "they," being ancestors, can come in and give us their gifts which are these stories, and that through the stories, somehow, even though people may be dead or gone or time is gone a long way in the past, that through the storytelling there was a belief that it all came back very immediately, that it came right back in the room with you. And so the storytelling in that sense was an act of . . . so that there wasn't anything lost, nothing was dead, nobody was gone, that in the stories everything was held together, regardless of time. And so, when I read the story about "The Twilight of the Gods" it was very upsetting, you see, for a person who was taught to believe that "No, these things go on and on and on." As long as we tell the stories, you know, then these things continue. The stories will only—these things will only die if we neglect to tell the stories. So I am still telling the stories.

*PS:* You also told us today an instance of the healing effect that stories can have. You mentioned a veteran who forgot to put on the brake when he parked his brand new car so that it rolled into a ravine and was wrecked, and who was then comforted by his fellow Pueblos who told him of similar accidents . . .

*LMS:* Yes, the stories are very important in many different ways. There are the usual ways that people find stories important in terms of history because, of course, the term in English is a combination of the word "story"—"his" "story," but at Laguna, the stories also serve to help the individual feel constantly a part of the group so that a person will never feel remote or lost no matter the time or situation. The way this functions is that, if something happens to you, as soon as something terrible happens to you, people come to you—and first of all, things are not kept private, I think that's important—so as soon as something terrible happens, people hear about it, and people come to you, whatever it might be, and the first thing people begin to do is they begin to tell you stories about other people and this has a very soothing effect—they don't talk about what just happened to you, but they'll say, "Well, now, that happened to my uncle, that happened to my uncle many years ago, the same sort of thing." And then, they will either tell you stories about the same sort of tragic thing, or, if this tragic thing that just happened to you took place in a certain geographical location, they may not tell you a story about a similar incident, but they'll say, "Well, bad things always happen at that place," and then they'll begin to tell about some kind of other terrible thing that happened at that place. And so people will come to you with all these other stories, and of course, the obvious immediate effect is they are taking your attention away from yourself, because you are hearing about other people and other incidents. It helps put things into perspective. We human beings have a tendency to think that we are the only ones that have ever experienced loss or sorrow. We're so self-centered. With the stories you begin to realize that what has just happened to you has happened before to different people. People will recount incidents worse than your own, so that by the time they get finished telling you all these other stories you realize you are not alone. You realize there are many people who have had the same thing happen to them. The best part is that you realize that for many years, in the future, even after you're gone, your story is joining all these other stories, and some day when something terrible happens to somebody else, they'll mention your story, too. So it is not as if it just happened to you or that there is nothing to be gained from your tragedy or loss. You have this sense that there's this ongoing story and your story has become part of it.

115

*PS:* You can still be of use to later generations . . .

*LMS:* Right. Through the story.

*PS:* You mentioned earlier today the feeling of self-worth. Do you feel that the so-called ethnic revival of the last 10 or 15 years has meant the same to the Indians as it has, for example, to the American blacks?

*LMS:* Yes, I think it has meant a lot to the people, both for the people who had their feeling of self-worth somehow undermined, or wounded, by schools, and also, I think, it has helped the older people who always believed—who always believed in the worth and the value of the Pueblo culture. I think it made them feel free to talk about the culture. The older people always felt that the Pueblo ways were as valid as the non-Indian ways which their children and grandchildren were being forced to learn, but they were afraid to say so, or they were afraid that maybe they would hinder their children or grandchildren if they tried to encourage them toward Pueblo language or toward Pueblo ways. This ethnic revival has freed them to teach things about the culture, the old stories, and things about the language which they might not have done so freely. They might have died without saying some of the things which are now being said. And in the religious ways, this revival has encouraged some of the older priests and religious persons to ask the younger people to come with them. And younger people, because of this revival, are not afraid or not ashamed. They want to come. So I think it has come in time for us, for the Pueblo people.

*PS:* Not too late, you'd say, but just in time . . .

*LSM:* Not too late, but *just* in time, just barely, which isn't to say that it's all going to be easy or that it's all going to be just perfect, or that no real damage was done by all these hundreds of years. I only wish that for some other Native American people it might have come sooner, because I suspect that perhaps for some groups, certainly for some individuals, it might be too late, but we make the best of what we can.

*PS:* Has there been a development among the Indians, as with the blacks after *Roots*, to try to find out who were your grandparents and so on?

*LMS:* A kind of research such as Alex Haley had to undertake isn't nec-essary, thank heavens, at Laguna. One of the things which is passed on from generation to generation among all the stories that are told, are stories about grandparents, great-grandparents, their great-grandparents, and their great-grandparents, and on and on and on. And the people have a great deal of patience with the naming of these ancestors, where they came from and which clan they were from and so forth. And so this was one of the things that's just second nature to the people, keeping track of these things. And of course, it is very easy because we have been living in this same area for so long. It's very easy even if some of your ancestors have gone from Paguate village to Laguna, or from Laguna to Seama—we are only talking about 6 miles at most. If someone were to die suddenly and not pass on a certain amount of information to you, it's still possible to get those things. Again that goes back to everyone knowing so much about everyone else. It's as if each person were a source, and so it's all right here.

*PS:* You have named your novel *Ceremony*. What does the word "ceremony" stand for for you?

*LMS:* Well, for me, it's the term we use when we refer to certain religious activities. I first heard it connected with the activities which the Navajos participate in in order to cure, healing, medicinal sorts of activities. And the Navajos would say in English, "Old so and so has been sick, so they're giving him a ceremony," or "They're having a ceremony for him." And so that's where I first heard the term, and that's how it will be used in English. Basically it refers to those kinds of activities. It can also refer to other sorts of activities, not necessarily healing ceremonies, but celebrations or giving thanks, those sorts of ceremonies.

*PS:* Could you say a little about how you feel Tayo is cured, how the ceremonies worked for him?

*LMS:* Well, it's fairly complex, I think, in the novel. He is first visited by Ku'oosh, and this old medicine man from Laguna is familiar with the scalp ceremony which was a purification ceremony which was done for warriors, or anybody that might have killed another human being in battle, because of course killing another human being was not taken lightly, it was a very devastating sort of thing, a tremendous thing—

*PS:* And at the same time American Indians joined up to take part in the war—

*LMS:* Right. The people at home were very, what you would say, patriotic.

*PS:* Patriotic Americans—

*LMS:* Patriotic Americans. They were some of the first people to join up. So very many of the Pueblo men went, joined up and went to the second World War. And also in later wars, the Korean war, the Vietnam war, many American Indians went. So, in the beginning, then, of the novel, certain Laguna rituals have been tried, to no avail, with this particular character. And he is sent, then, to this Navajo medicine man, who is a little bit notorious. The other Navajos don't agree with what he does.

*PS:* A somewhat questionable character—

*LMS:* Yes, a questionable character, questionable in terms of the purity of his ritual. Some of the other Navajos would say that he's taking liberties with the ritual, they didn't trust him. But the people in Tayo's family had heard that this medicine man was particularly successful with individuals suffering from the effects of things connected with Anglo-Saxon culture. Alcoholism, and those sorts of things. They were willing to try, and so Tayo goes to this medicine man. But truly, the thing that heals Tayo is not only that particular ceremony which involves the sand-painting, it is the greater ceremony which helps Tayo to get well. Tayo's healing is connected to the faith which this old medicine man had, a faith which went back to things far in the past, the belief that it's human beings, not particular tribes, not particular races or cultures, which will determine whether the human race survives. But all people have to constantly be working, otherwise we will manage to destroy ourselves—

*PS:* Working at being sane—

*LMS:* Yeah, working at being sane, and taking care of each other. And so, it's because this medicine man reminds Tayo of humanity, of something larger than just the individual and the individual community. He puts Tayo in touch with this larger feeling.

*PS:* That he is part of humanity—

*LMS:* Right, that he is part of humanity, and feeling a part again, not just of the tribe, but of humanity, is a very healing sort of thing, and that as human beings we need that. When they say that the human being is a social animal, that's not to be taken lightly, it's almost a spiritual sort of thing. And so once he's joined again, or reminded that he's always been joined—I think that's the important point, that he's always been joined together—once he is reminded of this and can find it again within himself, then the other things he does are acts which reiterate this closeness. They're important acts, but they only help to reiterate this—

*PS:* This closeness to the integrity he has in himself and has always had in himself—

*LMS:* So nothing happens, nothing is given or put into him that hasn't always been there. The only thing that changes is his awareness, his perception of himself in relation to the rest of the world.

*PS:* And wouldn't you also say that it's an important part of the healing process, and thus of your book, to see that evil is everywhere, not just in the Anglos, but also in the Pueblos, and for that matter, in Tayo himself, that it is—again back to your word humanity—it's common humanity?

*LMS:* Right. That's terribly important, I think, because it's especially easy to blame oneself and say, "It's only me, this evil, this bad is within me." That's too easy, too simple. And so is the opposite, which is just to blame others—to say, "It's white people," or, "It's those people, it's not me," and thereby withdraw in the same way. Either way isolates us from other human beings. If we say "It's all just me," then we're isolated. If we're saying "It's everybody else but me," it's the same sort of isolation. Radical Indian politicians like to say, "Well, it's all the white people's fault, you know, we didn't do any of this." That's such a simplistic view, because from the very beginning, the betrayals of our people occurred through deeply complicated convergences of intentions and world views. And there were persons, full-blood Indians, who cooperated with the enemy, or who cooperated with the invaders, and there were mixed blood or "half-breed" people who did—that's human nature.

*PS:* As you had with the blacks in Africa during slave trading times—

*LMS:* Right. Sure. It's something about us as humans, not about us as any particular race or group. It's nice to think that none of our people have the capability of doing anything treasonous. But unfortunately, as long as we're all human beings, there are certain human traits which turn up, and so it is important that Tayo discovers that the Destroyers and the destructive impulse don't reside with a single group or a single race, and that to manipulate people into war or other conflicts again is a human trait, it is a worldwide thing. It's not just one group of people, that's too simple.

*PS:* Yes, this was just what I would like to end on, this note that your book is not only about some American Indian people, but very much about Everyman who could have been in somewhat the same situation. Thank you very much.

*LMS:* Thank you.

# Interview with Elaine Jahner

Talking to Leslie is like taking a casual walk with a friend and using the visual details as reminders of shared concerns. It is quite a different matter from moving directly toward a goal with no attention at all to the passing landscape. In fact the image of an imagined walk became the point of references for an entire conversation.

We began by talking about her current work (more short stories and a filming project). I asked about the carryover effects from film to writing.

"Film," says Silko, "is a way of seeing very like the oral tradition. It operates on a highly refined, simultaneous, personal level. It makes me aware of the visual signals in the language and helps me realize a way of seeing, of organizing as a whole intead of through fragments of experience. Film gives the feeling that we get going for a walk, experiencing many things at once in a simple, elemental way.

"On a walk we see something; we experience it. Insight is in that instant. It can't be bought or sold or even given away. The nearest way to reproduce it is through film or perhaps fiction which can help us see a whole experience.

"The oral tradition with its cycles of stories creates whole experiences too, a foundation of experience on which to build. It presents all these different possibilities that affect how we see the structure of things. The transition from oral tradition to film with its juxtapositions is a natural one.

"People often ask me about my use of the novel; they assume that the novel is not a natural form for the Indian. But the cycles of stories in the oral tradition were like a novel. I just continue the old story telling traditions."

Because in some tribes English is still a second language, the question of the adequacy of the English language to express the consciousness of people whose primary language is not English arises frequently.

Excerpted from "The Novel and Oral Tradition: An Interview with Leslie Marmon Silko," *Book Forum: An International Transdisciplinary Quarterly* 5.3 (1981): 383–88, reprinted by permission of Elaine Jahner.

In our discussion, Leslie brought it up herself in a way that shows her love of language and its possibilities.

"English is a bastard language, inherently open and expansive. I love its expansiveness and inclusiveness. The nature of English is to defy academies. Look at the many people who have created a form of English that is their own, the Jamaicans for example. You can arrange and rearrange the language."

The use of conversations and interviews seems an appropriate way to convey Silko's ideas. Conversation springs from a relationship and the meaning of relationship is what concerns Silko most.

"Things about relationships. That's all there really is. There's your relationship with the dust that just blew in your face, or with the person who just kicked you end over end. That's all I'm interested in. You have to come to terms, to some kind of equilibrium with those people around you, those people who care for you, your environment. I notice things about feeling good about meeting a certain animal when I'm out walking around the hills ... Relationships are not just limited to man-woman, parent-child, insider-outsider; they spread beyond that. What finally happens in the novel, for example, is that I get way out of the Southwest in a sense and get into the kind of destructive powers and sadism that the Second World War brought out. Yet it is all related back to Laguna in terms of witchcraft."

*Part 3*

# THE CRITICS

# Introduction

Leslie Silko's short fiction was an important part of the American Indian literary renaissance identified by Kenneth Lincoln as taking place in the 1960s and 1970s.[1] That flowering of creative output coincided with scholarly and academic interest in multiethnic and women's studies. For a short time Silko was the only American Indian woman publishing fiction in national venues. In 1974, Greenfield Review Press brought out her volume of poems titled *Laguna Woman,* and the same year saw publication of seven of her short stories in the first anthology of short fiction by contemporary American Indian authors, Kenneth Rosen's collection titled *The Man to Send Rain Clouds.* Her work received critical attention from the time of these early publications. She was the subject of a pamphlet in Boise State University's Western Writers series as her first novel was being published, two documentary films were made about her in the 1970s,[2] and she has lectured and given interviews steadily between periods of isolation when she works on major projects.

The earliest criticism of Silko's fiction focused on explicating her work in the light of the culture, history, mythology, and customs of the family and community she grew up in, the Marmon family of Laguna Pueblo. Numerous reprintings of Silko's fiction in anthologies and translations testify to the capacity of her stories to engage the reader across cultural boundaries. Nevertheless, much in the stories that initially appears baffling or meaningless to the non-Laguna or non-Indian reader becomes more comprehensible in the light of some background study. James Joyce's fiction provides a comparable case: it may appeal deeply to any reader, but much will be obscure—whether the reader realizes it or not—without at least some rudimentary knowledge of Catholicism and Irish history. Some introduction to relevant features of the context out of which Silko writes is indispensable for any reading of her fiction, although it goes without saying that such contextual/cultural studies cannot exhaust the critical possibilities.

The articles by LaVonne Ruoff and Lawrence Evers, included in this volume, set a standard for this approach, and both of these early studies remain essential reading. Ruoff works with published sources, including the anthropological literature, to establish some of the details of traditional Keresan philosophy that inform the group of short stories gathered in *The Man to Send Rain Clouds*. It is worth noting that Ruoff's reading of "Yellow Woman" in the light of several stories collected by Franz Boas appears validated by Silko's decision to frame her own reprinting of "Yellow Woman" in *Storyteller* with her versions of the same traditional tales; indeed, the contextualizing function of the traditional material included in *Storyteller* testifies to Silko's engagement with the issue of how to present her material to a diverse readership. Evers's tracing of the historical background for "Tony's Story" underlines the importance of access to such material for understanding the artistry of the writer's rendering; it is clear from his discussion that while the documentary record coincides closely with the plot of her story, the two textual records are very far from being equivalent. Other studies noted in the bibliography that employ similar approaches to Silko's short fiction include the articles by Edith Blicksilver and Joan Thompson.

After the publication of *Storyteller*, criticism of Silko's short fiction focused exclusively on the eight stories included in that volume: five of the stories in Rosen's anthology plus "Storyteller," "Lullaby," and "Coyote Holds a Full House in His Hand." The mixed-genre fabric and experimental structure of *Storyteller* have intrigued critics, and several studies have concentrated on finding thematic or structural principles that unify the text into a coherent whole. Although these studies subordinate discussion of the short stories to consideration of the entire book, several are worth mention. The earliest efforts in this direction are the articles by Bernard A. Hirsch and Linda Danielson, who both find thematic motifs that weave the seemingly disparate elements of *Storyteller* into a unified text; subsequent studies have drawn on their groundbreaking work.

*Storyteller* is an intensely personal book, replete with the names of relatives, family photographs, and local anecdotes; and indeed is read by Arnold Krupat and Jennifer Browdy de Hernandez as autobiography. Lee Francis's reflections in this volume offer a personal perspective on "Tony's Story" and Laguna philosophy in general, and are a particularly valuable addition to Silko criticism in coming from a fellow Laguna. However, the personal tone of the book has met relatively little parallel reaction in the form of reader-response or subjective criticism. Two exceptions are Ambrose Lucero's commentary, one of the earliest essays responding to *Storyteller*, and a later piece by Alanna Brown.

A few studies have attempted to see Silko's work in the context of world literature. Reprinted in this volume, Kathryn Shanley's essay on "Storyteller" draws on Foucault to postulate a Yupik or Native perspective that can be achieved regardless of initiation into cultural particulars; her essay also contributes to the growing discourse on postcolonial theory. Dean Rader's reading of "Coyote Holds a Full House in His Hand," printed for the first time in this volume, uses a comparison with Kafka's "In the Penal Colony" to explore issues of the body as site for the inscription of meaning. Other critics who have taken up similar issues include Arnold Krupat, who discusses Silko with other writers he describes as "cosmopolitan" in *The Voice in the Margin;* Jacqueline Shea Murphy, who engages issues of gender representation; and Kathleen Manley, who finds principles of hypertext in the structure of *Storyteller.*

Another approach has been initiated by Robert M. Nelson; his study *Place and Vision* focuses on *Ceremony* but is an important model for seeing American Indian literature in the all-important context of physical and cultural geography. Paula Gunn Allen and Patricia Clark Smith's commentary uses a similar perspective and is also essential reading.

Although most of the dissertations and critical articles on Silko's writing have focused on her novels, the two books thus far published on her work center on her short fiction. Per Seyersted's pamphlet is based on research and extended personal interviews conducted before the publication of *Ceremony,* and gives most critical attention to her short fiction; it also contains a valuable bibliography of early publications. Melody Graulich's casebook on "Yellow Woman," in the Rutgers series on short fiction by women, reprints interviews and articles and includes an original article by Patricia Jones that emphasizes women's issues.

## Notes

1. Lincoln's book *Native American Renaissance* is listed in the bibliography of this volume. All the critics and studies mentioned in this introduction are listed in the bibliography; I have not duplicated the citations in notes here.

2. *From a Distance Outside of Time: An Interview with Leslie Marmon Silko,* with Ken McCullough, (South Carolina: Educational Television Network, 1976); *Running on the Edge of the Rainbow* (New York: Clearwater Publishing Co., 1982).

# Lawrence J. Evers

Do you see what happens when the imagination is superimposed upon the historical event? It becomes a story. The whole piece becomes more deeply invested with meaning.

—N. Scott Momaday, "The Man Made of Words"

On Good Friday in 1952 New Mexico state trooper Nash Garcia was killed and burned in his patrol car twenty miles from McCartys, New Mexico, deep in the Acoma reservation, and the following Monday two Acoma brothers, Willie and Gabriel Felipe, were arrested and charged with the murder. From the outset the killing stirred imaginations. Willie Felipe's confession printed on the front page of the *Albuquerque Journal* appeared a forced and inadequate explanation for the charred pile of bones and St. Christopher medal pictured sensationally above on the same page. Motive was the most persistent question in press coverage, the long hearings and trial, through the final psychiatric testimony in the case which gained the brothers a reduced sentence of life imprisonment early in 1953. The press, the court, the psychiatrists all looked for meaning in the event before they allowed it to sink into some slight chapter in the history of New Mexico. The small meanings they found were colored by the expectations of their professions and the majority community which they shared, and it remained for two Pueblo writers, in fictions published some twenty years after, to turn that small line segment of history into circles of form.

As fictions, Leslie Silko's "Tony's Story" and Simon Ortiz's "The Killing of a State Cop" have been noticed and praised.[1] Their editor writes: "It is interesting, and perhaps noteworthy, that two stories in this volume, by two different authors, deal with this same theme of violence and death of the white intruder."[2] The similarities of the stories

From "The Killing of a New Mexican State Trooper: Ways of Telling an Historical Event," *Critical Essays on Native American Literature,* ed. Andrew Wiget (Boston: G. K. Hall, 1985), 246–61; copyright Lawrence J. Evers, 1984, reprinted by permission of the author.

*are* remarkable, all the more so against the background of N. Scott Momaday's *House Made of Dawn.* And it was initially an attempt to understand the curious relations of these imaginative accounts which took me back round to examine the records of the case on which they were based.[3] Records of the "United States vs. William R. Felipe and Gabriel Felipe" help us to see the role of the individual imagination in the creation of fiction, but they are of interest in their own right as well. Like Browning's Old Yellow Book, they preserve an intriguing variety of perspectives on a single event.

# I

The barest account of the events of Friday, April 11, 1952, comes to us through confessions wrung by F.B.I. agents from the Felipes early in the morning of April 14.[4] Both Willie, thirty-two at the time of the killing, and Gabriel, twenty-eight, were born at Acomita, New Mexico, where they were living then—Willie with his wife, Gabriel with his mother and stepfather, Mariano Vicente. According to Gabriel's confession, the brothers borrowed their stepfather's pickup, bought two pints of Tokay wine at Los Ritos bar on Highway 66, and drove with their .30-30s north of Acoma toward Mount Taylor to hunt deer the morning of the killing. After an eerie hunt, Willie returned with a small deer, put it on the floor in the cab, and they returned to Los Ritos to buy sandwiches and more wine. There they turned west to Grants. It was about 2:00 P.M.

> We headed west on Highway 66 and I was driving. We had driven about 10 miles west from Los Ritos when I saw Nash Garcia parked in his state patrol car beside the highway. We drove on west about one mile and decided we had better not go to Grants with the deer in the pickup. William had deer blood on his pants so we decided to go home instead of going to Grants. I turned around and headed east on Highway 66, and I was driving about 65 or 70 miles per hour when we passed Nash Garcia still parked beside the highway. Garcia honked at us when we passed, and I stepped on the gas. And when we were about 1/2 mile east of where we passed Garcia, William looked back and said, "that patrol is following us." I looked and could see the state police car in the mirror. I drove on east to the McCarty road and turned south on McCarty road. Garcia followed us at a high rate of speed for about 7 or 8 miles, and I told William that Nash Garcia was the patrol chasing us and that he was the son-of-a-bitch that had put me in jail for drunk driving and for us to ambush Garcia and kill him. William said, "O.K., let's

kill him, but not here as this is not a good place to ambush him." We drove on about five miles with Garcia following us until we came up to a hill which had rocks and trees on it, and I said to William, "This is it." I drove the pickup off the road toward the hill and hid it behind a cedar tree. William jumped out of the pickup, took a .30-30 rifle and ran into the ditch about 15 feet from the pickup. Just as Garcia stopped I heard William shoot one shot and then three fast shots and Garcia yelled, "I give up. Don't shoot." Garcia opened the car door and stepped out of his car and fell beside his car.[5]

Loading the body into the patrol car, the brothers drove the car deeper into the backcountry, hid it in a grove of pinyons, and returned to spend the night at their mother's home. In the morning, Gabriel, carrying Garcia's revolver in his suitcase, went to Albuquerque with his mother and stepfather. Willie returned to the hidden patrol car, piled the front seat with dry cedar, and set the wood on fire. The following evening—Easter Sunday—he was arrested at Acomita. Gabriel remained free another day until, ironically, he was arrested on the streets of Albuquerque by a cousin of Garcia's.

The circumstances under which these confessions were obtained were questionable as their very language suggests, a matter I shall return to. However, in terms of the above reconstruction, the central motivation for the killing was clearly an old grudge given circumstantial intensity by alcohol and guilt at poaching a deer. Later in a statement given to psychiatrist Robert Navarre, Gabriel recalled the source of the grudge. He had been working for the railroad near Lincoln, Kansas, and had returned home.

> All of us Acoma Indians come home. I went to Grants to pick up a mattress, I got drunk, and I sit in a car with three other Indian boys. A patrolman come to where we were parked on the side of the street. This is the same patrolman I got in trouble with later [Garcia]. He asked us what we were doing. We say, "nothing." He say, "drinking?" We say, "no." He search us and find bottle. He arrest us for drunk driving. This patrol always bother Indians. We were by road, not driving.[6]

Garcia's prior record with Indians in general and Gabriel in particular was of scant interest to the Albuquerque press as they rushed to report the sensational killing and eulogize the first officer slain in line of duty in the state. Garcia, it was reported, had been a popular officer in Grants, and in the pages of the *Albuquerque Journal* and *Star* his stature grew. He entered law enforcement as a deputy sheriff in Albuquerque, joining the state police force about eight years before the killing. Garcia advanced to the rank of Captain and for a time was in charge of state police detachments in the Santa Fe area. Ben Chavez, an Albuquerque city patrolman, former neighbor, and friend of Garcia, praised him to the *Albuquerque Journal:* "When Nash was made Captain in 1948, he won it through merit. He was one of the best men in the district. A good man, a sincere man, faithful to his superiors, he believed in policework as a profession."[7] The remark punctuated two large pictures on the same front page which bore the caption:

> Held in ambush killing—Willie Felipe shows State Police Chief Joe Roach the remains of Patrolman Nash Garcia near Grants. Roach lowers his head and chokes back tears as he views the ashes—all that was left of his fellow officer when Garcia was shot down in a hail of bullets and then burned.

Garcia seems to have come to Grants in exile, though, after being demoted to patrolman. His brother Pete blamed the demotion on politics and jealousy and recalled that Garcia "was broken hearted when he was demoted and transferred two years ago."[8] Yet the press was mute about the circumstances surrounding the demotion and transfer, focusing rather on such comments from Garcia's superior officer as "He didn't have a chance to use his gun. They shot him down like a dog."[9] On April 15, a front page picture in the *Albuquerque Journal* showed Garcia with two small children. The caption read: "Nash was their godfather and hero." On April 17, the papers report a hero's funeral for Garcia. His bronze casket approached the church in a 1300 car procession while fifty uniformed state policemen and thirty city policemen and sheriff's deputies gave the final salute. "Hushed citizens along the street removed their hats at the passing of the bier," and "the crowd at the church overflowed onto the front steps." Joseph Montoya spoke at the graveside as the State of New Mexico buried a hero.

Heroes are not created idly. More often than not, they come to being to serve some political cause. So too in this case, though the emotional force generated by the death and memory of Nash Garcia, "godfather and hero," diffused in surprising directions. Sixties liberals might predict lynch mobs and a rebirth of Kit Carson style Indian control programs. But response was not so clear cut, a reflection of wavering federal Indian policy of the time. Indians were viewed with increased regard then, we recall, following their dramatic performances in World War II. Navajo was our unbreakable secret code, Ira Hayes toured the country with a Medal of Honor, even Willie Felipe wore a Bronze Star. And federal efforts to reward them with admission to the urban splendors of the fifties through relocation programs were well underway. Yet Indians remained wards. "I have lived with them. I know them. They are children," said one prospective juror during jury selection for the Garcia case.[10] More consistently in the documents of the case the brothers and all Indians are called "boys." They are viewed as possessing a kind of cultural immaturity, so that in assigning responsibility for the killing, the press looked not to the Felipes but rather to those who influenced them, their legal guardians.

Alcohol provided a convenient focus for the search. Early reports of the killing give the bottles of Tokay a special prominence, and liquor is clearly blamed for the act. Even "the grim-faced residents of Grants— where Garcia was well-liked—put part of the blame upon persons who sell liquor to Indians."[11] Accordingly, one of Governor Edwin L. Merchem's first responses to the case was to call State Liquor Director Elfego Baca onto the carpet. And Baca responded quickly. On April 18 charges were filed against Nepomucena Sanchez, owner of El Cerritos Bar, for allegedly selling liquor to the Felipes. Manuel Ortiz, operator of La Mesita Bar in the same area, was also charged with bootlegging liquor to Indians as similar investigations spread throughout the state.[12]

The political uses of the murder went well beyond a shakeup in the state liquor commission, however. The *Albuquerque Journal* editorialized in an early news story on the case: "Garcia's brutal slaying flung a challenge at federal and state law enforcement. It boils down to what the officers will do about the problem in Northwestern New Mexico with its complicated troubles of Indian lands and white cities."[13] The problem of course derived from the peculiar legal topography of reservation border area where a muddle of federal, state, private, and Indian allotment lands created jurisdiction troubles. Properly, federal officers had jurisdiction over federal and federal trust lands, while state officers (like Nash Garcia) reigned on state and private lands. Customary agreements with tribal officials (in this case the governor of Acoma Pueblo) allowed state officers to respect or ignore the boundaries as convenience dictated. In any case, the "challenge" posed by the press displaced any racial tensions generated by the murder with bureaucratic ones. Governor Merchem suggested that Bureau of Indian Affairs law enforcement efforts "have been nil," and righteously replaced Garcia with two men.[14]

Federal officials reacted defensively and in kind. The memory of a heroic Garcia, the need to find influences that made the "boys" go wrong, and a flurry of political bickering suppressed any attempt by the press to deal with the more complex cultural aspects of the case.

# II

The trial of the two brothers opened September 22, 1952, at Santa Fe with the Honorable Carl A. Hatch, U.S. District Judge, presiding in open court. U.S. Attorney Maurice Sanchez represented the government; Albuquerque attorneys Phillip Dunleavy and A. T. Hannett—himself a former governor of the state—represented the Felipes. Prior press treatments of the killing were felt in the courtroom. While a number of prospective jurors were excluded because they objected to the death penalty, each of the twelve Anglo males seated admitted freely to having followed the case in area newspapers. Judge Hatch repeatedly overruled Dunleavy's objections to this knowledge as prejudicial. When jury selection was complete, Hatch summarized: "All the jurors stated that they could and would lay aside anything they had read and decide the case solely upon the evidence."[15]

In all, the evidence presented at the trial from which the jurors were charged to decide the case bore striking resemblance to the newspaper accounts they were instructed to disregard. The prosecution labored to tell the events of the killing with gruesome realism. At one point Sanchez introduced a movie taken from a patrol car following the chase route that led to the scene of the killing, as he attempted to paint the crime as the "blackest in the history of the state."[16] Despite a few sensational remarks of their own and despite frequent objections, the defense brought a weary fatalism to the trial, echoing the apologetic motivations proffered in the Albuquerque newspapers.[17] The brothers had killed Garcia, admitted Dunleavy, but they did so possessing a "very low grade intelligence" and under the influence of alcohol. Therefore they were not responsible for their actions; they were temporarily insane.

To establish patterns of alcohol use and the level of Willie's intelligence, Dunleavy called not only expert professional testimony but also members of Felipe's family. He probed Willie's war record at length, as a key defense strategy appears to have been to establish the profound change service in the war had on Willie. Pabilita Vicente, Felipe's mother, testified that "when he came back, he was a changed boy. I could not understand that he was so different, that his behaviour wasn't good. . . . And it seemed like he learned that [to drink alcohol] in the army."[18] Mariano Vicente, Willie's stepfather, similarly testified to a "tremendous change" in Willie on his return from the war.[19]

Willie himself recalled that he was reluctant to go into the Army: "I was called by the draftboard and I didn't want to join the Army, and they had a little time in hunting me. But I finally got into the service when they found me."[20] Once inducted, Willie served the Infantry in the 37th Division well. His service earned him a Bronze Star awarded April 28, 1944, for meritorious service at Bougainville, Solomon Islands. The citation, introduced as evidence at the trial, reads in part:

> Throughout enemy attack PFC Felipe was a gunner in a light machine gun squad. His pillbox bore the brunt of the enemy's small arms and automatic fire, and was only fifty yards from the nearest enemy held pillbox. PFC Felipe manned his gun throughout the entire battle, delivering steady and murderous fire throughout. He refused all offers of relief. Later he volunteered on ammunition and food carrying parties over a route through open trenches and was subject to enemy sniper and knee mortar fire.[21]

Discharged in October of 1945, Willie re-enlisted within a year to serve as a truck driver. A superior noted on his papers: "likes Army, and would like to make it a career."

Yet a distinguished warrior does not make a distinguished truck driver. Following his reenlistment, questions were raised about Willie's inability to serve in his new role. In March of 1947 he was discharged for "inaptness." It was on this "inapt" image that the defense rested its case, coupling it with a final attempt to shift accountability to the brothers' guardians: "The real criminal was the bootlegger who gave these boys the liquor."[22] The whole of the defense argument was ruled irrelevant by Judge Hatch. In his instructions to the jury, Hatch ordered them not to consider drunkenness or mental ability as factors in determining temporary insanity, and the jury quickly found the brothers guilty of first degree murder. On October 17, 1952, Hatch sentenced them to die in the electric chair in Santa Fe.

# III

In an effort to substantiate an appeal, the defense had the Felipes transferred to the United States Department of Justice Medical Center in

Springfield, Missouri, for psychiatric examinations, and it was there that a deeper cultural context for the killing began to unfold. One of the first matters the federal psychiatrists reviewed were the confessions I have quoted. Dr. George Devereux wrote of the confessions:

> It is absolutely certain that this inmate [Willie] is materially unable to understand many of the words contained in his confession and the long sentences it contains. Regardless of whether the confessions are true or not, he signed a document which he did not understand as to content, and whose significance for his fate he was unable to evaluate properly.[23]

Trained in both anthropology and psychiatry, Devereux was unusually qualified to examine the brothers, and he pushed beyond the particular problem of the confessions to larger linguistic and cultural considerations which had been ignored in the trial.[24] He pointed out that one had to know Acoma culture to understand what the brothers meant by any given English word, thereby questioning the validity of previous testing of Willie:

> To us a "bear paw" is just a bear paw. To him this expression, which, I understand, appears in one of his Rorschack tests, has a special meaning: bear paws are used in Acoma curing rituals. If he says "mother," he can mean either his mother or his mother's sister, etc.[25]

But more directly related to the killing, argued Devereux, were the brothers' dreams and witch beliefs. He diagnosed Gabriel as a psychopath, one who compensated for a sense of inadequacy in fantasy through persecutory ideas of "being misunderstood," "picked on," and "envied." Gabriel was convinced that people envied him for his large flocks of sheep and therefore sought to harm him by gossip and by witchcraft. This Devereux notes is an "abnormal attitude for an Acoma Indian" in one important respect: Gabriel's feeling that witches had to be dealt with privately, instead of calling in one of the Acoma medicine societies who are supposed to deal with such matters. Gabriel, for example, told stories of his uncle's behavior that he considered normal:

> His uncle saw one night a large and a small fox—the latter being the "guardian" of the large fox—attack his flock. The uncle pursued them, and found two witches in human shape who had beside them foxskins, showing that they had just resumed human shape. (*Real* transforma-

135

tion, not just casting off a foxskin is meant.) They pleaded to be let off, but the uncle shot them.

> His uncle saw three deer: one male, two female, whose actions suggested that they were witches. He pursued them and when he saw them in human shape, despite their pleas, he shot them.[26]

These actions Gabriel considered natural, whereas, according to Devereux, a normal Acoma would have called in a medicine society: "The normal Acoma considers witchcraft a public matter. This inmate considered it a private grievance."[27] In addition to regular persecution dreams Gabriel told Devereux that he was bothered by hearing whistling sounds at night that were not heard by others: "although he was somewhat vague at this point, he seemed to say that ghosts converse by whistling."[28] In view of these factors and his entire examination, Devereux concludes his report on Gabriel with an inferential reconstruction of his state of mind during the killing:

> The evening before [the offense], the inmate was frightened by the ominous hooting of owls—birds of ill omen in Acoma culture. He was also quite drunk. During the hunt [the morning of the killing] he saw at thirty yards a large antlered deer—shot at it—thought he hit it, but the deer disappeared. When he went to the spot he saw no tracks, although he is a good tracker. This suggested to him—quite frighteningly—that he had had an experience with a witch-deer. . . . The pursuit itself [by Garcia] startled and frightened him a great deal, since being pursued is one of his principal nightmares. It is interesting to note that although they had outdistanced the police car, they stopped. One of Gabriel's nightmares is that of being pursued and being unable to get away and, for reasons of internal, neurotic motivation, *could* not get away. By the time he stopped the pick up . . . he was temporarily insane.[29]

As in his examination of Gabriel, Devereux argued that Willie Felipe was psychotic on the basis of his transformations of cultural beliefs about witchcraft into private, personal, and paranoic ideas.[30] People on the Acoma reservation hated and envied him and caused him trouble by witchery. "Sent" illness (witchcraft) killed his child. Fox-witches tore out the throat of several of his sheep but did not eat them. Like Gabriel, he believed that his maternal uncle had trouble with three witch-deer, and that the morning of Garcia's killing Gabriel shot at a witch-deer. But Devereux shows that Willie's problems were more deeply entwined with the psychological history of his family. Willie spoke poignantly of the return of an elder brother from the service:

> He lost his heart. The Indian doctors went out and brought his heart back and he was supposed to swallow it and chew it, but my brother chewed it and he did not get any better. The Indian doctors burned special weeds and my brother swallowed the smoke and then he was supposed to throw up his bad heart and bad spirits and feel better. The Indian doctors did this four times in four days, but he did not get better and he died in the state hospital in Colorado.[31]

Willie believed that his natural father Santiago Felipe, who had died some years before of a fall from a cliff, appeared to his maternal aunt and his sister with the top of his body transformed into a mountain lion, and that the aunt caused his father to die by supernatural means. Willie told Devereux that he knew this because when the corpse of his father was found in the cleft of a rock, he had an "old hole" in his side which had been plugged.

Willie believed that the killing of Garcia was not an act of the free will, but the result of having been witched. He had recurring anxiety dreams about being pursued. Sometime before the killing, he reported to Devereux that he had had a terrible dream of being pushed off a cliff. He considered this dream to be an omen of something terrible to happen.[32] Devereux recreated what did happen in Willie's mind on April 11, 1952, as follows:

> Each human being has a touchy point little related to reality. In this case of this man being pursued was about the worst thing that could happen to him, especially when it came on top of an anxiety dream and an encounter with a witch-deer—and under the influence of alcohol. On top of all this, he was pursued by a *black car*, which he related to the ominous black car which he had hallucinated sometime earlier near a salt lake. At this time the patient was in a state of *insane fear*, to such an extent that he is convinced that the black car was *flying* after him. (I carefully ascertained that he meant "flying" literally, and not in the sense of "going fast.") To the inmate this pursuit was a witch experience, triggering off temporary insanity. In reply to what he saw when he aimed, looking down the barrel, he replied, in obvious confusion: "Something black—just a black car—something black." When asked the color of the trooper's uniform he hesitated and had great trouble recalling that it was black. As far as the inmate knows now, he shot simply at something black: a black car which pursued him.[33]

In sum, Devereux argued in his report to the court that previous legal tellings of the killing were culturally blind, as they ignored the compelling psychic factors which moved the Felipes to kill Nash Garcia. He cautioned that while Indian beliefs are sometimes mistaken for delusions, in this case the danger was the reverse: that the delusional character of Indian beliefs, as held by the Felipes, might be mistaken for "normal" Acoma belief. The degree and manner of the brothers' witch beliefs marked them as psychotic rather than cultural in character.

Devereux's report was offered to Judge Hatch in an effort to obtain another trial for the Felipes. The new evidence of a supernatural context for the murder gained the Felipes not a second trial but a final headline and a reduced sentence.[34] On March, 3, 1953, Judge Hatch spared them the electric chair and sent them to prison for life.

# IV

Writers of fiction and storytellers are united in their need to imagine historical events. Even as the pages of the *Albuquerque Journal* yellowed and the Felipe brothers' trial record slipped into the federal storage center in Denver, memories of the Nash Garcia case lived in rumor along Highway 66. The rumors solidified into a legendary image of Garcia very different from the journalistic image I have reviewed. Leslie Silko recalls:

> This one rumor was that he hated Indians and that he'd been transferred to the Laguna area from near Cuba or Santa Fe because his superiors already knew he was psychotic abut Indians. Another story was that his own family admitted that there was something haywire with him, and he got what was coming to him.[35]

In a recent visit to Laguna-Acoma High School, Silko found that well over half the children she read to were aware of this image of Garcia. Five years old when the Felipe brothers were sent to prison, what Silko knows of the case is based on these tellings of the killing she heard as she grew up at Laguna. The rumor image of an Indian-hating Garcia is evident in "Tony's Story," as the bare bones of the event that we have viewed in newspaper accounts and the trial record: the returned veteran, the wine, the chase, the .30-30, the burning of the body. Throughout it is clear that Silko has very consciously shaped the event in her own mold.

A parched summer landscape is integral to Silko's design, and she shifts the time of the action from early spring to San Lorenzo Day late in summer. From the opening of the story, life on the reservation withers as the pueblo awaits overdue summer rains. But it is only as the brutal state trooper appears behind him on the highway that Antonio Sousea "knew why the drought had come that summer."[36] In the story's climactic scene Antonio is moved to act on that recognition, and he shoots the trooper. The sand soaks up the trooper's blood even as it had Leon's on the carnival grounds in the opening scene of the story.

> The tumbleweeds and tall yellow grass were sprayed with glossy, bright blood. He was on his back, and the sand between his legs and along his left side was soaking up the dark, heavy blood—it had not rained for a long time, and even the tumbleweeds were dying. (77)

As the trooper and his car burn, the story closes with rain clouds gathering in the west.

Silko also shapes her characters carefully. The Felipe brothers of fact become types no less a pair for their lack of a blood relation. Tony is the younger, yet a traditionalist, deferential even in his final action. Leon is aggressive, a war veteran. He talks too loudly, shakes hands like a whiteman, and drinks boldly in defiance of the whiteman's law. In conflict with the trooper, Leon looks to his "rights" and "letters to the BIA" for support; Tony to old Teofilo's stories and chants and arrowheads. As the "he" becomes an "it" for Tony, the trooper remains a "big Bastard" and a "state cop" to the end for Leon. Similarly, the historic Nash Garcia undergoes a transformation to become the state cop in "Tony's Story." Silko draws him as purely symbolic as the albino in N. Scott Momaday's *House Made of Dawn*. Like the albino, the state cop hides behind prominent dark glasses and speaks in a high pitched voice. And like the albino he is perceived as a witch.

The witch perception lies at the very center of Silko's telling of the event, giving it an eerie likeness to the Devereux report. The presence of the big cop lingers with Tony as he returns for the San Lorenzo Day carnival:

> Stillness breathed around me, and I wanted to run from the feeling behind me in the dark; the stories about witches ran with me. That night I had a dream—the big cop was pointing a long bone at me— they always use human bones, and the whiteness flashed silver in the

moonlight where he stood. He didn't have a human face—only little, round, white-rimmed eyes on a black ceremonial mask. (72)

Later when Tony looks at the cop he sees only "the dark image of a man" which he avoids, remembering his parents' caution "not to look into the masked dancers' eyes because they would grab me, and my eyes would not stop." (73–74) Pursued by the cop in the final scene, Tony must look at the cop and his eyes do not stop until the cop's body is in flames. Disposal of the witch-cop by burning is one of the few supernatural motifs Silko uses which Devereux does not mention in his analysis of Willie Felipe. Just as Willie Felipe has ominous dreams which foreshadow the killing of Garcia, so too Tony. As Felipe felt pursued by a black object and saw only a black object when he shot, so too Tony doesn't remember aiming and kills not a cop but a witch in a "strange form." But Silko was unaware of the Devereux report until well after publication of the story, and despite similarities, the two accounts of the killing are profoundly different. As I have noted, Devereux interpreted the Felipes' witch beliefs as aberrant by Acoma standards, as evidence of their psychosis. Linking the witch motif with the drought setting, Silko creates a psychological and cultural context in which Tony is drawn irreversibly to the killing. Tony's witch perception gives evidence of the persistence of cultural belief. By force of characterization and setting, Silko casts the act which rises from that belief in an affirmative tone.

## Notes

1. The stories were published in Kenneth Rosen, ed., *The Man to Send Rain Clouds: Contemporary Stories by American Indians* (New York: Viking, 1974). Two notable reviews of the book are Peter G. Beidler's published in the *Arizona Quarterly*, 30 (1974), 357–59, and Mick McAllister's in the *American Indian Quarterly*, 1 (1974), 210–11.

2. Rosen, p. xi.

3. I should like to acknowledge the help of my students Kathleen Cohill, Glenn Dick, and Marlene Hoskie in gathering information on the case. Ms. Ann Neff in the Office of the Clerk, United States District Court, District of New Mexico, kindly arranged to have the file of the "United States vs. William R. Felipe and Gabriel Felipe" transferred from the Federal Records Center in Denver, Colorado, to United States District Court in Tucson for my review. The file includes transcripts of the trial, the Court's correspondence regarding the case, and many of the exhibits introduced, which include the Felipes' confessions,

reports of their psychiatric examinations, photos of the scene of the killing, and other materials.

4. Plaintiff's exhibits 10 and 16, "U.S. vs. William R. Felipe and Gabriel Felipe," #16902 criminal.

5. Plaintiff's exhibit 16, 4–7.

6. "Report of Neuropsychiatric Examination of Gabriel Felipe," Nov. 11, 1952, Medical Center for Federal Prisoners, Springfield, Missouri. Gabriel Felipe's driver's license was revoked February 1, 1952, following his conviction January 25, 1952, for driving while intoxicated.

7. "Laud Slain Officer," *Albuquerque Journal,* April 15, 1952, p. 1.

8. "Job Came First," *Albuquerque Journal,* April 16, 1952, p. 13.

9. "Nash Garcia is Ambushed," *Albuquerque Journal,* 14 April 1952, p. 1.

10. Transcripts of "United States vs. William R. Felipe and Gabriel Felipe," p. 40.

11. *Albuquerque Star,* April 15, 1952, p. 1.

12. The same issue of the *Albuquerque Star,* April 18, 1952, disclosing Baca's actions reports, for example, that "Farmington's new mayor Tom Bolack vows drive to stamp out bootlegging," 24.

13. *Albuquerque Journal,* April 15, 1952, p. 1.

14. *Albuquerque Star,* April 19, 1952, p. 10.

15. Transcripts, p. 96.

16. Transcripts, p. 221.

17. For example, Dunleavy to Captain White, head of the New Mexico state police: "Are you familiar with the fact that less than two years ago the chief of the state police was convicted of putting a bicycle lock on the testicles of an accused person?" Transcripts, p. 168.

18. Transcripts, p. 362.

19. Transcripts, p. 368.

20. Transcripts, p. 380. Compare Ortiz's "Kaiser and the War," Rosen, pp. 47–60.

21. Citations of military documents are from copies introduced as evidence at the trial.

22. Transcripts, p. 167.

23. "Summary Psychiatric Evaluation of Gabriel Felipe," Dec. 26, 1952, p. 4.

24. One of Devereux's best known contributions in the area is *Reality and Dream: Psychotherapy of a Plains Indian* (New York: International Universities Press, 1951).

25. "Summary Psychiatric Evaluation of William Felipe," Dec. 22, 1952, p. 4.

26. "Evaluation of Gabriel Felipe," p. 1.

27. "Evaluation," p. 1.

28. "Evaluation," p. 3.

29. "Evaluation," p. 5.

30. Unless otherwise noted the following material is taken from Devereux's "Summary Psychiatric Evaluation of William Felipe."

31. Robert Navarre, "Report of the Neuropsychiatric Examination of William Felipe," Dec. 16, 1952, p. 2.

32. ". . . we must remember that his father was found dead in a cleft rock, after having fallen from a cliff. . . . Falling into a cleft rock also occurs in a rather terrible contest in one of the chief Acoma myths." Devereux, "Summary of Psychiatric Evaluation of William Felipe," p. 3.

33. "Summary," p. 6.

34. "'Delusions of Witchcraft' Cited in New Psychiatric Report on Felipe Brothers," *Albuquerque Journal*, Feb. 27, 1953, p. 8.

35. Personal communication, Mar. 30, 1976, Laguna, New Mexico.

36. Rosen, *The Man to Send Rain Clouds*, p. 73; hereafter cited parenthetically.

# Lee Francis

Back home it is not about "The Law." Rather, it's about The People. That is to say, if one's actions cause harm to another—be it another person, your family, your clan, your Nation—then do not do it! Not because it is "against the law"; rather, because by causing harm to another you end up harming yourself. You are not in harmony/balance with all of creation (both seen and unseen). Thus, in the real world, the two men responsible for killing Nash Garcia, the State Policeman in Leslie's story, were turned in by members of their Nation. They were tried and convicted and went to prison.

[Responding to the assertion that an egalitarian concept of law originated as an Indian idea]:

As far as I know, what is common to all the sovereign Native Nations on Turtle Island is [this]: we are elitist. My understanding of the word/concept of egalitarian is that "we are all the same. . . . we all are treated the same." [But] I am not the same as a Seneca. A Seneca is a Seneca. An Anishinabe is an Anishinabe. I will never be Anishinabe or Lakota or Muscogee—or even Acoma. I am Laguna. At the same time, a person who is not Laguna can never be Laguna. Thus, Native people are elitist. And so, if I buy into the notion of "egalitarianism" then it seems that I would also have to accept all that goes with being an egalitarianized "Indian" or Pan-Indian or Melting-Pot Indian. . . . As Robin Williams would say: "No. No. No. No. No People!" I, for one, am not a Pan or Pot—melted, fried, basted or boiled. In short, I would like to meet this "Indian" who had this idea about egalitarianism. I know for certain, that Indian was not Laguna!

I would challenge anyone to come to Laguna and, as a non-Laguna, proceed to declaim about democracy at Laguna. That person would be escorted off the rez without so much as a by-your-leave. The problem with my non-Native relations is that espousing egalitarianism and

"A Note on 'Tony's Story' in Laguna Context," contributed by Lee Francis, Ph.D., of Laguna Pueblo from an Internet discussion on NATIVELIT-L@cornell.edu:Wednesday, 19 June 1996; it is reprinted here by permission of Lee Francis.

democracy enables them to come onto my rez and patronize my elders, misbehave and be offensive in terms of respecting our "ways" (this is because they don't know our ways—because they aren't Laguna), all the while not having a clue as to why we are puzzled by their behavior.

As a child, when I went to one of the folks back home and asked "What do 'they' mean about democracy?" I was told. . . . "Look over there [towards an elder]. That one is _____ Clan. You are _____ Clan. There is no democracy. Only your clan. And for that one sitting there, there is only _____ Clan. That one's clan. You do not interfere with their clan. They do not interfere with yours. Both clans must walk together and at the same time remain apart." As a child, I of course walked away from my elder shaking my head and wondering what I was told. Some forty-plus years later, I think I may understand. And *no one* goes against the clan mothers. Theirs is the final word! So, I wonder . . . is that egalitarian? or elitist? I say, elitist.

# Dean Rader

In Franz Kafka's short story "In the Penal Colony," the prisoners of the colony suffer an unusual punishment. Instead of being executed, the prisoner must lie face down on the end of a machine called the harrow, at which point three different needles begin puncturing the skin and scrawling the prisoner's crime on his back. In short, the prisoners are not just punished for their crime—they wear it. They are marked by it.

A similar thematic is at work in Leslie Marmon Silko's "Coyote Holds a Full House in His Hand"—the final piece in *Storyteller*—though her story takes a comic rather than a tragic twist. The protagonist of the story is a middle-aged man from Laguna. When the story begins, he has just arrived in a Hopi village on Second Mesa, where he envisions a romantic rendezvous with a middle-aged Hopi widow, Mrs. Sekakaku, from whom he has received a series of perfumed letters and an invitation to visit for the annual Bean Dance. However, when he arrives at Mrs. Sekakaku's house, he decides that Mrs. Sekakaku has led her aunts and sisters to believe that he has been sending her plants, letters, and photographs without provocation. Furthermore, the chilly reception she extends him proves to him that her behavior is part of an elaborate scheme to "pretend he had come uninvited, overcome with desire for her."[1] Thus, instead of being invited for a romantic interlude, he is tricked into validating Mrs. Sekakaku's stories of a lovesick Laguna man.

He is doubly frustrated by this revelation because he had been looking forward to becoming physically intimate with Mrs. Sekakaku. On the bus from Laguna, he had repeatedly fantasized about "fingering the creases and folds and the little rolls" of Mrs. Sekakaku's thighs, and now such activities seem unlikely (262). But the Laguna visitor refuses to be had or to go home empty handed. Seeing an opportunity for satisfaction, he convinces Mrs. Sekakaku that he is a medicine man and assures her that he can cure her ailing aunt, but for the cure to work, all of her clanswomen must come to the house without men. Once the women

"Dealing (with) Coyote: Sexuality and Trickery in 'Coyote Holds a Full House in His Hand,' " published here for the first time, by permission of the author.

145

arrive, he lines them up by the fireplace and begins the ceremony. He has them lift their skirts up while, reverently, slowly, and erotically, he rubs juniper ash all over "each curve each fold each roll of flesh" of every woman's thighs, including Mrs. Sekakaku's and her aunt's (264). Not surprisingly, after he finishes rubbing everyone, taking extra time with Mrs. Sekakaku, the aunt claims she feels much better. For his payment, the women give him homemade pies and bread, and they even let him take a snapshot of them. He then quickly catches a bus back to Laguna, a happy and satisfied man.

Just as the prisoners in the penal colony wear the sign of their crime on their bodies, so, too, do the Hopi women wear a sign of transgression. Their "crime," from the Laguna man's point of view is twofold. First of all, they are part of the trick Mrs. Sekakaku plays on him: she invites him solely to impress and mislead them. Furthermore, they commit the harmless transgressions of desire and flattery: "all of them, the thin ones and the old ones, believed he was after them" (263). Because the Hopi women are happy to have their thighs rubbed by this strange man from Laguna who they think is attracted to them, an interesting reversal of desire takes place. Mrs. Sekakaku initially uses the Laguna man's desire to trick him into coming to visit her, whereas he uses the pride of Mrs. Sekakaku and the implicit desire of the Hopi women to trick all of them. Thus, Mrs. Sekakaku, Aunt Mamie, and the poor Hopi women wear the mark of their naïveté on intimate parts of their bodies. Of course, the irony of his curative ruse is that it is not just Aunt Mamie who is finally healed, but his aches as well are cured by the performance of the deceptive and erotic act.[2]

The importance of Silko's title emerges in this final scene of sexual satisfaction, trickery, and revenge. Silko never tells us the man's name, but his metaphorical name turns out to be Coyote, and we know he is a trickster even if he does not. Some of the most engaging and poignant Coyote myths include either implicit or explicit sexual overtones, and Silko's modern Coyote participates in this tradition with relish. In the myths of the Plains Indians and in the stories of the southwestern communities, Coyote's lechery and gluttony are legendary. Frequently, Coyote constructs elaborate schemes to fulfill his dual appetites of sex and food, and in this story both of the Coyote's lusts are sated by the Hopi women. However, Silko's title takes on its fullest significance when we consider it as a pun. "Coyote Holds a Full House in His Hand" is a delightful play on words. The obvious connotative reading works on the poker and gambling metaphor to which the title alludes. The Coyote figure in the story is not a medicine man. In fact, he is not even sure he remembers how to feign a ritual, so pretending to enact a cure solely to derive sexual and personal satisfaction is a huge gamble. When he is confronted with the unusual and wildly tempting jackpot of several Hopi women willing to have their thighs caressed, he is all too eager to wager. He literally gambles that what he holds in his hands will win him the reward he desires. The trope of holding makes the denotation of the title—that Coyote literally "holds" a full house (of women) in his hands—quite humorous indeed. The Coyote figure firmly and slyly holds each thigh of each woman in his hands, and this literalization of the metaphor makes Coyote's trick and Silko's character doubly intriguing. While the former connotation foregrounds Coyote's trickster history, the title's denotation participates in the ribald history of Coyote's sexual adventures. When the man rubs, squeezes, and grips the thighs of the women in the house, he not only "holds a full house in his hands," he completes the duality of Coyote the trickster and Coyote the lecher.

Additionally, Silko's tale allows the protagonist to enjoy revenge, a common theme in Coyote myths. Throughout the story, the Laguna man informs the reader that the Hopi men are known for their sexual prowess, so much so that Laguna women perhaps secretly desire them over their own men. He not only feels sexually inadequate compared to the Hopi men, but this feeling is exacerbated by his being en route to a sexual liaison with a Hopi woman on Second Mesa, the heart of Hopi territory. His hopes for a new outlook on life are dashed when he discovers that he has been tricked by a Hopi woman. Hence, when he is allowed, even encouraged, to rub intimate areas of the bodies of Hopi women, he not only gets "even again with the Hopi men" for their putative potency, he also finds his own masculine sexuality restored (265). Such a structural and metaphorical paradigm of sexuality lost and regained mirrors hundreds of Coyote tales and gives Silko's version an ironic and historical tension.

Though Silko's piece takes its primary thematic from the Coyote stories, it also participates in a number of other intertextualities that provide insights into the story's cultural resonances. According to Ramón A. Gutiérrez, the practice of isolating women in a single house was quite common in the pueblos during colonial times, and Silko's story participates in this tradition with a humorous twist.[3] As a symbol of their virginity, young women were physically segregated from men before marriage, but Gutiérrez argues that Pueblo women enjoyed significant empowerment through their sexuality and its link to the residence.

Thus, the Hopi female adage that "a man's place is outside of the house" suggests that Mrs. Sekakaku and her friends are not so much left behind by the men involved in the Bean Dance but that they have marshaled forces in their own domain (Gutiérrez, 20). Indeed, it could very well be that the protagonist is the victim of the *women's* scheme, not the other way around, for they certainly derive as much pleasure as he from the cure. Linda Danielson agrees, arguing that the tricks the two characters play on each other ultimately balance the story because "[e]ach of these Coyote characters in the course of the story fools the other, getting something he or she wants."[4] Thus, *Storyteller* ends the way it begins—with the contextualization and certification of the centrality of women.

Perhaps the most intriguing intertexts develop between the Coyote figure's "cure" and the description of two different ceremonies in Frank Waters's *Book of the Hopi*. Toward the beginning of his book, Waters recounts the creation story from Tòkpela (the first Hopi world) in which the first child born has his body rubbed with cedar ashes.[5] When the Coyote figure rubs ash over the legs of the Hopi women, the Laguna and Hopi texts juxtapose through the figure of Coyote, and their respective Laguna and Hopi experiences are transfigured. Additionally, this scene recalls one of the final moments of *House Made of Dawn* when, in a similar curative attempt, Abel smears his arms and chest with ashes as part of a Pueblo ritual.[6] But none of these texts carries the sexual overtones of Waters's report of the Hopi Márawu ceremony, a ritual performed entirely by women. Waters describes the Márawu as a celebration of the creation of the world, the Hopi emergence, and especially, human reproduction. According to the depiction in *Book of the Hopi*, the Hopi women enact a ritual similar to the one the Coyote figure performs:

> Both legs are painted black with the peculiar markings that give Márawu its name. Two circles, like garters, are drawn: one just above the knee and another high on the thigh. . . . These markings carry on the sex symbolism first expressed in Lakón, when the virginal Lakón maidens rubbed hands over the circular whorls on the Lakón shrine, expressive of their desire for impregnation and motherhood. (Waters, 289)

The similarities between the two texts are striking. The Coyote figure in Silko's story refers to garters on two different occasions, an act that suggests that the garter is a powerful sexual symbol. Perhaps he is so taken by garters and thighs because both mark the delineation between the public part of the body and the private part. Boundary and symbol intrigue Coyote: he wants to cross one and embody the other in dangerous ways. Both his trip to Hopi and his trick on the women are literal and metaphorical crossings of borders. Similarly, his application of ash on the thighs of the women holds symbolic and sexual relevance for him and for the women. Although he may not know the significance of the Márawu ceremony, the Hopi women certainly would, and, most importantly, so would the Hopi men, making his trick even more biting and satisfying. Because non-Hopis are forbidden to participate in or gain access to the details of the Márawu ceremony, it is difficult to confirm Waters's story; still, Waters's text provides a possible source for Silko's story.

Although Kafka's and Silko's stories share the thematic of marking the body out of revenge or punishment, Kafka's tale of inscription exposes a negative discourse, whereas Silko's and Coyote's are essentially positive. One should not think of crime and punishment in the literal sense here; Silko is playing with the motifs of trickery and trickster. Her goal is to place the protagonist, whom she portrays as lonely and unsure of himself, in a modern landscape to see what form his sexual subterfuge takes. Her story is successful because she unites the universal with the particular and allows the thread of language and ceremony to interweave the two.[7] We can relate to and sympathize with the feelings of inadequacy of this middle-aged man while at the same time we appreciate how fully he takes on the persona of the mythical Coyote. And in so doing, Silko's contemporary version resonates with the weight, force, and cultural significance of myth.

# Notes

1. Leslie Marmon Silko, *Storyteller* (New York: Seaver/Arcade, 1981), 262; hereafter cited in text by page number.

2. Although Coyote does not get exactly what he wants, he does not get caught either. This ability to exist between categories is one of the characteristics of the trickster; as Barbara Babcock notes, "at the center of his antinomian existence is the power derived from his ability to live interstitially, to confuse and to escape the structures of society and the order of cultural things"; see "'A Tolerated Margin of Mess': The Trickster and His Tales Reconsidered," in *Critical Essays on Native American Literature,* ed. Andrew Wiget (Boston: G. K. Hall, 1985), 154.

3. Ramón A. Gutiérrez, *When Jesus Came, the Corn Mothers Went Away: Marriage, Sexuality, and Power in New Mexico, 1500–1846* (Stanford, Calif.: Stanford University Press, 1991), 235–38; hereafter cited in text.

4. Linda Danielson, "*Storyteller:* Grandmother Spider's Web," *Journal of the Southwest* 30.3 (Autumn 1988): 351.

5. Frank Waters, *The Book of the Hopi* (New York: Viking, 1969), 9; hereafter cited in text. According to Waters, the following is part of the Tokpela creation myth: "On the first day the child was washed with water in which cedar had been brewed. Fine white cornmeal was then rubbed over his body and left all day. Next day the child was cleaned, and cedar ashes were rubbed over him to remove the hair and skin" (Waters, 9).

6. When Abel rubs his body with ashes, he is attempting to "cure" his psychological, emotional, and cultural malady: "His body was numb and ached with cold and he knelt at the mouth of the oven. He reached inside and placed his hands in the frozen crust and rubbed his arms and chest with ashes"; see N. Scott Momaday, *House Made of Dawn* (New York: Harper & Row, 1968), 210. Similarly, the rubbing of ashes by the protagonist of "Coyote Holds a Full House in His Hand" is also a sort of cure, but one that is laden with trickster overtones absent from Momaday's text.

7. See Bernard A. Hirsch, "The Telling Which Continues," *American Indian Quarterly* 12.1 (1988): 1–26.

# A. LaVonne Brown Ruoff

At one time, the ceremonies as they had been performed were enough for the way the world was then. But after the white people came, elements in this world began to shift; and it became necessary to create new ceremonies. I have made changes in the rituals. The people mistrust this greatly, but only this growth keeps the ceremonies strong. . . . That's what the witchery is counting on: that we will cling to the ceremonies the way they were, and then their power will triumph, and the people will be no more.

—Betonie in *Ceremony*

For Leslie Marmon Silko (Laguna), the strength of tribal traditions is based not on American Indians' rigid adherence to given ceremonies or customs but rather on their ability to adapt traditions to ever-changing circumstances by incorporating new elements. Although this theme is most fully developed in her novel *Ceremony* (1977), it is also present in her earlier short stories, "The Man to Send Rain Clouds," "Tony's Story," "*from* Humaweepi, the Warrior Priest," and "Yellow Woman," originally included in *The Man to Send Rain Clouds: Contemporary Stories by American Indians.*[1]

The history of Silko's own Laguna Pueblo, influenced by many different cultures, provides insight into why she emphasizes change as a source of strength for tribal traditions. According to their origin legends, the Laguna tribe (in existence since at least 1300), came southward from the Mesa Verde region. Some versions indicate that after pausing at Zia, they were joined by the head of the Parrot clan, who decided to take his people southward with them. After wandering farther, first

"Ritual and Renewal: Keres Traditions in the Short Fiction of Leslie Silko," Copyright 1979, MELUS, The Society for the Study of the Multi-ethnic Literature of the United States; reprinted by permission; revised version published in *American Women Short Story Writers: A Collection of Essays,* ed. Julie Brown (New York: Garland, 1995) and reprinted here by permission of A. LaVonne Brown Ruoff.

southward from the lake at Laguna and then northward back to the lake, they settled Punyana, probably in the late 1300s. After founding Old Laguna (Kawaik) around 1400, they issued invitations to other pueblos to join them. Those that responded were the Parrot clan from Zia, the Sun clan from Hopi, the Road Runner and Badger clans from Zuni, and the Sun clan from Jemez. The tribe occupied the site of what is now called Laguna (New Mexico) by the early 1500s. Additional immigration occurred during the 1690s, when the Lagunas were joined by Indians from the Rio Grande, probably fleeing both drought and the hostility of the Spanish after the Pueblo Rebellion in 1680 and the renewed uprising in 1696. These immigrants came chiefly from Zia, Cochiti, and Domingo, but a few came from Jemez, Zuni, and Hopi. Although some remained to join the Laguna tribe, others returned to their own pueblos when conditions improved. Over the years, a few Navajos intermarried with the tribe, bringing with them the Navajo Sun clan and *kachina* (spirits).[2]

The Spanish first entered the area in 1540 when Francisco de Coronado led an expedition to Zuni and two years later passed through the present site of Laguna on his way back to Mexico. Antonio Espejo, who commanded an expedition to New Mexico in 1582, visited the area in 1583. Between the appointment of Juan de Oñate as New Mexico's first governor in 1595 and the Pueblo Rebellion in 1680, there is little historical data on Laguna. Although the pueblo was not subjected to as many attacks from the Spanish as the Rio Grande pueblos, it was forced to surrender in 1692 after an attack by the troops of Governor Diego de Vargas (Ellis 3).[3]

Concerning the mixture of people who settled at Laguna, Parsons comments in *Pueblo Indian Religion* that "it is not surprising that Laguna was the first of the pueblos to Americanize, through intermarriage" (888). Around 1860 and 1870, George H. Pradt (or Pratt) and two Marmon brothers (Walter and Robert) came to the pueblo, married Laguna women, and reared large families. Silko indicates that her great-grandfather Robert and his brother had a government contract to set out the boundary markers for Laguna.[4] Walter, appointed government teacher in 1871, married the daughter of the chief of the Kurena-Shikani medicine men. The chief's son later took his place. According to Parsons, this group led the Americanization faction that was opposed by the pueblo hierarchy. The conservatives removed their altars and sacred objects from Laguna and moved to Mesita; around 1880, part of this group resettled in Isleta. While Robert Marmon served as governor, the two *kivas* (underground ceremonial meeting places) of Laguna were torn down by the progressives and what was left of the sacred objects was surrendered. There were no *kachina* dances for some time after the Great Split and the laying of the railroad on the edge of the village. When a demand arose later for the revival of the dances, Zuni influences were introduced into Laguna rituals (Parsons, *Pueblo* 2 888–890; Gunn 96). Parsons closes her description of Laguna with the comment that although the ceremonial disintegration was so marked when she first studied it (around 1920) that it presented an obscure picture of Keresan culture, it later (1939) offered "unrivaled opportunities to study American acculturation and the important role played by miscegenation" (*Pueblo* 890). Silko herself comments on these changes in her description of the impact of mixed-blood families on Laguna clan systems and the varying attitudes toward these families in the stories of that pueblo:

> People in the main part of the village were our clanspeople because the clan system was still maintained although not in the same form it would have been if we were full blood. . . . The way it changed was that there began to be stories about my great-grandfather, positive stories about what he did with the Laguna scouts for the Apaches. But then after World War One it changed. Soon after that there came to be stories about these mixed blood people, half-breeds. Not only Marmons but Gunns [John] and Pratts too. An identity was being made or evolved in the stories that Lagunas told about these people who had gone outside Laguna, but at the same time of the outsiders who had come in. Part of it was that the stories were always about the wild, roguish, crazy sorts of things they did (Evers and Carr, "Conversation" 30).

The continuing strength of Laguna traditions and the ability of her people to use alien traditions for their own purposes are strikingly portrayed in Silko's story "The Man to Send Rain Clouds." The title alludes to the belief that the dead are associated with cloud beings (storm clouds, or *shiwanna*, in Keres) who bring rain and who live in the six or four regions of the universe (Parsons, *Pueblo* 172). The story deals with an Indian family's observance of Pueblo funeral rituals despite the local priest's attempts to cajole them into observing Catholic ones. Ironically, the young priest is trapped by the Indians into taking part in their ceremony. The importance of ritual in Pueblo Indian life is emphasized at the beginning of the story when Leon and Ken, after finding old Teofilo dead, immediately observe the first stages of the funeral rites. Neglect of burial or death ritual can result in death or sickness because the ghost returns (Parsons, *Pueblo* 69). Before wrapping the body in a blanket, the men tie a gray prayer feather to the old man's long white hair (a custom similar to that of the Zuni) and begin to paint his face with markings so that he will be recognized in the next world—tasks ordinarily performed by a shaman.[5] The face painting is interrupted by an offering of corn meal to the wind and is concluded with the prayer "Send us rain clouds, Grandfather" (Rosen 6).

The pressure on Pueblo Indians to practice Catholicism is introduced when Father Paul stops Leon and Ken on their way home to ask about Teofilo and to urge them all to come to church. Using the age-old Indian technique of telling the non-Indian only what they want him to know, Leon and Ken answer the priest's questions about the old man's welfare ambiguously enough to keep him from learning about Teofilo's death. Only after the Indian funeral rites are almost completed does the family feel the need for the priest's services—to provide plenty of holy water for the grave so that Teofilo's spirit will send plenty of rainfall. Corn meal has been sprinkled around the old man's body to provide food on the journey to the other world.[6] Silko skillfully and humorously characterizes the conflict between the frustrated priest, who is denied the opportunity to provide the last rites and funeral mass, and Leon, who doggedly insists that these are not necessary: "It's O.K. Father, we just want him to have plenty of water" (Rosen 7). Despite his weary protests that he cannot do that without performing the proper Catholic rites, Father Paul finally gives in when Leon starts to leave. Realizing that he has been tricked into participating in their pagan rites and half suspecting that the whole thing may be just a spring fertility ceremony rather than a real funeral, he nevertheless sprinkles the grave with a whole jar of holy water. Leon feels good about the act, which completes the ceremony and ensures that "now the old man could send them big thunderclouds for sure" (Rosen 8). Thus, Silko emphasizes that these Pueblo Indians have not abandoned their old ways for Catholicism; instead, they have taken one part of Catholic ritual compatible with their beliefs and made it an essential part of their own ceremony.

"Tony's Story" deals with the return to Indian ritual as a means of coping with external forces. However, here the ritual concerns the shooting of a state policeman by a traditional Pueblo who becomes convinced that the policeman harassing him and his friend is a witch. Regarding her own views on the presence of witch stories in Laguna oral tradition and on the nature of witchery, Silko says that she never heard such stories until she went to Chinle on the Navajo Reservation. In expressing her agreement with Simon Ortiz, from Acoma Pueblo 20 miles south of Laguna, Silko states that when "everything is in good shape within the pueblo view, then there's not going to be any witchcraft. . . . Witchcraft is happening when the livestock are skinny"; instances are rare; but when they do occur, they are handled by everyone (Evers and Carr, 32). The treatment of witchery in this story is especially significant in view of Silko's later treatment of the theme in *Ceremony.*

Parsons defines the Pueblo concept of witchcraft simply as "power used improperly" (*Pueblo* 63). A witch may injure individuals or the entire community: "He may send an epidemic upon the town or he may sicken or kill a person by stealing his heart which is his life or by sending . . . into his body injurious things: insects, a piece of flesh from a corpse or a shred of funeral cloth or a splinter of bone, thorns, cactus spines, glass, anything sharp. . . . He is a potential murderer, a grave-robber, and a perpetual menace" (*Pueblo* 63). She emphasizes that to Pueblo Indians, witchcraft and immorality or crime are almost synonymous and that the witch possesses the traits people consider antisocial: envy, jealousy, revenge, quarrelsomeness, self-assertiveness, uncooperativeness, and unconventionality. Fear of witchcraft affects manners. You offer a visitor food or anything he may admire lest he take offense; you keep your affairs to yourself, do not meddle, and avoid quarrels. Particularly relevant to "Tony's Story" is Parsons's example of the Laguna war captains' shooting a woman thought to be a witch (Parsons, *Pueblo* 65,6).[7] Parsons concludes that at the time she was writing (about 1920), the right of a war captain to perform such an act would not be questioned in most Keresan or Tewan pueblos or in Zuni.[8]

In "Tony's Story," Silko uses the concept of witchcraft as power used improperly. She also uses many of the circumstances associated with witchcraft described above. The all-too-familiar story of the brutal policeman out to harass reservation Indians is made far more complex by Silko's use of the witchcraft theme as well as by her use of irony. Leon, the character beaten and hounded by the policeman without real provocation, is an ex-serviceman whose behavior sets him apart from the others of his pueblo. Although Leon, through his drinking and bold manner, inadvertently triggers the policeman's violence and although he threatens over and over to kill his attacker, he is nevertheless only a passive witness to the final shooting of the policeman. On the other hand,

155

his friend Tony, a traditional Pueblo only wishing to avoid trouble, becomes so convinced that the policeman is a witch that he shoots his adversary and then burns the body by setting fire to the police car. Silko makes clear that the times and the circumstances are such that a young man like Tony could become convinced that witchery is present. The ordinary life of the pueblo has been disrupted by the presence of the returning ex-servicemen, who always seem to cause trouble. Further, there has been a long dry spell—a sure sign in pueblo mythology that something has gone wrong.

The fact that Leon acts differently from Tony and from the others of his tribe indicates how far his experiences outside his pueblo have changed him. As the story opens he is oblivious to the danger of openly drinking in the midst of a festival crowd. Tony's comment that Leon now shakes hands hard like a white man demonstrates that the changes are not merely the result of his drinking. Leon himself admits both his separation from his past and his desire to regain it when he wonders whether he has forgotten what to do during the Corn Dance, in which he plans to participate. Tony's anxiety about Leon's drinking turns to fear when he sees a policeman in the crowd. Without provocation, warning, or explanation, the policeman smashes his fist into Leon's face, knocking him down, cutting his mouth, and breaking some of his teeth. The policeman's sudden violence vividly illustrates the misuse of power associated with witches.

The theme of witchcraft and the identification of the policeman as a witch is explicitly introduced in Tony's dream the night of the attack, when he sees the man point a long bone at him and when the man appears to have not a human face but "only little, round, white-rimmed eyes on a black ceremonial mask" (Rosen 72). Tony's dream serves as a form of clairvoyance, a technique used by many pueblo tribes for detecting witchcraft or witches.[9] As the harassment continues, the difference between the reactions of Leon and Tony becomes increasingly clear: Leon's non-pueblo dependence on verbal bravado and insistence on his legal rights seem to Tony to be dangerous ways to deal with witchery, which can only be overcome by dependence on Pueblo ritual. While Leon threatens to "kill the big bastard if he comes around here again," Tony tries to persuade him to forget the incident (Rosen 72). Leon's subsequent attempt to get redress from the pueblo council results only in an admonishment for drinking on the reservation. As Leon's methods for dealing with the policeman prove ineffective, Tony becomes more and more convinced of the power of witchery. The second confrontation with the policeman takes place after he has forced them off the road. Tony's fear of the policeman's power is so great that he cannot look into the man's eyes—just as, when a child, he was afraid to look into the eyes of the masked dancers lest they grab him. During this episode, the policeman gives his only explanation for tormenting Leon: "They transferred me here because of Indians. They thought there wouldn't be as many for me here. But I find them" (Rosen 74). Still trying to avoid the power of this supernatural force, Tony persuades Leon to go back home and rejects his friend's anger about the violation of his rights, which is not what the policeman was after: "But Leon didn't seem to understand; he couldn't remember the stories that old Teofilo told" (Rosen 74).

In his fear and anguish, Tony becomes increasingly isolated. He does not go to a *shaman* for help nor does he feel he can seek outside help. Old Teofilo, whose knowledge he trusted, is dead, and he is afraid to tell his family for fear he might subject them to harm. In fact, he ignores his father's warning to stay away from Leon, who is regarded as a troublemaker. Tony's attempts to communicate to Leon his perception of the nature of the danger represented by the policeman end in failure. When Tony offers his friend an arrowhead, a Pueblo protection against witchcraft,[10] Leon rejects it, choosing instead to put his faith in his request for help from the pueblo governor and in his own rifle.

The final confrontation takes place when Leon and Tony are driving toward a remote sheep camp. The role reversal, which dominates the final scene, is first indicated by the fact that this time it is Leon who spots the policeman, who is following them in his patrol car. The news interrupts Tony's reverie of what the land was like before the coming of the white man and convinces him that the witch must be destroyed. When the policeman forces them off the road and gets out to beat them with his billy club, he becomes for Tony the witch of his dream and the club, a camouflaged human bone.

Ironically, Tony, who advocated avoidance of trouble and who had objected to Leon's murder threats, shoots the policeman with Leon's gun and then takes charge of burning the police car and body. Tony calmly reassures the panic-filled Leon with the words, "Don't worry, everything is O.K. now, Leon. It's killed. They sometimes take on strange forms" (Rosen 78). As the car burns, rain clouds form, signaling the end of the drought.

At the moment that Tony decides to destroy the witch, he becomes a self-appointed pueblo war captain—a role in which he later involves Leon. The war captains represent the twin heroes Ma'sewi and

Uyuyewi, who appear in many Keres stories. The theme of the destruction of a witch by two young men is based on the exploits of these twins, such as their jointly killing two giantesses or as Ma'sewi's single-handedly drowning Pa'cayani, whose tricks brought drought and famine (Boas 13–16, 49–56, 236–237, 249–253; Parsons, *Pueblo* 245; Gunn 110; Lummis 209–212).[11] Although Ma'sewi, the elder twin, appears most frequently in Laguna stories as a monster slayer, here the younger man is given this role. The hero twins in the mythic past would have been praised for their witch killing. The formation of rain clouds immediately after the murder seems to indicate that nature approves of Tony's act, which has rid the pueblo of a menace. Nevertheless, Tony will be judged by neither Keres nor natural law but rather by non-Indian civil law. The conclusion of the story makes clear that the exorcism ritual is complete. What the conclusion leaves unclear are the consequences Tony will suffer for carrying out the ritual.[12]

In "*from* Humaweepi, the Warrior Priest," Silko presents the theme of the transmission of Pueblo religion and ritual through oral tradition. Here she focuses on the training given a young Pueblo boy that culminates in his initiation, at age 19, into the priesthood. The significance of the continuum of Pueblo beliefs passed down from one generation to the next is demonstrated through both the description of the boy's years of training by his uncle and his later telling his friend about a lesson taught by his uncle. Most important in this apprenticeship is learning to be part of the land and to express this sense of unity through ritual—to know the ways to live with plant life, animal life, and shelter used by animals, as well as the songs, chants, and prayers for all the seasons. In order to achieve this harmony with nature, Humaweepi must be separated from the pueblo, with its dances and Christian fiestas and its young people who dismiss as "nothing" what the old man taught. Learning to sleep in nests where deer had slept, to eat grass roots and dried wild grapes, and to live on the land during all the seasons is necessary for Humaweepi to reach the point where he is ready to take on animal power. The lesson repeatedly emphasized by the old man is that "human beings are special. . . . [T]hey can do anything" (Rosen 162). As the years pass, Humaweepi unconsciously learns through observing his uncle's religious rites, listening to his stories, and following his example. As the old man explains, "every day I have been teaching you" (Rosen 164).

When Humaweepi is ready for his initiation, the old man takes him high into the mountains, making him leave his cowboy boots on the way up and making him walk the rest of the way barefoot. After they reach a mountain lake, the old man sings and feeds corn pollen to the mountain wind, his voice becoming like the sound of the night wind in the trees. The scene is beautifully described by Silko: "The songs were snowstorms with sounds as soft and cold as snowflakes; the songs were spring rain and wild ducks returning" (Rosen 165). Humaweepi's moment of initiation comes when the old man shows him the gray bear-shaped boulder, half in the lake and half on the shore. Almost unconsciously, Humaweepi steps into the lake, places his beads on the bear's head, and sings the bear a song asking it to bestow its power on him as a man and warrior priest. All Humaweepi's training has led him to this ritual. By learning to live as animals have lived in nature, he has prepared himself to become a warrior priest who can be transformed into a bear—the special patron of Keresan, Zuni, and Tewan curing societies.[13] In her description of the instruction and of the initiation itself, Silko emphasizes nature and deemphasizes magic, for it is not magic formulas that enable Humaweepi to take on bear power but rather the gradual process of becoming one with nature.

In this story, Silko stresses the importance of the continuum of oral tradition in both religious instruction and in storytelling. Whereas the first part of this tale focuses on the uncle's preparation of Humaweepi for his initiation, the second part focuses on Humaweepi's own storytelling. As his uncle takes him up the mountain to the bear rock, Humaweepi realizes that some day he will be responsible for doing the things his uncle does. In the second part of the tale, Silko indicates that Humaweepi does this by transmitting stories to a friend rather than by transmitting rituals to an apprentice. The particular story told by Humaweepi in Part Two describes the animal power possessed by a holy man after initiation as demonstrated by his uncle's walking barefoot through the mountain snow like a wolf.

The old man, who abandons his yucca sandals partway up the mountain, insists that his feet do not get cold and that people grow to believe they need shoes only because fearful women instill the habit in them as children. "Does the wolf freeze his feet?" he asks (Rosen 168). When Humaweepi counters that the old man is not a wolf, his uncle reveals the strength of his power by appearing to become transformed: "The old man's eyes opened wide and then looked at me narrowly, sharply, squinting and shining. He gave a long, wailing wolf cry with his head raised toward the winter sky" (Rosen 168). In the distance, Humaweepi thinks he hears a wailing answer. Animal power, then, is not limited to bear power; although the bear is the most powerful, he can become transformed into other sacred animals as well. In the old uncle's words, "a man can do anything." For Pueblo men to fulfill this potential, the oral tradition must survive. By shifting the focus from ritual in the first part of the narrative to storytelling in the second part, Silko emphasizes that both are important to the continuum of oral traditions—that the traditions and the rituals on which these are based can die out if they become the exclusive property of only a select few who fail to transmit them.

The continuum of the oral tradition and the importance of story-telling are also demonstrated in Silko's "Yellow Woman."[14] Here, how-ever, the emphasis is on personal renewal, derived from experience out-side the pueblo, rather than on mastery of religious ritual. Adapting the traditional "yellow woman" abduction tales to contemporary circum-stances, Silko vividly illustrates the influence of these stories on the imagination of a modern Pueblo woman and the usefulness of the genre for explaining why this woman, and generations of women before her, would suddenly disappear with a stranger, only to return later with a story about being kidnapped. Many of the traditional tales emphasize the subsequent benefits that came to the pueblo as a result of these liaisons, as Silko indicates in her summary of them: "Yellow Woman went away with the spirit from the north and lived with him and his rel-atives. She was gone for a long time, but then one day she came back and brought twin boys" (Rosen 355).

Boas summarizes the basic elements of the traditional abduction sto-ries as follows: A woman is usually abducted by a dangerous *kachina*[15] when she goes to draw water. After encountering the abductor, the woman refuses to be taken away because she does not know what to do with her water jar. The abductor then threatens her with death, com-pels her to place the jar on the ground upside down, and then transports her by various means to his home, where he gives her impossible tasks to perform lest she be killed.[16] In some stories, Yellow Woman is described as the mother of the hero twins Ma'sewi and Uyuyewi, the names given not only to the twin children of the Sun and Yellow Woman but also to all such children of monster *kachinas* and the women they abduct. The children are usually born miraculously and raised after the death of their mothers (Boas 107; Gunn 150). Through bearing twins who subsequently become monster slayers or who simply bring new blood into the pueblo, Yellow Woman becomes a symbol of renewal through a liaison with outside forces. In addition to bringing new life to the pueblo, Yellow Woman renews it in other ways. For example, in the tale of Buffalo Man, Yellow Woman is abducted by him. After she is freed by her husband Arrow Youth, they are pursued by Buffalo Man and his herd. Arrow Youth succeeds in killing the abductor and all the other buffalo. Because Yellow Woman weeps for the death of her buffalo husband, Arrow Youth kills her as well. However, as a result of her abduction and pursuit by Buffalo Man, the pueblo is provided with much-needed meat (Boas 122–127, 261–262; Gunn 184–189).[17]

In general, the abductor is an evil force of great power, frequently associated with mountain spirits. Most common among the abductors in the printed accounts are Flint Wing (who lives on a mountaintop), Cliff Dweller (who lives on a high mesa), Whirlwind Man (who may be either an evil *kachina* or who may live among the good *kachinas* at Wenimatse), Whipper, and Buffalo Man (Boas 104–127). Although the abductor in Silko's "Yellow Woman" is the contemporary of all these figures, some of the details of her story more closely resemble the accounts of Cliff Dweller (Ma'etc' Tcowai) than of other abductors. For example, Cliff Dweller is associated with the north, the direction from which Silko says the abductor *kachina* came. In addition, both Cliff Dweller and the abductor in Silko's story leave their women temporarily to go hunting and bring back meat.[18]

Gunn describes Cliff Dweller as a wayward son who disregarded the teachings and prayers of his mother to become an outlaw and a kidnapper and murderer of women. He never married more than one wife at a time. To get her, he would go into the settlements, marry, and then take his wife to his cliff dwelling; if any refused, he would carry her off by force. When he became dissatisfied with his wife, he would throw her over the cliff and bring home another (Gunn 143).[19] In Boas's version, Yellow Woman goes to draw water but is carried away by Cliff Dweller, who tells her to stand north from him. He rolls the ring (for supporting the water jar on her head) toward her and thus transports her to his house on the cliff (104–105). In the versions given by both Boas and Gunn, Yellow Woman is ordered to grind an enormous amount of corn in a short time or else she will be killed. With the help of Spider Woman, Yellow Woman completes the task in the allotted time. After being given other superhuman tasks (which differ in the versions by Boas, Gunn, and Lummis), she realizes that she is going to be killed whether she completes them or not; consequently, she gets Spider Woman to help her escape by weaving a net to let her down from the cliff. In Boas's version, she escapes briefly, only to be killed by Cliff Dweller. Her sons, the hero twins, are born after her death. In Gunn's version,

Yellow Woman survives to bear the twins, and Cliff Dweller himself is killed (Boas 108; Gunn 143–152; Lummis 203–205).

Silko's sources for her "Yellow Woman" story are not the published accounts but rather the oral ones passed on by members of her family. As she makes clear in an interview:

> I figured that anybody could go to the anthropologists' reports and look at them. I have looked at them myself, but I've never sat down with them and said I'm going to make a poem or story out of this. . . . I don't have to because from the time I was little, I heard quite a bit. I heard it in what would have been passed off now as rumor or gossip. I could hear through all that. I could hear something else, that there was a kind of continuum. (Evers and Carr 30)

Silko has also indicated elsewhere that one of her sources was her great aunt Alice Little, who used to tell the young Marmon girls stories about Yellow Woman while babysitting them: "It seemed like, though, you keep hearing the same story all the time."[20]

According to Silko, the river in Laguna, where "Yellow Woman" opens, was always associated with stories as places to meet boyfriends and lovers:

> I used to wander around down there and try to imagine walking around the bend and just happening to stumble upon some beautiful man. Later on I realized that these kinds of things that I was doing when I was fifteen are exactly the kinds of things out of which stories like the Yellow Woman story [came], I finally put the two together: the adolescent longings and the old stories, that plus the stories around Laguna at the time about people who did, in fact just in recent times, use the river as a meeting place. (Evers and Carr 29)

She notes that the old adultery stories are better than ever and have become even more intricate, now that indoor plumbing has eliminated some of the excuses for going outside (Evers and Carr 33).

Although Silko's "Yellow Woman" is based on traditional abduction tales, it is more than a modernized version. Silko is less concerned with the events involved in Yellow Woman's abduction and her subsequent return home than with the character's confusion about what is real and what is not. Underlying this is the character's identification with Keres legends and her temporary rejection of the confining monotony of life within the pueblo.

Unlike the recorded traditional abduction tales, Silko's story does not begin with Yellow Woman's initial encounter with her abductor. Instead, it begins when Yellow Woman awakes after spending the night with the stranger she met by the river the previous afternoon. As the story opens, Yellow Woman becomes conscious of various strong physical sensations: the dampness with which her thigh clings to that of her abductor, the sight of the brown water birds, the sound of the water, the appearance of her sleeping lover, and the pangs of her own hunger. Indeed, one of the themes of the story is the power that physical sensations and desire have to blot out thoughts of home, family, and responsibility. Following the river southward to where she met her lover, she tries but fails to catch a glimpse of her pueblo. Her failure is one of the first indications that she has been separated from the world, which no longer seems real to her. Her reality consists of immediate physical sensations combined with vague memory of the legends told by her grandfather, which her own experience now parallels. The interrelationship between the myth of the past and the experience of the present begins when she touches her lover to tell him she is leaving—an unnecessary act if she really meant to leave. The connection between legend and experience is made explicit when he calls her "Yellow Woman," although he stresses that it was she who suggested the parallel the night before. Now, however, her sense of being part of the myth has weakened: she remembers only the touch of his body and the beauty of the moon (the moon is female in Keres mythology). Weakly she insists on her identity and his, separate from the legend. Although the abductor's name is revealed in the story, that of Yellow Woman is not: "I have my own name and I come from the pueblo on the other side of the mesa. Your name is Silva and you are a stranger I met by the river yesterday afternoon" (Rosen 34). That the stranger is the contemporary counterpart of the mythic abductors is underscored by the fact that his name, "Silva," is Spanish for "collection" or "anthology." Despite the young woman's denial that she and Silva are reliving the myth, the mention of it recalls to her the old Yellow Woman stories—not only the abduction tales but also such animal tales as the one about Coyote outsmarting Badger when both animals wanted to sleep with Yellow Woman.[21]

In contrast to the abductors in the recorded traditional stories who relied on threats to get Yellow Woman to go with them, Silva relies instead on his psychological dominance and on her physical desire for him. As Silva touches her and as she moves close to him, she is drawn once more into the world of the legend. Clearly she identifies with Yellow Woman when she wonders whether the legendary Yellow Woman had a life and identity outside the myths as she herself does. Her fear of going away with Silva melted away by her pleasure at the warmth of his body, she dimly perceives why the mythic Yellow Woman would go off so quickly with her abductor: "This is the way it happens in the stories, I was thinking, with no thought beyond the moment she meets the ka'tsina spirit and they go" (Rosen 35). Her resistance to Silva's will that she come with him is limited to her feeble protest that she does not have to go.

Their journey up the mountain intensifies her confusion about what is dream and what is fact. The farther away she goes from home and family, the more powerless she is to prove to herself that she is not Yellow Woman. She hopes to see someone else on the trail so that she can again be certain of her own identity. Although she tries to persuade herself that she cannot be Yellow Woman because the woman of the legend lived in the past and did not experience her modern world, she is nevertheless lured farther and farther into the high country by Silva, who always looks into her eyes and softly sings a mountain song. Only her hunger wrenches her thoughts from him back to her home, where her family would be cooking breakfast and wondering what had happened to her.

The second part of the story takes place high on the mountain where Silva has his home. He does not require her to perform superhuman chores once they arrive, as did the traditional abductors. Instead he sets her the task of frying some potatoes while he continues to watch her closely. As they eat, her thoughts return to the legend, and she asks if he has brought other women here before by telling them also that he was a mountain *kachina*. He does not answer. After showing her his view of the world (the Navajo reservation, the Pueblo boundaries, and cattle country), he arouses her fears when he matter-of-factly informs her that he is a cattle rustler. Although she wonders about this mountain rustler who speaks Pueblo, she convinces herself that he must be a Navajo because Pueblo men do not do things like that—an allusion to the old Navajo practice of raiding Pueblo settlements for food and women. Once again, he overcomes Yellow Woman's fears through seduction, laughing at her for breathing so hard while he caresses her. When she turns away, he pins her down and warns her, "You will do what I want" (Rosen 40). For the first time she realizes that he could destroy her as other abductors destroyed Yellow Woman in the legends. Nevertheless, her fear turns to tenderness as she watches him sleep.

When she awakens the next morning to find him gone, she is over-come by confusion, vainly seeking some evidence of his presence in the house to prove that he will return or even that he exists. Later in the day, after eating and napping, she awakens again to thoughts about her family. That she is going to remain with Silva is evident from her con-clusion that her family (including her baby) will get along without her. She feels the only difference her leaving will make is that a story about her disappearance will be created. Like Yellow Woman and her human counterparts, she will become the source for the continuation of the abduction tale in contemporary oral tradition.

Rather than walk home as she set out to do, she returns to Silva's house, where he has brought home a rustled beef carcass instead of the traditional deer meat. Silva tests her loyalty to him by asking whether she intends to come with him to sell the meat. Her questions as to whether anyone has tried to catch him and why he carried a rifle reflect her sense of danger; however, still under his spell, she agrees to accom-pany him.

Part Three of the story deals with the confrontation between Silva and an unarmed white rancher, an episode comparable to the tests in the traditional tales in which Yellow Woman's life is threatened or in danger; this time, the danger is indirect rather than direct. After the rancher accuses Silva of rustling, the latter orders Yellow Woman to go back up the mountain with the beef, which she starts to do, hearing at least four[22] shots as she rides quickly away. Reaching a ridge, she tries to see where she left Silva but cannot, just as she was unable to see her pueblo at the beginning of the story before she began the journey up the mountain. Her inability to see what she is seeking signals the end of her interlude with Silva. Unconsciously, she has decided to return home—just as her grandfather had said the legendary Yellow Woman usually did before her.

In the concluding section of the story, Yellow Woman makes her way back on foot to the river where she first met Silva. Although she feels sad about leaving him and is disturbed by his strangeness, her desire for him is rekindled when she comes to the spot where the leaves he trimmed from a willow mark their first meeting place. She convinces herself that she cannot return to him because the mountains are too far away but comforts herself with the belief that he will come back again to the riverbank. As she reaches her home, she is brought back to the realities of her own life by the smell of supper cooking and the sight of her mother instructing her grandmother in the white man's art of making Jell-O.

This acculturation explains why the only member of her family for whom she feels an affectionate kinship is her dead grandfather, who loved the Yellow Woman tales that he passed on to his granddaughter. As her link to the mythological and historical past, he would understand that her disappearance was not a police matter because she had only been stolen by a *kachina* mountain spirit. For him, this would have been explanation enough; for her family, however, which no longer possesses this sense of unity with the past, she is forced to create the story of being kidnapped by a Navajo. Thus, the grandfather's belief in the tales in which the lives of the Pueblo people were inextricably intertwined with their gods has been transmitted to his granddaughter, who uses them as an explanation for her temporary escape from routine. Her conviction that her own experiences will serve the pueblo as a new topic for storytelling and that she herself will have to become a storyteller to explain away her absence indicates that the process will continue.

In all four of these stories, Silko emphasizes the need to return to the rituals and oral traditions of the past in order to rediscover the basis for one's cultural identity. Only when this is done is one prepared to deal with the problems of the present. However, Silko advocates a return to the essence rather than to the precise form of these rituals and traditions, which must be adapted continually to meet new challenges. Through her own stories, Silko demonstrates that the Keres rituals and traditions have survived all attempts to eradicate them and that the seeds for the resurgence of their power lie in the memories and creativeness of her people.

# Notes

*Editor's note:* The original documentation format of this selection (MLA format of explanatory notes and bibliography of works cited) has been changed to a format of endnotes only for consistency with other essays in this volume.

1. Kenneth Rosen, ed., *The Man to Send Rain Clouds: Contemporary Stories by American Indians* (New York: Random House, 1974); cited hereafter as Rosen. All these stories except "*from* Humaweepi, Warrior Priest" were republished in Leslie Marmon Silko, *Storyteller* (New York: Arcade, 1981); cited hereafter as *Storyteller*.

2. See Florence H. Ellis, "Anthropology of Laguna Pueblo Land Claims," *Pueblo Indians, American Indian Ethnohistory: Indians of the Southwest*, vol. 3 (New York: Garland, 1974), 8–11, cited hereafter as Ellis; also Elsie Clews Parsons, *Pueblo Indian Religion*, vol. 2 (Chicago: University of Chicago Press, 1939), 888–890, cited hereafter as Parsons, *Pueblo*. I have followed Ellis's account rather than Parsons's, who spent very little time in Laguna. See also Elsie Clews Parsons, *Notes on Ceremonialism at Laguna*, Anthropological Papers of the American Museum of Natural History 9.1 (New York: Trustees of the AMNH, 1920), 83–131.

3. Also see John Gunn, *Schat-Chen: History Traditions and Naratives* [sic] *of the Queres Indians of Laguna and Acoma* (Albuquerque: Albright and Anderson, 1917), 22, 35, 47; cited hereafter as Gunn.

4. Lawrence J. Evers and Denny Carr, "A Conversation with Leslie Marmon Silko," *Sun Tracks* 3 (Fall 1976): 28–33, p. 29. Cited hereafter as Evers and Carr.

5. Turkey feathers are associated with the dead; see Parsons (*Pueblo* 275), and for a discussion of the Pueblo use of prayer feathers, see Parsons (*Pueblo* 285–292). I am unable to identify the face markings described by Silko. They are closest to the white, green, and blue that Boas says were used by the water clan; see Franz Boas, *Keresan Texts* (New York: American Ethnological Society, 1928), 295; cited hereafter as Boas.

6. Corn meal is even more associated with prayer than prayer sticks or feathers (Parsons, *Pueblo* 292). According to Boas's description of a Laguna funeral ritual, both water and food would be placed beside the corpse. After two days, the dead one, who by now has become a vapor, eats for the last time food provided first by a shaman and then sacrificed on the fire by the family (Boas 203–204). Parsons describes the latter sacrifice as occurring on the fourth day (Parsons, *Notes* 128–129).

7. The war captains represent the hero twins Ma'sewi and Uyuyewi. As the "out of town chiefs," they are in charge of all public functions (Boas 286).

8. In addition, witch effigies were "killed" in annual curing ceremonies; townspeople referred to these "witches" as living beings (Parsons, *Pueblo* 84–88).

9. Dreams are frequently but not always bad signs to a Pueblo. Bad dreams are seen as portents of death, and dreams of the dead are considered visitations of the dead (Parsons, *Pueblo* 84–88).

10. Parsons notes that one may use an arrow point or ashes against witchcraft; both are used to separate a person from a dangerous influence. Arrow points are thought to have power because they have been shot by lightning. The reasons for using ashes remain obscure (Parsons, *Pueblo* 106, 332).

11. Also see Charles Lummis, *The Man Who Married the Moon and Other Pueblo Indian Folk-Stories* (New York: The Century Co., 1894), 209–212; cited

hereafter as Lummis. Silko retells the story in her novel *Ceremony* (New York: Viking, 1977).

12. Simon Ortiz's "The Killing of a State Cop" deals with the murder of a policeman on reservation land by a Pueblo Indian. In addition, N. Scott Momaday's *House Made of Dawn* includes an incident in which the central character, Abel, a veteran of World War II, kills an albino tormentor, thinking he is a witch. According to Lawrence Evers, these fictional treatments are based on the murder of Nash Garcia, a New Mexican policeman, on Good Friday, 1952, in Grants, New Mexico. See "The Killing of a State Trooper: Ways of Telling an Historical Event," *Critical Essays on Native American Literature*, ed. Andrew Wiget (Boston: G. K. Hall, 1985), 246–261.

13. When Keresan, Zuni, and Tewan doctors, called bears, draw on the bear paws, which are the equivalent of a *kachina* mask, they become bears. Doctors and *shamans* have the power literally to turn into bears just as bears may get rid of their skins and become people. Animals are considered the givers of medicinal plants, which are named for them. Because they are considered guardians or protectors, their stone images are primarily displayed on altars and are kept in homes. Keresan and Tewan doctors may give animal images to their patients to protect them against the witches who have made them sick (Parsons, *Pueblo* 188–190).

14. Many of the critical essays in *"Yellow Woman": Leslie Marmon Silko*, ed. Melody Graulich (New Brunswick, NJ: Rutgers University Press, 1933) focus on Silko's storytelling. Helen Jaskoski examines how *Storyteller* takes its form and theme from the traditional relationship between storyteller and audience; see "Words Like Bones," *CEA Critic* 55.1 (1992): 70–84.

15. The *kachina* (ka'tsina in Keres) spirits as a class are always kind and helpful; they live in the northwest at Wenimatse, a beautiful mountain region where the spirits gamble, dance, hunt, or farm. The term also refers to spirits who can be impersonated by masks. See Parsons, *Pueblo* 174; Boas 276–277; Anthony F. Purley, "Keres Pueblo Concepts of Deity," *American Indian Culture and Research Journal* 1 (1974): 29–32.

16. According to Boas (218–219), "Yellow Woman" is a generic term used to specify heroines in Keres stories. Parsons points out that Kachina Girl or Yellow Woman (Ko'tchina'ko) is paired with the male *kachina* and that this supernatural pair is associated with the colors yellow and turquoise. The practice of pairing, whether of the same or opposite sex, carries an assurance of companionship rather than of number (Parsons, *Pueblo* 101–102).

17. This story is the subject of Silko's poem "COTTONWOOD, Part Two: Buffalo Story," *Storyteller* 67–76.

18. Although Flint Wing lives on a northern mountaintop and goes hunting, the tales about his abduction of Yellow Woman are less similar to Silko's story than are those about Cliff Dweller (see Boas 111–118, 258–259; Gunn 122–125).

19. A reference to the Navajo Cliff or Throwing Monster (tse'nenaxli), whose name comes from his habit of catching people in his long sharp claws and throwing them to his children down among the rocks; see Gladys Reichard, *Navaho Religion: A Study of Symbolism* 2 vols. (New York: Pantheon, 1950), 1:7–4; 2: 420. When Silva says the Navajo people know him too, he may be alluding either to their knowledge of the abduction stories or to the fact that both Cliff Dweller of the Keres legends and Cliff Monster of the Navajo kill by throwing their victims off cliffs (Boas 108; Gunn 52; Lummis 203–205).

20. Leslie Marmon Silko, "Poetry and Prose Reading," MLA-NEH Summer Seminar on Contemporary Native American Literature (Flagstaff, AZ, June 1977). Also see Silko's comments on storytelling in Kim Barnes, "A Leslie Marmon Silko Interview," *Journal of Ethnic Studies* 13 (Winter 1986): 83–105.

21. A reference to the tale recorded by Boas in which Coyote and Badger want to sleep with a brown-haired, light-complexioned Navajo girl, who will permit them to do so only after they bring her rabbits. Each tries to outwit the other (167–169, 271–272). These two animals are very frequently linked in Pueblo stories. See the chapters on "Badger" and "Coyote and Kin" in Hamilton A. Tyler, *Pueblo Animals and Myths* (Norman: University of Oklahoma Press, 1975).

22. The number four occurs often in Keres tales. However, Parsons notes that among many Indian peoples, it is the favored numeral. It is used so much, especially in folktale and ritual where freedom of repetition is unrestricted, that it frequently means no more than "some" or "several" (Parsons, *Pueblo* 1:100). Boas associates it with the characteristic number in individual Laguna families (8.1: 217).

# Kathryn W. Shanley

In his article entitled "The Translation Dilemma", Jeffrey F. Huntsman raises a crucial question regarding the translation and study of Native American literatures: what do we stand to gain and/or lose by making "pretty judgments"?

> [O]utsiders can make too much of a given phrasing because they fail to understand fully the force—or lack of force—the phrase may have for its ordinary users. To cite a set of trivial but effective examples: If we compare French *j'ai faim* (lit. "I have hunger") with Irish *Ta ocras orm* (lit. "It is hunger on me") with English *I am hungry*, should we dwell on the imagistic effectiveness of the Irish phrase, the intimate identification of person and plight of the English, or the subtle and philosophical detachment of the French? And what then are we to make of the Navajo, which translates literally "Hunger is trying to kill me"? Such pretty judgments would be utterly foolish, of course, because each phrase is the most commonplace formulation available and invokes not the tiniest *frisson* of poetic delight in a native speaker.[1]

That there is, then, a somewhat "illegitimate" delight to be found in the practice of "pretty judgments" is not a surprising, new idea; and, I suppose, the pursuit of novelty solely for the delight it can bring is harmless enough. But, isn't poetic delight in a native speaker beside the point anyway? Or, is it? Once we determine to read for reasons other than delight, once we "own up" to the politics at work in reading (deriving meaning) as we do, we must recognize, as Foucault states it, that "the exotic charm of another system of thought is the limitation of our own, the stark impossibility of thinking *that*."[2] Put another way, the stark impossibility of "thinking" in cultural terms other than our own results either from our limited experience or from our recognition (how-

Originally published as Kate Shanley Vangen, "The Devil's Domain: Leslie Silko's 'Storyteller,' " in *Coyote Was Here: Essays on Contemporary Native American Literary and Political Mobilization*, ed. Bo Scholer (Aarhus, Denmark: SEKLOS, University of Aarhus, 1984), 116–23; reprinted by permission of the author.

ever subconscious) that the limitation preserves our own position of power and privilege—even if it is only our privilege to enjoy ourselves with immunity from responsibility toward those people who are the objects of our pleasure. Foucault further states that delight and humor are only possible because we have somehow done away with "the site, the mute ground upon which it is possible" to understand the cultural terms that would see the situation as common.

Leslie Silko, in her story entitled "Storyteller," restores the mute ground of the Alaskan native. She tells us: "The stories must be told" by native people themselves and the "time has come" for the telling.[3] At the same time as Silko creates a protagonist who can and does find a way to tell her story, she implicitly shows how the colonialist culture's discursive system closes off the people's stories. At a time in literary history when Indian texts, both traditional and contemporary, are entering the academic fashion scene, "Storyteller" teaches a new way of listening (reading)—a reading that refuses the ease of "pretty judgments." Because every Indian writer, by definition, faces what Elaine Jahner terms "a tyranny of expectations"—that is, Indian and non-Indian communities alike expect to find "representative" Indian voices, knowing the mind of one's reader becomes crucial to the Indian writer.[4] Yet, that reader's mind must not be allowed to dictate the writer's own creative shapings of language and experience to the extent that meaning is no longer possible in his or her own terms; therefore, it is important to the writer from the so-called Third World that the whole world be seen as the First World, the world we all inhabit. The gap between what "they" think and what "we" think, when approached thus—as their lack or our loss—betrays the limited thinking on the part of many Western intellectuals when they speak of so-called Third and Fourth World peoples and their literatures. Silko's way of writing reveals a sophisticated understanding of the dynamics at work in reading non-Western writings, how discursive systems of language and thought dictate the grounds upon which meaning is built as well as the meanings themselves. The discursive grounds on which Silko chooses to do battle are the Church and the State—"confession" to sin and to crime.

Leslie Silko writes out of her experience as a woman of Laguna Pueblo and "white" heritage raised in the southwestern United States. As a young woman she taught in Alaska; "Storyteller" resulted from that experience. Neither a speaker of Laguna nor a speaker of Yupik, Silko nonetheless imbues the English language with the *langue* of a tribal world view. The protagonist of the story, a tribal native of the Arctic northlands, represents political possibility in a way that challenges a system of acculturation that refuses to privilege authentic Indian voices, all the while ostensibly demanding them—a system, in other words, that seeks to rob a people of the power of words. Although she has probably never seen a skyscraper or ridden an escalator or been to a beauty parlor, the girl is able to discern what discourses are available to her and able to "legitimize" her own story through those discourses without compromising her own content and form appreciably.

The girl in the story watches the sky from her jail cell, looking for a "sign" and feeling affirmed by what she "reads." Her history unfolds as she is reminded of the many lessons she has had in the reading of "signs" and the telling of stories. The first time she leaves her village, she leaves to attend the mission school. Through an incident with the matron at the school the gender aspect of Christianization is manifested and speaking English is the "sign" that Christianization is complete:

> The dormitory matron pulled down her underpants and whipped her with a leather belt because she refused to speak English.
> "Those backwards village people," the matron said, because she was an Eskimo who had worked for the B.I.A. a long time, "they kept this one until she was too big to learn." The other girls whispered in English. They knew how to work the showers, and they washed and curled their hair at night. (p. 20)

At the same time that the Eskimo girls are taught, not only how to, but that they must, speak English, they are taught how to make themselves into sexual 'signs' in the discursive system of the Church. The girls at the mission school are genderized to see themselves as objects, rather than to see themselves as sexual persons who interact with men within their tribal communities according to traditions evolved over many hundreds of years. Although the reader is only given a glimpse of the mission school experience in the story, it is enough to evoke a striking contrast between the Eskimo woman and the image of the ideal woman in capitalistic society—the woman who is schooled to buy and sell herself as a sexual "sign" on the commodity market.

How women are expected to behave, the "sins" they must avoid, the protagonist knows well: "Village women did not even look through the door to the back room [of the store]. The priest had warned them" (p. 23). Further, the English language is inextricably bound in the girl's mind to the Church's concept of sin, for as the story progresses the narrator tells us, "But English was of no concern to her any more, and neither was anything the Christians in the village might say about her or the old man" (p. 23). As far as the villagers are concerned, the girl and/or the old man have committed a sexual sin by living together in a relationship other than that which is sanctioned by the Church; not speaking English apparently falls into a similar category—it is a sin of *langue*. Thus, the religious mores of the colonizer have been internalized by the colonized people through the concept of sin and in the medium of the English language. And, since absolution from sin requires confession— the public acknowledgment of wrongdoing, the stage is set for the girl's usurpation of the Church's discourse in order that the whole story be told. Although she does not accept the concept of sin as the Church and the church-influenced community would have her do (that is, in terms of a virgin/whore dichotomy), she does confess to a "sin" or crime that the community instead terms "accident." She also does what the priest cannot bring himself to do: she bears witness to the systematic injustice under which her people suffer, particularly those of her people who refuse to accept acculturation into the colonizer's socio-linguistic system.

Neither innocent of sexual experience nor free of desire, the girl in the story can hardly be seen as virginal in the discursive term of Judeo-Christian religion. (In fact, in another Native American tribal tradition, the girl's conduct and attitude might be quite unacceptable; however, the virgin/whore dichotomy would not be the operating paradigm, I dare say, in *any* Native American tribe.) The denial of sexual knowledge, a denial that is an essential component at work in seeing woman as virgin, would be unheard of among a people who view themselves as connected to nature, rather than above nature. In other words being sexual would not be considered "animalistic" behavior in a pejorative sense. Taken to the extreme, the kind of thinking that insists upon controlling and containing woman's sexuality thus leads to an equal and oppositely directed movement, a kind of "pornography." Susan Griffin, in her book, *Pornography and Silence*, describes the mind-set well:

> [I]n the pornographic mind, all along, the virgin *is* a whore. For this woman, we must remember, is a figment of the pornographic imagination. She does not stand for the absence of knowledge, the way we might suppose. She stands for a lie. Her image signifies the denial of sexual knowledge and desire which the pornographic mind has tried to forget but which it cannot forget.[5]

*Part 3*

The denial of any kind of knowledge, but particularly of sexual knowledge, suggests a subject/object relationship that serves to distance the subject from responsibility toward the object. For my purposes, then, the term, "pornography," refers to a psychological distance created to allow for "illegitimate" pleasure, pleasure with another person that ignores the other's reality altogether. So, when the girl says, "I killed him . . . but I don't lie," she is insisting on exposing the full range of her knowledge, her deed and the reasons for her deed (p. 31). Her story is an "insurrection of subjugated knowledges" in form as well as content.[6]

The girl in the story at first cannot understand why it is that the Gussucks came to her tiny village, but gradually she realizes that their mission is genocidal to the cultural life of her people, if not to physical life altogether. That realization comes to her through the story her grandmother tells her about her parents' death; sexual encounters with the red-headed man provide her with an understanding of the "mind" behind their deaths and what she must appeal to in that "mind" in order to have her revenge. As she gains the powerful understanding of the oppressor, she also gains strength in her voice.

When she enters the store and dares to go where the men are, she violates the dictum that women do not even look where they cannot go, that women enter the devil's domain when they lay claim to sexual knowledge. The power of story increases within her:

> The storeman was watching her because he didn't let Eskimos or Indians sit down at the tables in the back room. But she knew he couldn't throw her out if one of his Gussuck customers invited her to sit with him. She walked across the room. They stared at her, but she had the feeling she was walking for someone else, not herself, so their eyes did not matter. The red-haired man pulled out a chair and motioned for her to sit down. She looked back at the storeman while the red-haired man poured her a glass of red sweet wine. She wanted to laugh at the storeman the way she laughed at the dogs, straining against the chains, howling at her.
>
> The red-haired man kept talking to the other Gussucks sitting around the table, but he slid one hand off the top of the table to her thigh. She looked over at the storeman to see if he was still watching her. She laughed out loud at him and the red-haired man stopped talking and turned to her. He asked if she wanted to go. She nodded and stood up. (p. 23)

Her laugh acts as a "sign" of sexual knowledge that indicates to both the red-haired man and the storeman that she has over-stepped her bounds.

The red-haired man's sexual ritual—the lighting of candles, the playing of phonograph records, and the taping of an image on the wall above the bed—require no particular response from the girl. Though he speaks to her, mostly about how people have been talking about her, she does not answer and it doesn't matter that she does not speak. The discourse of the "illegitimized" person, the whore, is relegated to the realm of silence. When she discovers that the image above the bed is the image of a woman copulating with a dog, she tells the old man who "laughs softly to himself" and comments, "It doesn't surprise me" (p. 24). The old man's assessment of the Gussucks is confirmed. "Gussucks kept dogs inside their houses with them; they did not seem to mind the odors which seeped out of the dogs. 'They tell us we are dirty for the food we eat—raw fish and fermented meat. But we do not live with dogs,' the old man once said" (p. 22). The Gussucks, as the old man suggests, do not understand how to maintain a proper relationship with animals; in their arrogance they use everything and anything for the pleasure it brings them without regard for the life-spirit in other living things. The old lady also tells the girl how the Gussucks came "firing their big guns at the walrus and seals" destroying the source of the people's sustenance. The old lady tells the priest about the murder of the girl's parents, how they were sold poisoned wine, but she is not surprised either "when the priest did nothing" (p. 25). The priest and the red-haired man and the storeman are in the same camp—they are all destroyers.

It is through the old man, finally, that the girl learns the importance of the story:

> One night she listened to the old man tell the story all night in his sleep, describing each crystal of ice and the slightly different sounds they made under each paw; first the left and then the right paw, then the hind feet. Her grandmother was there suddenly, a shadow around the stove. She spoke in her low wind voice and the girl was afraid to sit up to hear more clearly. Maybe what she said had been to the old man because he stopped telling the story and began to snore softly the way he had long ago when the old woman had scolded him for telling his stories while others in the house were trying to sleep. But the last words she heard closely: "It will take a long time, but the story must be

told. There must not be any lies." She pulled the blankets up around her chin, slowly, so that her movements would not be seen. She thought her grandmother was talking about the old man's bear story; she did not know about the other story then. (p. 26)

As the other story falls to the girl's charge, the old man provides the story's form; the old woman provides the content. It is the story of the wounded caribou. In the girl's story Red signifies crime, the murder of a people and the rape of a land. Red is the color of the tin from the petroleum barrels, the "sign" the girl looks toward for guidance across an otherwise colorless landscape. "But the red tin penetrated the thick white color of earth and sky; it defined the boundaries like a wound revealing the ribs and heart of a great caribou about to bolt and be lost to the hunter forever" (p. 28).

After nailing the red tin on the shack, the girl begins to watch the river ice over. She waits for the right time. The landscape conspires with her against the Gussuck and his denial of knowledge. "The wind had blown the snow over the frozen river, hiding thin blue streaks where fast water ran under ice translucent and fragile as memory . . . It was time" (p. 28). She functions as tribal historian, preserving tribal memory. She traps the storeman with the limitation his discourse creates in his thinking. To him the girl is whore—exploitable, expendable, disarmed and, most importantly, silenced. But he, ". . . he was sure he could outrun her" (p. 30). Later, when she is asked to offer her side of the story to the law, she is not believed. The attorney also believes she is disarmed:

> The attorney exhaled loudly; his eyes looked tired. "Tell her that she could not have killed him that way. He was a white man. He ran after her without a parka or mittens. She could not have planned that." He paused and turned toward the cell door. "Tell her I will do all I can for her. I will explain to the judge that her mind is confused." She laughed out loud when the jailer translated what the attorney had said. The Gussucks did not understand the story; they could not see the way it must be told, year after year as the old man had done, without lapse or silence. (pp. 31–32)

She has successfully resurrected the native voice, the voice that speaks out of a connectedness to the land. The story hinges on an incredible irony: the survival of the girl and her people—survival, that is, in spiritual and cultural terms specific to them as a people—depends on her ability to tell the story; yet, in order for her story to be told, she must enter the terms of the dominant culture's discourse as categorically condemned—as murderer and fornicator.

Although the reader of literature from the Western tradition is accustomed to heroes who stand up against injustices of all kinds in a variety of ways, the Indian hero who does so in Western literary tradition does so in essentially two ways: as tragic hero or innocent victim. From the beginning of the narration, Silko refuses to allow an easy identification of or with the protagonist as either one. First, she plays on the kind of Christian sentiment and liberal sensibility that so easily grants the Indian the status of victim and/or tragic hero—a status which, once granted, affects a catharsis that acts as a substitute for meaningful action. The girl appears mad in that she watches the winter landscape "until one day she got excited and started calling the jailer. She realized she had been sitting there for many hours, yet the sun had not moved from the center of the sky" (p. 17). Although Indians are noted for their connectedness to the land, this is not the connectedness of a Chief Seattle mourning the passing of people; nor is it the defiant refusal to speak of an institutionalized Chief (as in *One Flew Over the Cuckoo's Nest*). Silko's protagonist reads nature as vengeful and threatening. Exotic charm is not allowed; instead, the reader must face what may be unintelligible to the Western mind—what in Christian cultures is relegated to the devil's domain, what in anthropology is termed the "participation mystique."[7] Further, the ghost of her grandmother, the voice in the dark functions as the core of the story; to the girl the grandmother's voice is a real, actual part of the whole puzzle she is piecing together, solving.

Later, the reader learns that the girl leaves the old man "whose hands were always hunting, like ravens circling lazily in the sky, ready to touch her"—not because she feels sexually violated, but because "she was restless and strong . . . [and] had no patience with [him] who had never changed his slow smooth motions under the blankets" (p. 20). The protagonist is neither tragic heroine nor innocent victim. By not allowing easy identification with the protagonist, identification with woman as victim or Indian as victim, Silko forces an awareness of how little *is* known about Alaskan Native women. In Paula Gunn Allen's article, "Lesbians in American Indian Cultures," she speaks of the void in Indian women's history, "The tribes became more male-oriented and more male-dominated as acculturation accelerated. As this process continued . . . less and less about women in any position other than that sanctioned by the missionaries was likely to be recorded."[8] The discourse of the Church has everything to do with the silencing and the invisibility of Indian women.

Women and Indians share a vital connection to natural cycles that is devalued by the Gussuck; thus, the Gussuck must degrade himself (by picturing himself as the dog copulating with the woman in the pinned-up image) in order to interact with women or Native peoples. He must enter the devil's domain, the heart of darkness, the "illegitimate" realm of his own system of values, if he desires intercourse with "illegitimate" epistemologies. Clearly, he suppresses or denies a sense of responsibility toward the object of his pleasure; instead, the victim is blamed, hated. As the narrator tells us of the storeman, "He hated the people because they had something of value, the old man said, something which the Gussucks could never have. They thought they could take it, suck it out of the earth or cut it from the mountains but they were fools" (p. 29). Nature as Indians know it, nature as women know it, the Gussuck believes he controls. He cannot relate to nature on any other terms.

Finally, Silko gives readers who long for the exotic charm of another culture's system of thought, a parody on their own "thought" by conspicuously illustrating the Eskimo's many "words" for the color yellow: the "yellow machines" (p. 18), the "yellow stains melted into the snow where the men urinated" (p. 22), the "yellow stuffing that held off the cold" (p. 29), and the "blinking yellow flame in the mica window of the oil stove" (p. 24). At the same time, she gives very little culturally-specific information—that is, information that any person who is observant and sensitive could not glean from a visit to the northlands—other than the story within the story; and, much of the story is history, available at the nearest good library. That does not mean that the point-of-view, the sensibility that shapes the story is not Indian. On the contrary, Silko's Indian world view is precisely what enables her to counter-image the Eskimo girl in the story as well as she does.

I began with a brief discussion of the politics at work in the reading process, how "illegitimate delight" is often derived from the making of "pretty judgments." In the reading process genuine discovery is possible in the movement away from what is exotic (therefore delightful) and toward what is unintelligible (therefore frightening). Silko's "Storyteller" creates just such a movement. It is not a Yupik story translated into English; it is a story written *as if it were* a Yupik story. It is a story which prepares the reader of Indian literatures to read the Yupik story should it ever be encountered, should it ever be written. Perhaps such a story exists on the court transcripts of some municipality or in the journal of some missionary as a mediated account. The girl in Silko's story, whether such a person has existed or not, either dies because her story can only be heard as the "confession" to a crime or lives because her story can only be heard as the unintelligible mutterings of a mad person; either way it's not a "pretty" ending. The reader is left, finally, with the task of envisioning political and linguistic alternatives—new discourses, if you will—that dare to see the Eskimo woman as other than a darker version of her Christian sister, other than a criminal, other than a mad woman. These new discourses would make legitimate the storyteller and would insist that the story be told, but "It will take a long time."

# Notes

*Editor's note:* The following notes have been reformatted from the original printing for consistency with other essays in this volume.

1. Jeffrey F. Huntsman, "The Translation Dilemma," *Smoothing the Ground*, ed. Brian Swann (Berkeley: University of California Press, 1983).
2. Michel Foucault, *Power/Knowledge: Selected Interviews and Other Writings, 1972–1977* (New York: Pantheon Books, 1980).
3. Leslie Marmon Silko, *Storyteller* (New York: Seaver, 1981); cited hereafter by page number.
4. Elaine Jahner, "The Novel and Oral Tradition: An Interview with Leslie Marmon Silko," *Book Forum: An International Transdisciplinary Quarterly* 5.3 (1981): 383–388.
5. Susan Griffin, *Pornography and Silence: Culture's Revenge Against Nature* (New York: Harper and Row, 1981).
6. Michel Foucault, *The Order of Things* (New York: Random House, 1980).
7. Benjamin Whorf, "A Linguistic Consideration of Thinking in Primitive Communities," *Language, Thought and Reality* (Cambridge, MA: Technological Press of Massachusetts Institution of Technology, 1956).
8. Paula Gunn Allen, "Lesbians in American Indian Cultures," *Conditions Seven*, 1981.

# Chronology

| | |
|---|---|
| 1870s | Brothers Walter and Robert G. Marmon settle in Laguna. Robert marries Marie Anaya Marmon of Laguna; Leslie Marmon is their great-granddaughter. |
| 1948 | Leslie Marmon born 5 March in Albuquerque, New Mexico. |
| 1954–1963 | Attends elementary school at Laguna, New Mexico, and middle and secondary schools in Albuquerque. |
| 1965–1969 | Attends University of New Mexico. First marriage to Robert Chapman, birth of son Robert. Graduates with honors. |
| 1969 | Publication of "Tony's Story" in *Thunderbird*, University of New Mexico student literary magazine |
| | Publication of "The Man to Send Rain Clouds" in *New Mexico Quarterly*. |
| 1969–1970 | Studies law at University of New Mexico with support from American Indian law program fellowship. |
| 1970–1973 | Fellowship for graduate study in English at University of New Mexico. Teaching at Navajo Community College in Tsaile, Arizona. Marriage to John Silko, birth of son Cazimir. |
| 1971 | Fellowship from National Endowment for the Arts. |
| 1974 | Publication of first book, *Laguna Woman,* a collection of poems. |
| | Seven short stories appear in *The Man to Send Rain Clouds,* first collection of short fiction by contemporary American Indian writers. |
| | Publication of "Lullaby" in *Chicago Review* and *Yardbird Reader*. |

|          | Publication of "A Geronimo Story" and "Laughing and Laughing" in *Come to Power: Eleven Contemporary American Indian Poets.* |
|----------|---|
|          | Receives grant from National Endowment for the Humanities. |
|          | Receives award for poetry from *Chicago Review.* |
|          | Receives grant from Rosewater Foundation. |
| 1974–1975 | Lives in Alaska. Writes first novel, *Ceremony.* |
| 1975     | Publication of "Storyteller" in *Puerto del Sol.* |
|          | "Lullaby" appears in *The Best American Short Stories 1975.* |
| 1976     | "An Old-Time Indian Attack Conducted in Two Parts" published in *Yardbird Reader*; later reprinted in *The Remembered Earth.* |
| 1976–1978 | Joins faculty of University of New Mexico, teaches creative writing. |
| 1977     | Publication of first novel, *Ceremony.* |
| 1978     | Lectures in Norway. |
|          | Subject of documentary film *Running on the Edge of the Rainbow.* |
|          | Moves to Tucson, Arizona. Joins faculty of University of Arizona, teaches in creative writing program. |
| 1978–1980 | Correspondence with James Wright; selected letters are later published in *The Delicacy and Strength of Lace.* |
| 1979     | Lecture at the English Institute, Harvard, 1 September: "Native American Literature and the Uses of English." |
| 1979–1981 | Founds Laguna Film Project; films "Arrowboy and the Witches," a 60-minute videotape version of the story titled "Estoy-eh-muut and the Kunideeyahs" in *Storyteller.* |
| 1980     | Builds stone cottage at Dripping Springs. |
|          | Publication of "Coyote Holds a Full House in His Hand" in *Tri-Quarterly.* |
| 1981     | Publication of *Storyteller*; mixed-genre text incorporating |

short fiction, traditional oral tales, poems, photographs, critical commentary, autobiography, and family and community history.

Receives MacArthur Foundation Grant for five-year term. Begins full-time work on book that eventually becomes *Almanac of the Dead*.

Publication of English Institute lecture under title "Language and Literature from a Pueblo Indian Perspective"; subsequent reprinting in *Yellow Woman and a Beauty of the Spirit: Essays on Native American Life Today*.

1983   Publication of "Private Property" in *Earth Power Coming*, edited by Acoma poet Simon Ortiz and published by Navajo Community College.

1986–1987   Paints mural 12 feet high by 36 feet long on wall in downtown Tucson, Arizona.

1991   Publication of second novel, *Almanac of the Dead*.

1993   Publication of *Sacred Water*, a collection of photographs and reflective essays centered on the ecology of southern Arizona.

1994   Publication of second editions of *Laguna Woman* and *Sacred Water*.

Receives Native Writers' Circle of the Americas lifetime achievement award.

1996   Publication of *Yellow Woman and a Beauty of the Spirit: Essays on Native American Life Today*.

# Selected Bibliography

The primary sources section lists Silko's published books, important uncollected essays, interviews, and films. I cite first printings of the short stories and note their inclusion in the two important collections, *Storyteller* and *The Man to Send Rain Clouds*; I have not tried to list all of the many reprintings of individual stories in anthologies, textbooks, and other collections. The list of secondary sources emphasizes criticism of the short fiction, including works that focus on *Storyteller*, and also cites studies that model important approaches to her work generally. I have not listed separately all the critical essays included in the casebook on "Yellow Woman."

## Primary Sources

### Books

*Laguna Woman: Poems by Leslie Silko*. Greenfield Center: N.Y.: Greenfield Review Press, 1974. Rev. 2d ed., Tucson, Ariz.: Flood Plain Press, 1994.
*Ceremony*. New York: Viking, 1977.
*Storyteller*. New York: Seaver/Arcade, 1981.
*Almanac of the Dead: A Novel*. New York and London: Simon and Schuster, 1991.
*Sacred Water*. Tucson, Ariz.: Flood Plain Press, 1993. 2d ed., 1994.
*Yellow Woman and a Beauty of the Spirit: Essays on Native American Life Today*. New York: Simon and Schuster, 1996.
With James Wright. *The Delicacy and Strength of Lace: Letters between Leslie Marmon Silko and James Wright*. Edited by Anne Wright. St. Paul: Graywolf Press, 1985.

### Short Stories: First Printings

"The Man to Send Rain Clouds." *New Mexico Quarterly* 38.4/39.1 (Winter-Spring 1969): 133–36. Reprinted in *The Man to Send Rain Clouds* and *Storyteller*.
"Tony's Story." *Thunderbird* (University of New Mexico literary journal) (1969): 2–4. Reprinted in *The Man to Send Rain Clouds* and *Storyteller*.

"Bravura." In *The Man to Send Rain Clouds: Contemporary Stories by American Indians.* Edited by Kenneth Rosen. New York: Random House, 1974. 149–54.

*"from* Humaweepi, the Warrior Priest." In *The Man to Send Rain Clouds: Contemporary Stories by American Indians.* Edited by Kenneth Rosen. New York: Random House, 1974. 161–68.

"A Geronimo Story." In *Come to Power: Eleven Contemporary American Indian Poets.* Edited by Dick Lourie. Trumansburg, N.Y.: The Crossing Press, 1974. 81–94. Reprinted in *The Man to Send Rain Clouds* and *Storyteller.*

"Laughing and Laughing." In *Come to Power: Eleven Contemporary American Indian Poets.* Edited by Dick Lourie. Trumansburg, N.Y.: The Crossing Press, 1974. 99.

"Lullaby." *Chicago Review* 26.1 (Summer 1974): 10–17 and *Yardbird Reader* 3 (1974): 87–95. Reprinted in *Storyteller.*

"Yellow Woman." In *The Man to Send Rain Clouds: Contemporary Stories by American Indians.* Edited by Kenneth Rosen. New York: Random House, 1974. 33–45. Reprinted in *Storyteller.*

"Storyteller." *Puerto del Sol* 14.1 (Fall 1975): 11–25. Reprinted in *Storyteller.*

"Coyote Holds a Full House in His Hand." *TriQuarterly* 48 (Spring 1980): 166–74. Reprinted in *Storyteller.*

"Private Property." In *Earth Power Coming: Short Fiction in Native American Literature.* Edited by Simon J. Ortiz. Tsaile, Ariz.: Navajo Community College Press, 1983. 21–30.

## Uncollected Essays

Foreword to *Border Towns of the Navajo Nation,* by Aaron Yava. *Yardbird Reader* 3 (1974): 98–103. Reprinted in *Border Towns of the Navajo Nation,* by Aaron Yava. Alamo, Calif.: Holmganger Press, 1975, n. p.

"An Old Time Indian Attack Conducted in Two Parts." *Yardbird Reader* 5 (1976): 77–84. Reprinted in *The Remembered Earth: An Anthology of Contemporary Native American Literature.* Edited by Geary Hobson. Albuquerque: University of New Mexico, 1979. 211–15.

"Leslie Silko, Laguna Poet and Novelist." In *This Song Remembers: Self-Portraits of Native Americans in the Arts.* Edited by Jane Katz. Boston: Houghton Mifflin Co., 1980. 186–94.

"They Were the Land's." Review of *Creek Mary's Blood,* by Dee Brown. *The New York Times Book Review,* 25 May 1980, 10, 22.

"Grace Abounding in Botswana." Review of *Whites,* by Norman Rush. *New York Times Book Review,* 23 March 1986, 7.

"Pablo, Domingo, Richard and Sara." Review of *Stones for Ibarra,* by Harriet Doerr. *New York Times Book Review,* 8 January 1984, 8.

"Here's an Odd Artifact for the Fairy-Tale Shelf." Review of *The Beet Queen* by Louise Erdrich. *Impact/Albuquerque Journal Magazine,* 7 October 1986,

10–11, and *SAIL—Studies in American Indian Literatures* 10 (Fall 1986): 178–84.

"*Reservation Blues* by Sherman Alexie." Review. *Nation*, vol. 260, 12 June 1995, 856.

"Landscape, History and the Pueblo Imagination." In *The Ecocriticism Reader: Landmarks in Literary Ecology.* Edited by Cheryl Glotfelty and Harold Fromm. Athens: University of Georgia Press, 1996. 264–75.

With Lawrence J. Evers. "A Conversation with Frank Waters." *Sun Tracks: An American Indian Literary Magazine* 5 (1979): 61–68.

With Helen M.. Ingram and Lawrence A. Scaff. "Replacing Confusion with Equity: Alternatives for Water Policy in the Colorado River Basin." In *A River Too Far: The Past and Future of the Arid West.* Edited by Joseph Finkhouse and Mark Crawford. Reno: Nevada Humanities Commission, 1991. 83–103.

## Interviews

"A Conversation with Leslie Marmon Silko." With Lawrence J. Evers and Denny Carr. *Sun Tracks: An American Indian Literary Magazine* 3.1 (1976): 28–33.

"Leslie Silko: Storyteller." With James Fitzgerald and John Hudak. *Persona* (1980): 21–38.

"Stories and Their Tellers." With Dexter Fisher. In *The Third Woman: Minority Women Writers of the United States.* Edited by Dexter Fisher. Boston: Houghton Mifflin Co., 1980. 18–23.

"The Novel and Oral Tradition: An Interview with Leslie Marmon Silko." With Elaine Jahner. *Book Forum: An International Transdisciplinary Quarterly* 5.3 (1981): 383–88.

"Two Interviews with Leslie Marmon Silko." With Per Seyersted. *American Studies in Scandinavia* 13 (1981): 17–33.

"A Leslie Marmon Silko Interview." With Kim Barnes. *The Journal of Ethnic Studies* 13.4 (1986): 83–105.

"Leslie Marmon Silko." With Laura Coltelli. In *Winged Words: American Indian Writers Speak.* Edited by Laura Coltelli. Lincoln: University of Nebraska Press, 1990. 135–53.

"Leslie Marmon Silko." With Donna Marie Perry. In *Backtalk: Women Writers Speak Out.* Edited by Donna Marie Perry. New Brunswick, N.J.: Rutgers University Press, 1993. 314–40.

"*Almanac of the Dead*: An Interview with Leslie Marmon Silko." With Laura Coltelli. In *Native American Literatures.* Edited by Laura Coltelli. Pisa: SEU—Servizio Editorale Universitario, 1994. 65–80.

"An Interview with Leslie Marmon Silko." With Stephen Pett. *Short Story* 2.2 (Fall 1994): 91–96.

## Recordings

*From a Distance Outside of Time: An Interview with Leslie Marmon Silko*. With Ken McCullough. South Carolina: Educational Television Network, 1976. Videorecording.

"The Laguna Regulars and Geronimo." Mohawk Nation: *Akwesasne Notes*, 1977. Audiotape reading of "A Geronimo Story."

*Running on the Edge of the Rainbow*. Words and Place Videocassette Series. New York: Clearwater Publishing Co., 1982. Videorecording.

*Arrowboy and the Witches*. 1986. Videorecording.

"Leslie Marmon Silko." Vol. 3 of *Native American Novelists*. Princeton, N.J.: Films for the Humanities and Social Sciences, 1995. Videorecording.

# *Secondary Sources*

## Reference Works

Clements, William M. "Leslie Marmon Silko." In *Dictionary of Literary Biography: American Novelists Since World War II*, 3d ser., vol. 143. New York: Gale Research, 1994. 196–205.

Coltelli, Laura. "Silko, Leslie Marmon." In *Native American Women: A Biographical Dictionary*. Edited by Gretchen M. Bataille. New York: Garland Publishing, 1993. 233–34.

Cook-Lynn, Elizabeth. "American Indian Short Fiction." In *Critical Survey of Short Fiction: Essays*. Vol. 2. Edited by Frank N. Magill. Englewood Cliffs, N.J.: Salem Press, 1981. 567–74.

Jahner, Elaine. "Leslie Marmon Silko." In *Dictionary of Native American Literature*. Edited by Andrew Wiget. New York: Garland, 1994. 499–511.

Jaskoski, Helen. " 'Lullaby' by Leslie Marmon Silko." *Masterplots 2*. Englewood Cliffs, N.J.: Salem Press, 1986. 1416–19.

"Leslie Marmon Silko." In *Great Women Writers: The Lives and Works of 135 of the World's Most Important Women Writers, from Antiquity to the Present*. Edited by Frank Northen Magill. New York: Holt and Co., 1994. 495–99.

"Silko, Leslie Marmon." In *World Authors 1985–1990*. Edited by Vineta Colby. New York and Dublin: H. W. Wilson, 1995. 821–23.

## Critical Studies

Anderson, Laurie. "Colorful Revenge in Silko's 'Storyteller.' " *Notes on Contemporary Literature* 15.4 (1985): 11–12.

Benediktsson, Thomas E. "The Reawakening of the Gods: Realism and the Supernatural in Silko and Hulme." *Critique: Studies in Contemporary Fiction* 33.2 (1992): 121–31.

Blicksilver, Edith. "Traditionalism vs. Modernity: Leslie Silko on American Indian Women." *Southwest Review* 64.2 (1979): 149–60.

Browdy de Hernandez, Jennifer. "Laughing, Crying, Surviving: Leslie Marmon Silko's *Storyteller*." *A/B:Auto/Biography Studies* 9.1 (1994): 18–42.

Brown, Alanna Kathleen. "Pulling Silko's Threads through Time: An Exploration of Storytelling." *American Indian Quarterly* 19.2 (1995): 171–79.

Cohen, Robin. "Landscape, Story, and Time as Elements of Reality in Silko's 'Yellow Woman' " *Weber Studies: An Interdisciplinary Humanities Journal* 12.3 (1995): 141–47.

Danielson, Linda L. "*Storyteller*: Grandmother Spider's Web." *Journal of the Southwest* 30.3 (Autumn 1988): 325–55.

————. "The Storytellers in Storyteller." *SAIL—Studies in American Indian Literatures*, 2d ser., 1.2 (1989): 21–31.

Dasenbrock, Reed Way. "Forms of Biculturalism in Southwestern Literature: The Work of Rudolfo Anaya and Leslie Marmon Silko." *Genre* 21.3 (1988): 307–19.

Evers, Lawrence J. "The Killing of a New Mexican State Trooper: Ways of Telling an Historical Event." In *Critical Essays on Native American Literature*. Edited by Andrew Wiget. Boston: G. K. Hall, 1985. 246–61.

Fleck, Richard F. "Sacred Land in the Writings of Momaday, Welch, and Silko." In *Entering the 90s: The North American Experience: Proceedings from the Native American Studies Conference at Lake Superior University, October 27–28, 1989*. Edited by Thomas E. Schirer. Sault Ste. Marie, Ontario: Lake Superior University Press, 1991. 125–33.

Graulich, Melody, ed. *"Yellow Woman," Leslie Marmon Silko*. Women Writers: Texts and Contexts. New Brunswick, N.J.: Rutgers University Press, 1993.

Hirsch, Bernard A. " 'The Telling Which Continues': Oral Tradition and the Written Word in Leslie Marmon Silko's *Storyteller*." *American Indian Quarterly* 12.1 (1988): 1–26.

Hoilman, Dennis. "The Ethnic Imagination: A Case History." *Canadian Journal of Native Studies* 5.2 (1985): 167–75.

Jaskoski, Helen. "From the Time Immemorial: Native American Traditions in Contemporary Short Fiction." In *Since Flannery O'Connor: Essays on the Contemporary Short Story*. Edited by Loren Logsdon and Charles W. Mayer. Macomb, Ill.: Western Illinois University, 1987. 54–71.

————. "Words Like Bones." *CEA Critic* 55.1 (1992): 70–84.

————. "Teaching with *Storyteller* at the Center." *SAIL— Studies in American Indian Literatures*, 2d ser., 5.1 (Spring 1993): 51–61.

Krumholz, Linda Joan. " 'To Understand This World Differently': Reading and Subversion in Leslie Marmon Silko's *Storyteller*." *Ariel: A Review of English Literature* 25.1 (1994): 89–113.

Krupat, Arnold. "The Dialogic of Silko's *Storyteller.*" In *Narrative Chance: Postmodern Discourse on Native American Indian Literatures.* Edited by Gerald Vizenor. Albuquerque: University of New Mexico Press, 1989. 55–68.

———. *The Voice in the Margin: Native American Literature and the Canon.* Berkeley: University of California Press, 1989.

Langen, T. C. S. "Estoy-eh-muut and the Morphologists." *SAIL—Studies in American Indian Literatures,* 2d ser., 1.1 (1989): 1–12.

Lappas, Catherine. " 'The Way I Heard It Was . . . ': Myth, Memory, and Autobiography in *Storyteller* and *The Woman Warrior.*" *CEA Critic* 7.1 (1994): 57–67.

Lincoln, Kenneth. *Native American Renaissance.* Berkeley: University of California Press, 1983.

Lucero, Ambrose. "For the People: Leslie Silko's *Storyteller.*" *Minority Voices: An Interdisciplinary Journal of Literature and the Arts* 5.1–2 (1981): 1–10.

Manley, Kathleen. "Decreasing the Distance: Contemporary Native American Texts, Hypertext, and the Concept of Audience." *Southern Folklore* 51.2 (1994): 121–35.

McAllister, Mick. "Homeward Bound: Wilderness and Frontier in American Indian Literature." In *The Frontier Experience and the American Dream: Essays on American Literature.* Edited by David Mogen, Mark Busby, and Paul Bryant. College Station: Texas A & M University Press, 1989. 149–58.

McBride, Mary. "Shelter of Rufuge: The Art of Mimesis in Leslie Marmon Silko's 'Lullaby.' " *The Wicazo Sâ Review* 3.2 (1987): 15–17.

Nelson, Robert. "He Said / She Said: Writing Oral Tradition in John Gunn's 'Kopot Ka-nat' and Leslie Silko's *Storyteller.*" *SAIL—Studies in American Indian Literatures,* 2d ser., 5.1 (1993): 31–50.

———. *Place and Vision: The Function of Landscape in Native American Fiction.* New York: Peter Lang, 1995.

Perez Castillo, Susan. "The Construction of Gender and Ethnicity in the Texts of Leslie Silko and Louise Erdrich." *The Yearbook of English Studies.* Vol. 24. Cambridge: Modern Humanities Research Assoc., 1994. 228–36.

Riley, Patricia. "The Mixed Blood Writer as Interpreter and Mythmaker." In *Understanding Others: Cultural and Cross Cultural Studies and the Teaching of Literature.* Edited by Joseph Trimmer and Tilly Warnock. Urbana, Ill.: National Council of Teachers of English, 1992. 230–42.

Rosen, Kenneth, ed. Introduction to *The Man to Send Rain Clouds: Contemporary Stories by American Indians.* New York: Random House, 1974. ix–xiv.

Ruoff, A. LaVonne Brown. "Ritual and Renewal: Keres Traditions in the Short Fiction of Leslie Silko." *MELUS* 5 (1978): 2–17. Revised and reprinted in *American Women Short Story Writers: A Collection of Essays.* Edited by Julie Brown. Wellesley Studies in Critical Theory, Literary History, and Culture No. 8; Reference Library of the Humanities 1737. New York: Garland, 1995. 167–89.

Ruppert, Jim. "Story Telling: The Fiction of Leslie Silko." *The Journal of Ethnic Studies* 9.1 (1981): 53–58.

Sands, Kathleen Mullen. "Indian Women's Personal Narrative: Voices Past and Present." In *American Women's Autobiography: Fea(s)ts of Memory.* Edited by Margo Culley. Madison: University of Wisconsin Press, 1992. 268–94.

Seyersted, Per. *Leslie Marmon Silko.* Boise State University Western Writers Series No. 45. Boise, Idaho: Boise State University, 1980.

Shea Murphy, Jacqueline. "Words Like Bones: Narrative Performance and the Reinscribing of Violence in Leslie Marmon Silko's *Storyteller.*" *Journal of Narrative and Life History* 3 (1993): 223–38.

Smith, Patricia Clark with Paula Gunn Allen. "Earthy Relations, Carnal Knowledge: Southwestern American Indian Women Writers and Landscape." In *The Desert Is No Lady: Southwestern Landscapes in Women's Writing and Art.* Edited by Vera Norwood and Janice Monk. New Haven: Yale University Press, 1987. 174–96.

Thompson, Joan. "Yellow Woman, Old and New: Oral Tradition and Leslie Marmon Silko's Storyteller." *The Wicazo Sâ Review: A Journal of Indian Studies* 5.2 (1989): 22–25.

Vangen, Kate Shanley. "The Devil's Domain: Leslie Silko's 'Storyteller.' " In *Coyote Was Here: Essays on Contemporary Native American Literary and Political Mobilization.* Edited by Bo Scholer. Aarhus, Denmark: SEKLOS, University of Aarhus, 1984. 116–23.

# Index

# The Author

Helen Jaskoski's books include *Early Native American Writing: New Critical Essays* (Cambridge University Press), *Poetry/Mind/Body* (University Press of America), and a short novel, *The Tar Pit Murders* (Regents Press). She has published numerous articles and reviews on multiethnic American literature and on poetry therapy, and she was founding editor of the second series of *SAIL—Studies in American Indian Literatures*. A published poet as well as fiction writer, she is a member of Multi-Cultural Women Writers of southern California.

She is currently professor of English and comparative literature at California State University Fullerton, where she has also taught in the religious studies, ethnic studies, and liberal studies programs. She has served as Fulbright professor of American literature, Marie Curie-Sklodowska University, Lublin, Poland; as resident director, California State University International Program, Florence, Italy; as professor of English in the summer master of arts program, University of California at Irvine; as professor for the Bread Loaf School of English, Middlebury College, Vermont; as adjunct professor of English, Mount St. Mary's College, Los Angeles; and as lecturer and visiting professor, California State University Los Angeles.

# The Editors

Gary Scharnhorst is professor of English at the University of New Mexico, coeditor of *American Literary Realism,* and editor in alternating years of *American Literary Scholarship: An Annual.* He is the author or editor of books about Horatio Alger Jr., Charlotte Perkins Gilman, Bret Harte, Nathaniel Hawthorne, Henry David Thoreau, and Mark Twain; and he has taught in Germany on Fulbright fellowships three times (1978–1979, 1985–1986, 1993). He is also the current president of the Western Literature Association and the Pacific Northwest American Studies Association.

Eric Haralson is assistant professor of English at the State University of New York at Stony Brook. He has published articles on American and English literature—in *American Literature, Nineteenth-Century Literature,* the *Arizona Quarterly, American Literary Realism,* and the *Henry James Review,* as well as in several essay collections. He is also the editor of *The Garland Encyclopedia of American Nineteenth-Century Poetry.*